P9-AFN-072

California
Preschool
Curriculum
Framework

Volume 3

History–Social Science
Science

Publishing Information

The *California Preschool Curriculum Framework, Volume 3*, was developed by the Child Development Division, California Department of Education (CDE). This publication was edited by Faye Ong and John McLean, working in cooperation with Laura Bridges, Child Development Consultant. It was designed and prepared for printing by the staff of CDE Press, with the cover designed by Juan D. Sanchez. The document was published by the Department of Education, 1430 N Street, Sacramento, CA 95814-5901. It was distributed under the provisions of the Library Distribution Act and *Government Code* Section 11096.

ISBN: 978-0-8011-1733-6

Ordering Information

Copies of this publication are available for purchase from the California Department of Education. For prices and ordering information, please visit the Department Web site at http://www.cde.ca.gov/re/pn/rc/ or call the CDE Press sales office at 1-800-995-4099.

Notice

The guidance in the *California Preschool Curriculum Framework, Volume 3*, is not binding on local educational agencies or other entities. Except for the statutes, regulations, and court decisions that are referenced herein, the document is exemplary, and compliance with it is not mandatory. (See *Education Code* Section 33308.5.)

Contents

CHAPTER 3
Science 135

A Message from the State Superintendent of Public Instruction

I am pleased to present the *California Preschool Curriculum Framework, Volume 3,* a publication I believe will be a major step in working to close the school-readiness gap for young children in our state. Created as a companion to the *California Preschool Learning Foundations, Volume 3,* this framework presents strategies and information for educators to enrich learning and development opportunities for all of California's preschool children.

Like the third volume of the preschool learning foundations, this third volume of the curriculum framework focuses on two learning domains: history–social science and science. It includes guiding principles; the vital role of the family in early learning and development; the diversity of young children in California; and the ongoing cycle of observing, documenting, assessing, planning, and implementing curriculum. The preschool curriculum framework takes an integrated approach to early learning and describes how curriculum planning considers the connections between different domains as children engage in teacher-guided learning activities.

Chapters 2 and 3 focus on the learning domains. Each chapter provides an overview of a domain, the foundations for that domain, principles in planning curriculum, and curriculum strategies illustrated by vignettes. The strategies pertain to both the learning environment and teachers' interactions with children. These chapters offer key principles and a rich variety of ideas for early childhood educators to support the learning and development of preschool children. Additionally, there are specific principles and strategies for teaching children who are English learners.

Three themes are interwoven throughout this volume: early childhood educators need to be intentional in supporting learning in all domains, young children learn through play, and young children's families are their first teachers. Young children benefit greatly from comprehensive and integrated curriculum planning that includes history–social science and science. As young children play, they express themselves by exploring ideas about the past, where they live, fairness and respect for others, their families' cultural traditions, and how to use money to purchase things. They also are naturally interested in scientific inquiry, the properties and characteristics of nonliving objects and materials, living things, and the earth and materials. Observation of young children's play gives insights into how to build on their interests and expand their learning. Early educators also enrich young children's learning through ongoing collaboration with families. Together, early educators and family members can create meaningful learning experiences for children in preschool and at home.

The preschool curriculum framework speaks to new early childhood educators as well as experienced ones. It recognizes the best practices already used by preschool programs and provides new ideas that bring the preschool learning foundations to life for everyone responsible for the care and education of young children. Volume 3 completes the preschool curriculum framework and should prove to be instrumental in preparing children for school.

Tom Torlakson

TOM TORLAKSON
State Superintendent of Public Instruction

Acknowledgments

The development of the preschool curriculum framework involved many people. The following groups contributed: project leaders; principal writers; community college faculty advisers; advisers on English-language development and cultural diversity; universal design advisers; additional consultants and reviewers; project staff and advisers from the WestEd Center for Child and Family Studies; staff from the California Department of Education; early childhood education stakeholder organizations; participants in the formative and review focus groups; and participants in the Web-posting process.

Project Leaders

The following staff members are gratefully acknowledged for their contributions: **Peter Mangione** and **Katie Monahan**, WestEd.

Principal Writers

Special thanks are extended to the principal writers for their expertise and contributions.

Chapter 1: Introduction to the Framework

Peter Mangione, WestEd

Mary Jane Maguire-Fong, American River College

Marie Jones, American River College

Chapter 2: History–Social Science

Janet Thompson, University of California, Davis

Ross Thompson, University of California, Davis

Kelly Twibell, University of California, Davis

Chapter 3: Science

Osnat Zur, WestEd

Community College Faculty Advisers

Special thanks are extended to the faculty advisers for their expertise and contributions:

Caroline Carney, Monterey Peninsula College

Amy Obegi, Solano Community College

Advisers on English-Language Development and Cultural Diversity

Particular thanks are extended to the following advisers for their involvement in the project:

Gisela Jia, City University of New York, Lehman College

Antonia Lopez, National Council of La Raza

Alison Wishard Guerra, University of California, San Diego

Universal Design Advisers

The following universal design experts are gratefully acknowledged for their contributions:

Maurine Ballard-Rosa, California State University, Sacramento

Linda Brault, WestEd

Additional Consultants and Reviewers

Particular thanks are also extended to the following consultants for their involvement in the project:

Gay Macdonald, University of California, Los Angeles, Early Care and Education

Susan Wood, California Institute of Technology (Caltech), Children's Center

WestEd Center for Child and Family Studies—Project Staff and Advisers

Linda Brault
Melinda Brookshire
Caroline Pietrangelo Owens
Teresa Ragsdale
Amy Schustz-Alvarez
Charlotte Tilson
Ann-Marie Wiese

California Department of Education

Thanks are extended to the following staff members: **Richard Zeiger,** Chief Deputy Superintendent of Public Instruction; **Lupita Cortez Alcalá,** Deputy Superintendent, Instruction and Learning Support Branch; **Camille Maben,** Director, Child Development Division; **Cecelia Fisher-Dahms,** Administrator, Quality Improvement Office, Child Development Division; **Desiree Soto,** Administrator, Northern Field Services, Child Development Division; and **Laura Bridges,** Consultant, Child Development Division, for ongoing revisions and recommendations. During the lengthy development process, many CDE staff members were involved at various levels. Additional thanks are extended to **Deborah Sigman,** Deputy Superintendent, District, School, and Innovation Branch; **Gavin Payne,** former Chief Deputy Superintendent; **Gail Brodie, Sy Dang Nguyen, Luis Rios, Mary Smithberger,** and **Charles Vail,** Child Development Division; and **Meredith Cathcart,** Special Education Division.

The following individuals are also acknowledged for their contributions to the vignettes:

Aleksandra Klitinek, Prekindergarten Teacher, New York City Department of Education

Gloria de Napoli Peropat, LCSW-R, Prekindergarten Social Worker/Early Childhood Specialist, New York City Department of Education

Early Childhood Education Stakeholder Organizations

Representatives from many statewide organizations provided input that affected various aspects of this curriculum framework.

Action Alliance for Children
Alliance for a Better Community
Asian Pacific Islander Community Action Network (APIsCAN)
Association of California School Administrators
Baccalaureate Pathways in Early Childhood & Education (BPECE)
Black Child Development Institute (BCDI), Sacramento Affiliate
California Alliance of African American Educators (CAAAE)
California Association for Bilingual Education (CABE)
California Association for the Education of Young Children (CAEYC)
California Association for Family Child Care (CAFCC)
California Association of Latino Superintendents and Administrators (CALSA)
California Child Care Coordinators Association (CCCCA)
California Child Care Resource and Referral Network (CCCRRN)
California Child Development Administrators Association (CCDAA)
California Child Development Corps
California Commission on Teacher Credentialing (CCTC)
California Community College Early Childhood Educators (CCCECE)
California Community Colleges Chancellor's Office (CCCCO)
California Council for the Social Studies (CCSS)

California County Superintendents Educational Services Association (CCSESA)

California Early Childhood Mentor Program

California Early Reading First Network

California Federation of Teachers (CFT)

California Head Start Association (CHSA)

California Kindergarten Association (CKA)

California Preschool Instructional Network (CPIN)

California Professors of Early Childhood Special Education (CAPECSE)

California School Boards Association

California Science Teachers Association (CSTA)

California State PTA

California State University Office of the Chancellor

California Teachers Association

Californians Together

Campaign for High Quality Early Learning Standards in California (CHQELS)

Child Development Policy Institute (CDPI)

Child Development Training Consortium (CDTC)

Children Now

The Children's Collabrium

Coalition of Family Literacy in California

Council for Exceptional Children/California Division for Early Childhood (Cal-DEC)

Council of CSU Campus Childcare (CCSUCC)

Curriculum Alignment Project (CAP)

Curriculum & Instruction Steering Committee (CISC)

Desired Results access Project

Early Learning Advisory Council

English Language Learners Preschool Coalition (ELLPC)

Federal/State/Tribes Collaboration Workgroup

Fight Crime: Invest in Kids California

First 5 Association of California

First 5 California, California Children & Families Commission

Head Start State-Based Training and Technical Assistance Office for California

Infant Development Association of California (IDA)

Learning Disabilities Association of California

Los Angeles Universal Preschool (LAUP)

Mexican American Legal Defense and Educational Fund (MALDEF)

Migrant Education Even Start (MEES)

Migrant Head Start

National Council of La Raza (NCLR)

Packard Foundation, Children, Families, and Communities Program

Preschool California

Professional Association for Childhood Education (PACE)

Special Education Administrators of County Offices (SEACO) Committee

Special Education Local Plan Area (SELPA) Committee

TeenNOW California

University of California, Child Care Directors

University of California, Office of the President (UCOP)

Voices for African American Students, Inc. (VAAS)

ZERO TO THREE

Public Input

Ten focus groups consisting of 115 participants provided valuable feedback, and others offered suggestions during a public review of the draft that was posted online.

Photographs

Many photographers contributed to a large pool of photographs that were taken over the years and collected by WestEd. Special thanks are extended to WestEd and the photographers. The following child care agencies deserve recognition for allowing photographs to be taken of staff members, children, and families:

American River College, Sacramento

Note: The names, titles, and affiliations of the individuals named were current at the time the publication was developed.

Antelope Elementary School, Antelope Elementary School District, Red Bluff

Brooklyn Early Education Center, Los Angeles Unified School District, Los Angeles

Chinatown Community Children's Center, San Francisco

El Jardín de Los Niños, University Preparation School at California State University, Channel Islands

Friends of St. Francis Child Care, San Francisco

Fruitvale Elementary School, Oakland Unified School District, Oakland

Harrison Elementary School, Los Angeles Unified School District, Los Angeles

Hoopa Valley Tribal Head Start, Hoopa Valley Tribe, Hoopa

Kidango Ohlone Lab Center, Fremont

Supporting Future Growth, Site III, Child Care Center, Oakland

Little People's After School Learning Land, Sacramento

Oakland Head Start Lion Creek's Crossing, Oakland

Oakland Head Start West Grand Avenue Center, Oakland

Poplar Avenue Elementary Campus Preschools, Thermalito Family Involvement & Literacy Center Preschool, Thermalito Union School District, Thermalito

Roosevelt Infant Center, Los Angeles

Small Wonders Daycare, Buellton

Walnut Park Elementary, Los Angeles Unified School District, Huntington Park

West Street Elementary School, Corning Union Elementary School District, Corning

CHAPTER 1

Introduction
to the Framework

Young children enter preschool with a sense of wonder and a love of learning. They have an insatiable appetite for knowledge when they have learning experiences that are engaging and enjoyable. Positive experiences in which children are able to make choices and explore can help them to feel competent and confident. How can we offer them engaging and enjoyable learning experiences that fuel their intellectual engines and build their confidence? How can we connect children's fascination with learning to history–social science and science domains? How can we integrate learning in those two domains with learning in all other domains and make the most of children's time in preschool? With these questions in mind, the California Department of Education (CDE) developed this third volume of the curriculum framework for preschool programs, which include any early childhood setting where three- to five-year-old children receive education and care.

Like volumes 1 and 2 of the preschool curriculum framework, volume 3 provides an overall approach for **teachers**[a] to support children's learning through environments and experiences that are:

- developmentally appropriate;
- reflective of thoughtful observation and intentional planning;
- individually and culturally meaningful;
- inclusive of children with disabilities or other special needs.

a. In this document, the term *teacher* is used to describe any adult who has education and care responsibilities in an early childhood setting. Teachers include adults who interact directly with young children in preschool programs and family child care home settings, as well as those who provide special education services. In family child care, teachers may be referred to as caregivers.

The framework presents ways of setting up environments, encouraging and building upon children's self-initiated play, selecting appropriate materials, integrating learning experiences across domains, and planning and implementing teacher-guided learning activities. As much as possible, the writers of this document have used everyday language to describe curriculum concepts and strategies that pertain to history–social science and science. However, some technical terminology appears in the text. The use of technical terms reflects the need for precise language and offers the reader the opportunity to connect practice to theory and abstract ideas. To aid the reader, technical words that appear in **boldface** are defined in the glossary.

What children learn in the history–social science and science domains during the preschool years is presented in the *California Preschool Learning Foundations, Volume 3*.[1] As preschool teachers plan learning environments and experiences, the foundations provide background information to:

- understand children's developing knowledge and skills;
- consider appropriate ways to support children's learning and development.

In essence, curriculum planning should offer children learning opportunities that are attuned to their developing abilities and connected with their experiences at home and in their communities. The National Association for the Education of Young Children's accreditation criteria state that a curriculum includes the goals for the knowledge and skills to be acquired by children and the plans for learning experiences through which such knowledge and skills will be acquired.[2] A preschool curriculum typically defines a sequence of integrated experiences, interactions, and activities to help young children reach learning goals. In contrast, a curriculum framework provides general guidance on planning learning environments and experiences for young children. Thus, as a curriculum framework, this document provides:

- principles for supporting young children's learning;
- an overview of key components of curriculum planning for young children, including observation, documentation, and reflection;
- descriptions of routines, environments, and materials that engage children in learning;
- sample strategies for building on children's knowledge, skills, and interests in the domains of history–social science and science.

Two domains are the focus of volume 3 of the CDE's preschool learning foundations and this volume of the preschool curriculum framework: history–social science and science.

California's Preschool Children

A fundamental consideration in planning curriculum for individual children is being responsive to the competencies, experiences, interests, and needs each child brings to the preschool setting. The state's preschool population includes children who are culturally diverse, speak languages other than English, possess different abilities, and come from diverse socioeconomic backgrounds. When teachers and other program staff collaborate with families, they make curriculum individually and culturally meaningful. An increasingly prominent factor in the diversity of California's children is their early experiences with language. Language and literacy development contributes to young children's learning and long-range success in many different ways. Children who enter preschool with competence in a language other than English rely on their home language as they learn English. While building competence in English and continuing to build competence in their home language, children are able to draw on all of their knowledge and skills as they engage in learning in every domain. In response to the need to support children with diverse early language and literacy experiences, the CDE has developed the preschool English-language development foundations; a chapter in the *California Preschool Curriculum Framework, Volume 1*, on curriculum planning that supports English-language development;[3] and *Preschool English Learners: Principles and*

Practices to Promote Language, Literacy, and Learning[4] (hereafter referred to as the PEL Resource Guide). The third volume of the curriculum framework offers strategies that are aligned with the English-language development foundations, the first volume of this curriculum framework, and the content of the PEL Resource Guide.

Socioeconomic diversity is another trend that requires attention. The percentage of children who live in low-income homes is high; almost 20 percent live below the poverty level.[5] At the same time, the benefits of high-quality preschool are more pronounced for children from low-income backgrounds than for other population subgroups. Children from diverse socioeconomic backgrounds are more likely to benefit from preschool when the curriculum is attuned to their learning strengths and needs.

Children with disabilities or other special needs are another part of California's preschool population. Children with disabilities or other special needs benefit from learning in inclusive environments with typically developing children. Studies have shown that children in inclusive environments, with appropriate support and assistance, achieve more than children in segregated environments.[6] Inclusive environments benefit not only children with disabilities or other special needs, but also children who are typically developing. As the following information suggests, the diversity of young children means that every preschool program needs a flexible approach to curriculum in order to be responsive to all children who enter its doors.

Demographics

Compared with most other states, California has an extraordinarily diverse population of children, particularly those under the age of five. For 2009–10, more than six million children were enrolled in California's K–12 schools; 50.37 percent were Hispanic, 27.03 percent were white, 8.51 percent were Asian, 6.85 percent were African American, and 2.53 percent were Filipino.[7] Similarly, in 2008 there were more than three million children ages zero to five living in California, and 53 percent were Hispanic, 28 percent were white, 10 percent were Asian American, and 6 percent were African American.[8] This trend is anticipated to continue over the next several decades.

English learners

Data for the 2008–09 school year indicate that, in California, there are more children who are English learners enrolled in younger grades than in older grades.[9] In the 2010 California Report Card, Children Now estimated that 40 percent of children in California's kindergarten classrooms are English learners.[10] Children Now also reports that "Over one-third (39 percent) of California's zero-to-five population live in families where the most knowledgeable adult does not speak English well."[11] These families are referred to as living in "linguistically isolated homes."[12] In an earlier report, Children Now and Preschool California indicated that young children living in linguistically isolated homes are less likely to be enrolled in preschool programs.[13]

The broad range of languages spoken by children in the state is clearly a significant factor in developing curriculum for preschool children who are learning English. During the 2009–10 school year, 84.6 percent of California children in kindergarten through twelfth grade who were learning English spoke Spanish, followed by Vietnamese (2.5 percent), Filipino (1.4 percent), Cantonese (1.4 percent), Hmong (1.1 percent), and Korean (1.0 percent).[14]

Many families may come from similar geographic regions outside the United States but may not necessarily speak the same language.[15] Preschool offers an important opportunity for children whose families speak a different language at home to learn English while continuing to learn their home language. Competence in two languages will allow children to become adults who can contribute to both the global economy and their local communities. Preschool programs can best support young children by planning curriculum that fosters English-language development and supports the children's continuing development of their families' language.

Socioeconomic status

The National Center for Children in Poverty documented that, in 2008, approximately 45 percent of children in California under the age of six lived in a low-income family.[16] In addition, compared with other states, California ranks 20th in the nation in the number of children under age eighteen living in poverty.[17] According to the National Center for Children in Poverty, younger children (birth to six years) are more likely to live in a low-income household than older children.[18] Young children of immigrant parents are 20 percent more likely to live in a low-income family than children of native-born, English-speaking parents. Young African American, Hispanic, and Native American children in California are also more likely than white children to live in very-low-income families.[19]

Children with disabilities or other special needs

In 2009–10, over 78,000 children in the birth-to-five age range with identified disabilities attended preschool in California.[20] This number does not include children at risk of a disability or developmental challenges. Children with disabilities represent the diversity of California's entire preschool population and require unique considerations in the preschool setting. Three-, four-, and five-year-old children with identified disabilities have individualized education programs (IEPs) that are consistent with the CDE's preschool learning foundations. Under the Individuals with Disabilities Education Act (2004), all children must have access to the general curriculum and have their progress measured accordingly.[21] In California, the CDE's preschool learning foundations inform curriculum planning. Together, the foundations and curriculum framework offer a comprehensive approach to planning access to inclusive learning opportunities for all children.

Overarching Principles

All three volumes of the preschool curriculum framework were developed with eight principles in mind—principles that are grounded in early childhood research and practice. The following principles emphasize individually, culturally, and linguistically responsive learning experiences and environments for young children:

- Relationships are central
- Play is a primary context for learning
- Learning is integrated
- Intentional teaching enhances children's learning experiences
- Family and community partnerships create meaningful connections
- Individualization of learning includes all children
- Responsiveness to culture and language supports children's learning
- Time for reflection and planning enhances teaching

These principles have guided the development of each volume of the preschool curriculum framework. Because these principles play a central role in the overall development of the curriculum framework, they are repeated in each volume. Explanation of the principles follows.

Relationships are central

Relationships with others are at the center of young children's lives. Caring relationships with close family members provide the base for young children to engage with others, to explore with confidence, to seek support when needed, and to view interactions with others as likely to be positive and interesting. Recognizing the power of early relationships, preschool teachers and programs build strong relationships with children and families. Just as important, preschool teachers nurture the social–emotional development of young children through those relationships. Research shows that healthy social–emotional development helps young children learn, for example, to sustain attention more easily, to make and maintain friendships, and to communicate needs and ideas. Under the guiding eye of teachers in close partnership with families, young children build their ability to engage in relationships with adults and other children. Preschool offers children a variety of opportuni-

ties for social interactions (with familiar adults, peers), group participation, and cooperation and responsibility. A climate of caring and respect that promotes nurturing relationships between children and within the community of families supports children's learning in all domains.

Play is a primary context for learning

Play is at the heart of young children's explorations and their engagement in learning experiences.[22] During play, children maximize their attention span as they focus on self-selected activities that they regulate themselves. When children make their own choices, engage other children in interaction, and spend time amusing themselves on their own, they learn much about themselves, their own capabilities, and the world around them. At the preschool level, play and learning should be seamless. Children need to be *engaged* to learn. As Zigler observes, children bring more than their brains to school.[23] When children's hearts, minds, and bodies are engaged, adults can help them learn almost anything they are ready to learn. In a program where play is valued, children's interests, engagement, creativity, and self-expression are supported through a balance of child-initiated and teacher-guided activities. The environment reflects an appreciation for the value of pretend play, imaginary play, dramatic play, and physically challenging play. Play not only provides the context for thinking, building knowledge, being attentive, solving problems, and increasing social and physical skills, it also helps children to integrate their emotional experiences and internalize guidance from their teachers. For some children, it may be necessary to make special adaptations to create access to learning through self-initiated activities and play.

Learning is integrated

Learning engages young children in every possible way. Young children continually use all their senses and competencies to relate new experiences to prior experiences and to understand things and create meaning. Their learning is integrated while often having a specific focus. For example, during book reading children use their knowledge and thinking abilities, emotional responses, understanding of language, physical skills, and the full range of experiences at home and in the community to make new connections and understand. Children come to preschool as experts about many things—among them, their families, their home language(s), and their belongings. When learning builds on what children know and allows them to expand their skills playfully, they are happy to participate in any learning experience or activity, to recite any rhyme, to count any set, to take on any appropriate new physical challenge. That is why offering children experiences that are personally meaningful and connected is so important. In addition, since children learn using all of their sensory modalities in an integrated way, it is essential to strengthen the modalities with which individual children need special help and build upon their

areas of strength. Integrated learning is further described in the section titled "Curriculum Planning."

Intentional teaching enhances children's learning experiences

Effective curriculum planning occurs when teachers are mindful of children's learning and are intentional in their efforts to support it. In the National Association for the Education of Young Children (NAEYC) publication titled *The Intentional Teacher,* Ann Epstein offers the following description:

> [T]he intentional teacher . . . acts with knowledge and purpose to ensure that young children acquire the knowledge and skills (content) they need to succeed in school and in life. Intentional teachers use their knowledge, judgment, and expertise to organize learning experiences for children; when an unexpected situation arises . . . they can recognize a teaching opportunity and are able to take advantage of it, too.[24]

With an understanding of early learning and development, the teacher supports learning in areas identified by California's preschool learning foundations. The intentional teacher is flexible in order to accommodate differences in children's learning strengths and needs. Intentional teaching strategies span from planning learning environments, experiences, and routines to spontaneous responses suggested by the moment-to-moment focus of the children.

Family and community partnerships create meaningful connections

Strong connections with families grow from respecting and valuing the diverse views, expectations, goals, and understandings that families have for their children. Programs demonstrate respect

Relationships are central.
Play is a primary context for learning.
Learning is integrated.
Intentional teaching enhances children's learning experiences.
Family and community partnerships create meaningful connections.
Individualization of learning includes all children.
Responsiveness to culture and language supports children's learning.
Time for reflection and planning enhances teaching.

Eight Overarching Principles

for families by partnering with them to exchange information about their children's learning and development and to share ideas about how to support learning at home and at preschool. Partnerships with families extend to the community where the families live, come together, and support one another. Building connections to the surrounding community allows a program to become known and make use of community resources. Getting to know the community also gives teachers insights into the learning experiences and competencies that children bring to the preschool setting and informs efforts to make preschool meaningful and connected for children.

Individualization of learning includes all children

Each child is unique. Preschool teachers use their understanding of each child's blend of temperament, family and cultural experiences, language experiences, personal strengths, interests, abilities, and dispositions to support the child's learning and development. By recognizing and adapting to each child's individual development, teachers are able to offer learning experiences that

are meaningful, connected, and developmentally attuned to each child. Creating an environment in which all children feel welcome is important. When children with disabilities or other special needs are included, the partnership with families is especially important. The family is the primary bridge between the preschool staff and special services the child may be receiving.

The family, teacher, and other program staff can team together and include other specialists in the preschool setting. Adapting to an individual child may mean modifying the learning environment to "increase a child's access, potential and availability for learning through thoughtful organization of materials and space."[25] Specifically designed professional support and development opportunities, as well as specialized instructional strategies, can help teachers deliver individualized education and care to meet the needs of all the children in a program.

Responsiveness to culture and language supports children's learning

Responsive preschool programs create a climate of respect for each child's culture and language when teachers and other program staff partner and regularly communicate with family members. They work to get to know the cultural strengths each child brings to preschool. An essential part of being culturally and linguistically responsive is to value and support each child's use of home language, for "continued use and development of the child's home language will benefit the child as he or she acquires English."[26] Equally important are nurturing interactions with children and their families in which "teachers attempt, as much as possible, to learn about the history, beliefs, and practices of the children and families they serve."[27] In addition to being responsive to the cultural history, beliefs, values, ways of communicating, and practices of children and families, teachers create learning environments that include resources such as pictures, displays, and books that are culturally rich and supportive of a diverse population, particularly the cultures and languages of the children and families in their preschool setting.[28, 29] Community members also add to the cultural richness of a preschool setting by sharing their art, music, dance, traditions, and stories.

Time for reflection and planning enhances teaching

Preschool teachers are professionals who serve an important role in society. In nurturing the development of young children, teachers engage in an ongoing process of observation, documentation and assessment, reflection and planning, and implementation of strategies in order to provide individualized and small group learning experiences. As increasing numbers of children with diverse backgrounds, including children with disabilities, participate in preschool programs, collaboration, teaming, and communication are essential to extend the benefits of preschool to all children. Curriculum planning requires time for teachers to reflect on children's learning and to plan strategies that foster children's progress in building knowledge and mastering skills. Preschool programs that support intentional teaching allocate time in teachers' schedules to allow them to reflect and plan both individually and as a team. With appropriate support, teachers are able to grow professionally through a continuous process of learning together and exploring ways to be responsive to young children's learning interests and needs.

Organization of the Framework

This preschool curriculum framework builds on the *California Preschool Learning Foundations, Volume 3*, which describes the knowledge and skills that preschool children typically demonstrate with appropriate support in the following two domains:

- History–social science
- Science

In this introduction, curriculum planning for these domains is presented in an integrated manner. Within this integrated approach to planning learning activities and environments, each specific domain is the focus of a chapter. Each chapter provides a look at integrated curriculum through the lens of the particular domain addressed by that chapter. For example, chapter 3, "Science," highlights how promoting the use of different forms of communication to record and document information may include encouraging children to create a representation by drawing, making a three-dimensional model, or taking a photo. While learning how to record scientific information, children will also practice their developing skills related to the Visual Arts strand of the Visual and Performing Arts domain as well as the Measurement strand of the Mathematics domain. Information on strategies to support children's learning may appear in more than one domain chapter because the same strategy or similar strategies apply to multiple areas of growth and development. In essence, this curriculum framework is designed to allow the reader to examine the breadth and depth of each domain in the context of integrated learning.

The domain chapters begin with an overview of principles and strategies for supporting preschool children's learning, and of the environments and materials that promote learning. Each domain is divided into strands that define its scope. In each chapter, the strands are introduced and followed by a "Bringing It All Together" vignette, an "Engaging Families" section to support home–school connections, and a "Questions for Reflection" section to encourage teacher reflection.

Each strand is further divided into substrands. Each substrand section includes:

- a brief overview of the substrand;
- sample interactions and strategies (e.g., conversations, activities, experiences, routines) for helping children make progress in the specific area of learning identified by the substrand;
- vignettes that illustrate the strategies in action. (It is important to note that the interactions illustrated by the vignettes might take place in any language; individual children would appropriately engage in such communication using their home language.)

The sample strategies range from spontaneous to planned. Some sample strategies focus on how teachers build on children's interests during interaction and instruction; some rely on planning and teacher initiation; and others reflect a combination of teacher planning and spontaneous responses to children's learning. Taken together, they offer a range of ways in which early childhood educators can support children's learning and development. The sample strategies are intended to include a broad range of teaching approaches and to reflect a variety of ways to address the individual needs of a diverse group of children. However, the sample strategies are neither exhaustive nor meant to be used as recipes to follow. Rather, they are starting points, or springboards, for teachers as they plan and implement their own strategies. It is noteworthy that some strategies for one domain can just as easily be used to support learning in another domain.

The fact that many strategies overlap across domains reflects the integrated nature of young children's learning. For example, in chapter 2, there is a recommendation on page 83 to listen to children's narrative descriptions to support the development of children's sense of time. This strategy includes inviting children to talk about past and current experiences and then expanding on children's initial statements with descriptive language. Of course, encouraging children to create narrative descriptions would also promote language and literacy learning and social–emotional development. In addition, inviting children to illustrate their narrative descriptions would foster learning in the Visual and Performing Arts domain. The possibilities for a strategy designed to support learning in one domain to lead to learning in other domains are endless. Part of the art of teaching is to discover possible connections between domains and then to use those insights to guide children through integrated learning experiences.

Each domain chapter includes "Teachable Moments" to address the balance between planning for children's learning and being spontaneous and responsive when a child or a small group of children may be absorbed with solving a problem, excited about a new idea, or show emerging understanding of a concept. Planning creates the context for teachable moments. Therefore, this framework offers information on "Planning Learning Opportunities" in various places.

Intentional teaching includes planning interactions, activities, environments, and adaptations. Teachers plan such learning opportunities based on what they learn from the children's families and their observations and assessments of children. When teachers plan learning opportunities, they anticipate how the children might respond. But the plan needs to be flexible to allow the teacher to be responsive to how the children actually engage in learning. The teacher observes the children and listens for the teachable moments made possible by the plan.

English-Language Development and Learning in All Domains

The English-language development foundations and recommended curriculum strategies address the need to give additional focused support to preschool children whose home language is not English. Chapter 5 in volume 1 of the preschool curriculum framework states a reality: "Children who are learning English as a second language form a substantial and growing segment of the preschool population in California served by state child development programs."[30] Children's progress with learning English varies greatly from child to child. Some children enter preschool with practically no prior experience with English. Other children have some experience with English but still do not possess the basic competence necessary to demonstrate knowledge and skills outlined in other domains when the curriculum is provided mainly in English. And there are other children who are learning English as a second language who may be fairly sophisticated in their understanding and use of English.

Given the great variation among children who are learning English as a second language in preschool, their knowledge and skills in the English-language development domain are described at the *beginning, middle,* and *later* levels. In other words, the English-language development foundations reflect a continuum of second-language (English) learning regardless of an individual child's age. This continuum shows that children who are learning English while simultaneously developing their home-language abilities use their knowledge and skills in their first language to continue to make progress in all other domains. Children who are English learners also vary greatly in the level of proficiency in their first language—which, in turn, influences their progress in English-language development.

In an integrated curriculum, the key to supporting all children is to plan learning activities and environments based on an ongoing understanding of each child's interests, needs, and family and cultural experiences. For young children who are learning English, this approach means focused attention to each child's unique experiences in acquiring a second language and an understanding of how to use a child's first language to help her understand a second language. In applying an integrated approach, teachers take advantage of every moment to provide children with opportunities to communicate with greater understanding and skill while engaged in play or in adult-guided learning activities. The curriculum framework for English-language development is based on a number of key considerations for supporting children learning English in preschool settings. The chief considerations are are as follows.

1. Children who are learning English as a second language possess a home language on which effective teaching strategies can be based.
2. Children who are learning English as a second language may demonstrate language and literacy knowledge and skills in their home language before they demonstrate the same knowledge and skills in English.
3. Children who are learning English as a second language may need additional support and time to make progress in all areas that require English knowledge and skills; therefore, the English-language development curriculum framework presents strategies to support children who are learning English in particular ways so that teachers can both provide scaffolding for children's learning experiences and utilize multiple modes of communication (e.g., nonverbal cues).
4. The English-language development foundations and curriculum recommendations focus mainly on language and literacy learning, because that learning is, by nature, language-specific; in addition, children who are learning English will demonstrate competence in other domains in their home language (e.g., history–social science and science).
5. An intentional focus on the process of learning English as a second language is necessary at all times in an integrated approach to curriculum in early care and education settings.

The level of additional support and the amount of time English learners need to demonstrate the knowledge and skills described by the foundations in domains such as history–social science and science will be influenced by the children's development in both their first language and English. The language the child speaks at home as well as the amount of rich experience the child has in the home

- allow children to participate voluntarily;
- create opportunities for interaction and play with peers.

Children need to feel comfortable with everyone in the preschool setting and with use of their home language and nonverbal communication to express themselves while learning and trying to use English. As volume 1 of the *California Preschool Curriculum Framework* states: "Language is a tool of communication used in all developmental domains. Children who are English learners need to be supported not only in activities focused on language and literacy, but across the entire curriculum."[31] All children, particularly children at the *beginning* and *middle* levels of English-language acquisition, may show knowledge and skills in other domains, such as the visual and performing arts or mathematics, using their home language. The preschool Desired Results Developmental Profile (DRDP) is an assessment instrument that recognizes this possibility by considering children's demonstration of knowledge and skills in their home language as evidence of developmental progress.[b]

language will likely affect the amount and type of support the child needs. For example, if a child's home language and culture include learning traditional stories at an early age, the child may understand and use concepts of time in the home language. This experience may foster history–social science learning in the preschool program. Likewise, talking in the home language with a parent or grandparent about growing vegetables in a garden may later help a child participate in a science project introduced by a preschool teacher. Depending on the experiences individual children have outside of the preschool program, they may make progress with some foundations earlier than with other foundations. For example, older preschool children may need additional time to make progress in learning scientific vocabulary such as *observe, predict, measure,* and *experiment.*

The California Department of Education's DVD titled *A World Full of Language: Supporting Preschool English Learners* emphasizes that a climate of acceptance and belonging is an important starting point for providing additional support to children who are learning English as a second language. In effective programs, intentional efforts:

- focus on the children's sense of belonging and need to communicate;

---

b. It is important to use the appropriate Desired Results instrument. For children who are typically developing, the Desired Results Developmental Profile (DRDP) is the appropriate assessment instrument (visit http://www.wested.org/desiredresults/ for more information). For children with disabilities receiving preschool special education services, the appropriate instrument is determined by the Individualized Education Program (IEP) team, which includes the family and the child's preschool teacher. All three-, four-, and five-year-old children with an IEP who receive preschool services, regardless of instructional setting, must be assessed using either the DRDP or the DRDP *access,* which is an alternative version of the DRDP with measures that have an expanded range for assessing preschool-age children with disabilities. Visit http://draccess.org/ for more information.

Because first- and second-language development varies among English learners, the English-language development foundations and the language and literacy foundations are to be used in tandem with the curriculum framework. It is recommended that, when planning curriculum for all areas of learning, teachers begin by reading and considering the English-language development foundations and the curriculum framework guidance as they gauge each child's current comprehension and use of English. Teachers then develop a plan for how to integrate and use the suggested activities or strategies to support areas of learning that take into consideration the diversity of English learners. As described in the English-language development foundations, intentional teaching requires an ongoing awareness of the home-language development of each child and the English learner's ability to use English in activities suggested in the other chapters of the *California Preschool Learning Foundations, Volume 3*.

Universal Design for Learning

The guidance in this preschool curriculum framework applies to all young children in California, including children with disabilities or other special needs. In some cases, preschool children with disabilities or other special needs demonstrate their developmental progress in diverse ways. Recognizing that children follow different pathways to learning, this framework incorporates a concept known as *universal design for learning*. Universal design provides for multiple means of representation, multiple means of expression, and multiple means of engagement.[32] *Multiple means of representation* refers to providing information in a variety of ways so the learning needs of all children are met. For example, it is important to speak clearly to children with auditory disabilities while also presenting information visually, such as with objects and pictures.

Multiple means of expression refers to allowing children to use alternative ways to communicate or demonstrate what they know or what they are feeling. For example, when a teacher seeks a verbal response, a child may respond in any language, including American Sign Language. A child with special needs who cannot speak may also respond by pointing, by gazing, by gesturing, by using a picture system of communication, or by any other form of alternative or augmented communication system.

Multiple means of engagement refers to providing choices in the setting or program that facilitate learning by building on children's interests. The information in this curriculum framework has been worded to incorporate multiple means of representation, expression, and engagement.

Although this curriculum framework presents some ways of adapting or modifying an activity or approach, it cannot offer all possible variations to ensure that a curriculum meets the needs of a particular child. Of course, the first and best source of information about any child is the family. Additionally, there are several resources available to support inclusive practice for young children with disabilities or other special needs. The resources, Web sites, and books listed in the *California Preschool Curriculum Framework, Volume 1*, appendix D, are recommended for teachers' use.

Curriculum Planning

Curriculum planning to support children as active meaning makers

Preschool children possess an amazing capacity to organize vast amounts of information. When we watch a preschooler alone in play, in play with friends, or engaged in a conversation, we see a mind actively working to make meaning.

Preschool children experience the world and build knowledge in an integrated manner, during simple moments of play and interaction with objects and with other people. They constantly gather information and strive to make sense of it. Their minds take in words, numbers, feelings, and the actions and reactions of people, creatures, and objects and integrate new information into an increasingly complex system of knowledge. Effective curriculum for young children

engages their active minds and nurtures their enthusiastic search for meaning and understanding.

Integrated curriculum

Research studies clearly show that young children construct ideas, concepts, and skills within everyday moments of play and interaction with others. For young children, learning is a *dynamic* process that happens whenever young children encounter the world around them. Young children actively, purposefully, and energetically seek to figure out what new objects and materials are like and how they work. Play involves children's dynamic push to discover, to uncover, to figure out, and to make sense of the world. Play deserves careful consideration, because play and learning often mean the same thing. Indeed, play can be a rich context in which children construct ideas, skills, and concepts. During play, children discover and integrate new ideas, refine their thinking, and master emerging skills. Observing children at play is similar to observing scientists at work—children analyze, design, test, experiment, and negotiate ideas and strategies in order to figure out new and better ways of doing something.

Imagine four young children who are eager and engaged in play amidst an assortment of wooden blocks. They may appear to be "just playing"; however, upon closer inspection, this moment of play reveals a web of ideas, hypotheses, and theories under construction, as well as an energetic debate. The children are negotiating how to connect the blocks to make roads that will surround their carefully balanced block structure. The structure has walls of equal height, which support a flat roof. There are 10 towers, built with cardboard tubes. Resting on each tube is a shiny, recycled jar lid, each one a different color. Two children are figuring out between themselves when to add or take away blocks in order to make a row of towers that increases in height. To anyone who listens and watches, it is evident that the children are building a foundation for addition and subtraction. To make each wall just high enough to support a flat roof, they count aloud the number of blocks they are using for each wall, showing an emerging understanding of the math concept of cardinal numbers. When they hear the signal that lunch is about to be served, one child finds a clipboard with pen and paper attached, draws a rudimentary outline of the block structure on the paper, and then asks the teacher to write, "Do not mess up. We are still working on our towers."

In this moment of play, children explore concepts that are foundational to math, science, literacy, language, the arts, and history–social science. For example, they are building concepts of number, quantity, pattern, equality, print, representation, and conflict negotiation. The learning is integrated, purposeful, and self-motivated, with children developing important skills in a project they initiated. With thoughtful planning, and by observing and listening

to the children's play, teachers set the stage for this learning. As part of curriculum planning, the teachers made sure that the block area was well organized and stocked with engaging materials. As a result, the block area holds its usual basic inventory of materials, but it also holds objects such as cardboard tubes, recycled jar lids of different colors, and a clipboard with pen and paper that are new and challenging to the current group of children, to provoke more complex ideas and theories and thereby support integrated learning.

Children learn many concepts and skills within purposeful play and projects. As stated earlier, play is a guiding principle for early childhood teaching and learning. Curriculum for young children means teaching in a way that supports them in building concepts and skills in an integrated way as they gather information, experiment with it, and confront problems within the natural course of play and interaction with others. Rather than being a series of fact-filled lessons, each intended to teach a specific skill or concept, effective curriculum for young children supports their natural, inquisitive nature as they investigate the surrounding world. For example, young children are eager to investigate language—how it works and the power it holds to engage others. They explore art media with rapt attention—diving in to explore the unique physical properties of each medium (e.g., pencils, paint, or clay)—and begin to figure out what they can do with each one. With the eagerness of a scientist, they explore and experiment with objects from both the natural world and the physical world. With a passion no less intense than that of a debate team, they exchange ideas and strategies with others and orchestrate increasingly more elaborate pretend play with peers and

adults. Children's play reflects the foundations of each academic content area: history–social science, science, visual and performing arts, physical development, health, language and literacy, and math. In the early childhood period, children construct their knowledge by forging new connections in the brain that hold ideas, skills, and concepts related to multiple academic disciplines.

To support young children's learning, teachers may use a variety of strategies (e.g., interactions, **scaffolding**, explicit instruction, modeling, demonstration, changes in the environment and materials, and adaptations, which are especially important for children with disabilities).[33] By adapting the physical environment, the materials, and the planned activities, teachers support individual children's strengths and abilities and guide their learning. For example, to support the learning of a child who relies on a wheelchair for mobility, teachers check to make sure the classroom furnishings are arranged so that the child always has clear pathways and access to all interest areas and that the tables and shelving are set up to allow the child to see, reach, explore, and manipulate all the learning materials. Only when teachers provide such adaptations do all children enjoy equal access to the play materials

and the opportunity to actively construct ideas and skills with other children.

Integrated curriculum sometimes begins with a project or an investigation that has a specific focus of interest and that draws together the children, their families, and the teachers in pursuing this interest. A project or an investigation holds possibilities for children to develop ideas and skills related to multiple academic disciplines. For example, as children gather materials for a project, they might use their emerging concepts of number and quantity. Or during the project, teachers might invite children to dictate stories about what occurred, giving children a chance to tell a story in a sequence and to experience print, letters, and words. Children might also create and solve problems in the project, negotiating complex ideas with the help of others—an early lesson in history–social science, for example. The following vignette from a class of children ranging from three to five years of age illustrates integrated curriculum in a project that extends over time. This vignette recounts how children make evident to the teachers their ideas, concepts, and skills that relate to the history–social science domain and how the teachers document children's ways of exploring and making sense of the experiences.

Teachers Josh and Connie decided to build on an issue that had arisen with children in the prior year. Connie had witnessed a conversation between two girls, each of whom had donned long, ruffled dress-up gowns in the pretend play area. The two girls were talking animatedly about being princesses as they selected their gowns. One girl had light skin and straight blonde hair, and the other had dark-brown skin and short, black, curly

dent at length, noting in this and similar conversations how children were constructing ideas about themselves and others that had the potential of either supporting or undermining issues of fairness and mutual respect. They began to see that, within such exchanges, the children were trying to figure out, through pretend play, the range of attitudes, values, and beliefs that influenced everyday encounters with others. Josh and Connie acknowledged that beliefs and attitudes about others surfaced in the children's play in ways that they could not always anticipate. They wondered how they could help the children in their class think about values and beliefs concerning diversity of skin color, language spoken, or attitudes that resulted in judging others simply by their appearance.

hair. The blonde girl said to the dark-haired girl, "You can't be Cinderella! I can be Cinderella, but you can't! You don't look like Cinderella." Her playmate, stunned by this pronouncement, replied indignantly, "I can too be Cinderella!" For a second there was silence as the two girls stared at each other. The girl with dark features, whose friend had denied her the role of Cinderella, looked away, lifted her long, ruffled skirts, and began to step lightly around the playhouse. She said nothing more. After a few minutes, she slipped out of her dress and ventured off to a new play area.

Surprised by this brief exchange, teacher Connie said nothing, but later told co-teacher Josh about what she had seen. She regretted that she had done nothing in the moment and was embarrassed at how awkward she felt as she watched this moment play out. The teachers discussed the inci-

The pattern of enrollment in a preschool often leads to a diverse array of cultures and ethnicities. This diversity provides a rich cultural context that can give rise to much learning for children and adults alike. However, it is not uncommon for children to say things to one another that reflect ideas, assumptions, and beliefs that are inaccurate, unfair, potentially disrespectful, and even hurtful. After several conversations about this observation, the teachers decided to invite the children and their families to participate with them in a project to address some of these sensitive and potentially hurtful issues.

Josh recalled an idea he had studied in one of his early childhood education classes—to use persona dolls with young children. He explained to Connie how they might use a persona doll to develop curriculum to address this issue. Persona dolls—handmade dolls that range in size up to three feet tall—are made with specific features designed to give the doll a chosen identity. The persona doll is also given a name and a story. In this way, children hear about the family with whom the doll lives, her racial or ethnic background, and a few of her likes and dislikes. Josh explained that persona dolls provide a comfortable way to launch conversation topics that might otherwise feel insensitive, awkward, or rude. He recounted several stories about how teachers used persona dolls to support children in learning more about racial, family, linguistic, or ability differences.

Josh and Connie decided to introduce a persona doll to their classroom, with the intention of creating a curriculum project that could offer possibilities for exploring self-identity, the identity of others, empathy, fairness, and conflict resolution. They also looked forward to building their own understanding about how to respond when children (or even teachers) were caught in uncomfortable moments of having said or done something that devalued someone else. They decided on these questions to organize the curriculum project: "How will the children

respond when we invite a persona doll to join our class? How might this experience generate deeper understanding of differences and respect for differences in children? And how might this experience also help teachers and families to discover ways to talk about and to value differences among people, such as race and family customs?"

Josh located a vendor who sold persona-doll kits. He and Connie decided to order the child-size kit that included fabric and patterns for constructing a dark-skinned child with brown eyes and tightly curled black hair. They sent a letter to children's families explaining the persona doll and asking for a volunteer who might be able to sew the doll out of view of the children in the class. One of the children's aunts, a seamstress, agreed to sew the doll, and one of the parents volunteered to weave hair extensions into the doll's hair.

The teachers discussed possibilities for what the doll's name and story would be. They decided to name her Ashia. They also decided that she would be new to the community served by the preschool, that she would be scared about meeting new friends, that she would be from a home in which she currently lives with just one parent—her mother, who is of European American heritage—and that her father lives in his homeland, a small country in Africa. Ashia's story would be that she and her mother recently moved from her father's country and that her father, with whom she communicates regularly, remained behind and is living with his mother, Ashia's grandmother. Ashia misses them both.

Teachers Josh and Connie used a simple question to plan Ashia's introduction to the classroom. On their plan, they wrote, "How will children respond to Ashia's arrival?" The teachers decided to introduce Ashia during a large-group morning circle. Connie, who would be leading the group gathering, held Ashia on her lap as she greeted the arriving children. Josh ushered in the last of the children and then settled at the edge of the group, with video camera in hand, to document children's responses to Ashia. Ashia's face was nestled into Connie's shoulder, and Connie patted Ashia's back gently as the children arrived. When all the children were seated, Connie turned Ashia toward the children and said, "I would like you to meet my new friend. Her name is Ashia. Today is her first day of school, and she is a bit nervous." Estella, one of the four-year-old children, blurted out, "She's not real. She's fake!" Another four-year-old echoed Estella's comment: "She's just a doll. She's fake." Connie looked thoughtfully at Ashia and then asked the two children who had spoken, "Can you tell us why you say she isn't real?" Estella repeated her original claim: "Because she is fake." A nearby child offered, "Because she don't have bones." Connie nodded in reply, "You are giving my question a lot of thought, I can tell, but you know what? She is a real doll, actually a very special real doll to me, and I am hoping she can be real for you, too." Connie continued, "When Ashia's mom dropped her off this morning, she told me that Ashia is very tired and also very scared. Ashia is tired because she and her mother recently moved from a place far away, where she used to live with her mother, her

father, and her grandmother. It was a country in the continent called Africa. To get here they had to take a long plane ride." Joaquin spoke up in excitement, "I was on a plane once. We visited my tia." The teacher smiles at Joaquin and adds, "I remember that. You went to Arizona and were gone for a whole week. It took Ashia and her mom two whole days to travel to California, where we all live and where she and her mother now live." Connie picked up a globe that was sitting behind her on a table. She pointed to California and drew a line with her finger to Arizona, saying, "This is where Joaquin traveled when he went on a plane to see his aunt." She then put her finger back on California and drew a line across the globe until she reached the African continent. "This is how far Ashia and her mom had to travel—a long, long way—so she is still very tired. And do you remember that I said she was sad, too? Well, she made the long trip with her mother, and she had to say good-bye to her father and grandmother, who stayed behind." Grant interjected, "I miss my grandma. She lives far away." Connie smiled at Grant and said, "Sometimes I get sad like that, too, Grant."

Connie scanned the children's faces before continuing, "So some of you know what it feels like to miss someone who is far away. And you know what? Ashia is also nervous, because she had many friends where she used to live, and in our class she doesn't know anyone." Some hands flew up quickly amid a chorus of voices: "I will be her friend." "She can be my friend." "We can take her out to show her the yard. That will make her happy!" Connie reached below her *chair for a backpack and unzipped it, saying, "Since Ashia is missing her home, her mother thought it would be helpful if she could leave some of Ashia's special items in her classroom."*

Connie pulled out a photo of a row of brilliantly colored houses and explained, "These are homes from Ashia's neighborhood where she used to live. If you'd like, we can put this photograph in the block area, and some of you can show her the blocks we have. Maybe you can try to make a house with Ashia that looks like her grandma's home, where she used to live." Next, Connie pulled out a set of four small copper cups. "One, two . . . Wow, there are more! Count with me," she says, slowing down so that the children can join in the count. "Ashia's mom told me that Ashia used to play with these cups at her grandma's house and that her grandma wanted her to take them with her to California. I'm wondering, do you think Ashia might enjoy finding this set of four cups in the playhouse?"

The environment as curriculum: Interest areas to support children's play and child-initiated learning

The play environment of a preschool setting is a primary source for early childhood curriculum. Well-stocked play areas, often called interest areas or activity areas, provide young children with a vast array of possibilities for learning. Driven to explore novel objects, people, and events, young children relate to well-planned play environments just as scientists relate to their laboratories or artists relate to their studios. When teachers thoughtfully organize the space in the setting into small, well-stocked interest areas, young children use such spaces like mini-laboratories or mini-studios. In each interest area, children find both familiar materials and novel materials, the latter added as a way to pique new interest or to add challenge and complexity to the children's learning that is an integral part of their play.

Children enter these play areas and explore what they might do with the easily accessible materials. As children play, they form hypotheses about what they can make the items do. They experiment, invent, and devise theories to make sense of their experiences, all embedded within their play. Play-based interest areas, both indoors and outdoors, each with a distinct focus, are designed to offer a basic inventory of materials with which children can apply emerging skills and develop concepts while they play.

As teachers plan curriculum, they consider ways to provoke more complex and coherent ideas by adding materials to an area. When adapting the curriculum to support all learners, teachers modify the play space or the materials available in the play space to make sure that each child in the program has access. Such ongoing additions and changes to the play spaces are essential to curricu-

lum planning. By thoughtfully planning the interest areas and allocating long periods of uninterrupted time for self-initiated play, teachers provide children with important opportunities to develop many foundational concepts and skills. Examples of interest areas in a preschool environment include the following:

- Dramatic play area
- Block area
- Art area
- Book area
- Writing area
- Math area
- Science area
- Family display area
- Music, movement, and meeting area

The example of the curriculum project of inviting Ashia, the persona doll, to become part of the group can demonstrate other ways that teachers use interest areas to support learning.

The next items Connie pulls from the backpack are several books. "These must be some of Ashia's favorite books." Connie flips through the books, summarizing, "This one looks good. It is about a little girl who lives in her house with her grandma, and she is going to visit her mother who lives in another town. And this one looks like one we want to read, too. It's about a little boy who misses his father who lives far away. How about we put Ashia's books in the book/story area so that she can read them there with her new friends?" Connie pulls a few more things from the backpack: a change of clothes and a long piece of brightly printed cloth. "Okay, she has a change of clothes, but this is something special. Ashia's mother wanted to make sure we knew about this." Connie spreads out the brightly colored cloth. "This is a special

piece of cloth Ashia's mother called a kanga. It is something you wear, like a scarf, and Ashia's grandmother gave it to her. So this cloth is very special to Ashia. Her grandma, her father, and her mother carried her in it when she was a baby. So we will have to find a very special place for this, where Ashia can find it. Maybe she can show you how to use it to carry the baby dolls." Kelly looked concerned, "But she doesn't have a place to put her clothes. She doesn't have a cubby like we do." "You're right," acknowledges Connie, "Maybe after circle time, you can help make a name card that we can put on a cubby for her things."

Daily routines as curriculum

Curriculum plans include ideas for involving children in daily routines and making routines an important context for learning, in general, and for social–emotional development, in particular. Daily routines provide natural opportunities for children to apply emerging skills, take on responsibilities, and cooperate. Teachers integrate engaging learning opportunities into the everyday routines of arrivals, departures, mealtimes, naptimes, handwashing, and setup and cleanup, both indoors and outdoors. Children enthusiastically apply emerging skills as they contribute to carrying out daily routines: for example, when they are helpers who ring the bell to let the other children know to come inside; when they count how many children are ready for lunch; when they move a card with their photo and name from the "home" column to the "preschool" column of a chart near the room entry; when they put their name on a waiting list to paint at the easel; and when they help set the table for a meal, making sure that each place has a plate, utensils, and a cup. Such routines offer opportunities for children to build language skills, to learn the rituals of sharing time with others, and to relate one action in a sequence with another. Over the course of the project with the persona doll Ashia, the teachers look for ways to extend children's learning within the daily routines.

Before the large-group discussion, Connie asked the children for ideas on where Ashia might store her backpack. Ariel suggested that Ashia hang it with the other backpacks on the hooks near the entry. Cody pointed to a low table near the entry area and said, And she could sign in where we do, too." On this low table near the entry, children know they will always find the "sign-in binder" and a ring of cards with the names of all the children. On arrival, children explore making their version of their signatures, similar to what their family members do as they sign in their children. Paloma countered, But Ashia doesn't have a name there! We need to put her name there, so she can find her name, too. And we need to put her picture on her card, too." Connie agreed, saying, "These are good ideas. We will need to take a photograph of Ashia, make a name card for the sign-in book, and put her name and photo by one of the coat hooks. Where else will we need to add her name?"

"Oh, there's one more item here," said Connie, as she pulled out a blue scarf. "When Ashia's mother brought her to school today, she asked that I make sure that Ashia wear this scarf when she is playing in the sandbox. Sand is harmful to Ashia's soft, curly hair. Her mom was hoping each of you could

help her remember to keep her scarf on while playing near sand." Janelle, who has hair bundled into neatly tied braids adorned with beads, much like Ashia's, smiles, saying softly, "I can help her." Connie nods, "Oh, I'm sure Ashia would love that, Janelle." Connie and Josh have frequently heard Janelle's mother reminding her daughter to wear her hat when playing in the sand. "And you know what? Ashia's mom brought a basket of beautiful scarves, in case any of you would like to cover your hair, too, while you are playing in the sandbox." A chorus of excited voices rang out: "I do, I do!" and "I want to use one!" Connie dismissed the group with this comment: "I'll put the basket near the door to the yard, so those who want to put on a scarf before going outside can do so." A few minutes later, to the teachers' surprise, almost every child—boys and girls—had made a beeline to the basket to select a scarf and surrounded a teacher with a request for help in tying the scarf prior to entering the yard.

The scarf basket became a regular part of the transition ritual. Ashia's arrival spawned several other new daily routines. In the writing area, teachers added a low hook, from which hung a clipboard where children could sign up when they wanted a special photo taken with Ashia. They also added two new job cards on the helper chart to designate who would be in charge of helping to take Ashia outside. Each new routine invited the children to use emerging skills. Teachers overheard the following conversation between four-year-olds Alicia and T'syana, whose names were the first to go on the job chart as "Ashia's helpers." Alicia, whose first language is Spanish, handed a scarf to T'syana, who also uses Spanish with her family, saying, "*Venga*, T'syana. Come here." Alicia motioned for teacher Josh to place the scarf on Ashia's head. When he was done, she thrust her scarf into his hand and pointed to her own head. Josh tied a scarf on each girl's head. T'syana grabbed Ashia's left hand, Alicia grabbed the other, and together they walked Ashia outside.

The Daily Schedule

The daily schedule balances child-initiated play and teacher-guided activities. The latter involves teachers planning, introducing, and guiding specific activities to enhance children's learning during small- and large-group times. In contrast, child-initiated play refers to children's responses to ideas and materials introduced by teacher that the children are free to explore without teacher guidance. Child-initiated play also includes those times when children create, organize, and engage in activities completely on their own.

Child-initiated play

In the previous examples, teachers added many new and engaging items to the interest areas—items the teachers hoped might provoke the children's thinking and learning in new directions. These novel materials held possibilities for children to increase their understanding of people, customs, and places that may have been unfamiliar to them. Though introduced by the teachers, the materials encouraged child-initiated play. In essence, they created opportunities for the children to initiate learning on their own. The teachers also made sure that, within the schedule of the day, children had ample time to experiment, invent,

work together with others, and explore ways to incorporate the new materials into their play. A daily schedule that ensures ample time for children to initiate their own play in well-developed interest areas is critical to the teaching and the learning. Young children need ample time to engage in play, in the company of peers, in order to build their ideas, to pose problems, to try out solutions, and to negotiate and exchange ideas. When children initiate, organize, and develop their own play in the interest areas, it is called *child-initiated learning*. At times children choose to play alone, but frequently, child-initiated play takes place in small groups of their own choosing.

The first few weeks after Ashia's entry into the classroom, teachers began to notice how Ashia's presence presented opportunities to explore concepts related to fairness and to engage children in solving problems. One day, teacher Josh observed the following scene as a small group of children played in the housekeeping area. He wrote an account in order to share it later with Connie.

Ashia was seated in the rocking chair. Josiah picked up two baby dolls and announced, "This one's for me, and this one's for you, Ashia." Josiah placed one of the dolls on Ashia's lap. When he turned around and began to take some pretend food items from the cupboard, Thomas walked over to Ashia and removed the doll from Ashia's lap. Angelica, who up to this point had been watching and not engaged in the play, reached out with her arm toward Thomas. Angelica, who has a hearing loss and who signs to communicate, extended her palm in front of Thomas in a gesture for him to stop. Thomas handed Angelica the doll, and she immediately placed it back in Ashia's arms.

Josh added this brief interpretation to his note: "Angelica saw herself as part of the play and conveyed her intention very clearly to Thomas. Thomas responded, without argument, to her request. This was a big step for him, as he did not resist her request nor try to maintain hold of the doll. This is a good example of both Angelica and Thomas displaying how they are learning to resolve a conflict and share materials."

Teacher-guided activities in small groups

In a schedule with ample time for children to initiate play in well-stocked interest areas, there are times when teachers organize and guide specific activities for children. Such teacher-guided curriculum activities are clearly distinct from child-initiated curriculum activities. Teacher-guided activities occur in two contexts—small groups and large groups. A small group would consist of one teacher working with a group of four to eight children. A large group is typically a gathering of all the children in an early childhood setting. Each context serves a different purpose and requires different preparation and different teaching strategies.

For some aspects of the curriculum, teachers may choose to organize an activity with a small group of children. Although initiated and guided by the teacher, an effective small-group encounter of this nature should still be rich in possibilities for children to contribute and negotiate ideas with each other. Teacher-guided activities in small groups work best in quiet spaces away from distractions of the full group and provide a manageable context for children to discuss and explore ideas and experiences. The teacher listens to children's ideas, helps orchestrate the give-and-take of ideas among children, and poses ideas or problems for children to wonder about, explore together, or even solve. Away from the distractions of a large group, teachers can easily observe, listen, and converse with children in a small group, as well as note how individual children think, express ideas, relate with others, and use their emerging skills.

Such teacher-guided conversations can enrich children's learning in all domains, particularly the children's language learning and vocabulary development. In addition, teachers can intentionally guide the development of specific skills by planning small-group activities (e.g., songs, games, shared reading) for short periods

of time that playfully engage children in using specific emerging skills—such as sound and sound pattern recognition. In programs that have children who are English learners, small groups can foster learning between children (also known as peer learning). The PEL Resource Guide provides several suggestions for promoting peer learning[34] and for providing individual children with scaffolding that helps them engage in new and more complex thinking.

Small-group activities have several advantages over large-group activities. With small groups of children, teachers can readily observe, listen, and document children's developmental progress. Teachers can also individualize the curriculum and use questions or prompts to scaffold each child's thinking in more complex ways. In the following example, teachers and children who are getting to know the persona doll Ashia engage in a small-group discussion as part of this ongoing project. The conversation itself is a context for curriculum and provides opportunities for children to reveal their ideas and hypotheses.

As they observed children's play with Ashia, teachers Josh and Connie noticed recurring conflicts over who would play with Ashia. These conflicts were much like the disputes that occur when children share real friends. Estella, one of the older girls, had become particularly attached to Ashia. The teachers wondered whether this had something to do with Estella's recent separation from one of her parents. One teacher had overheard Estella saying as she played with Ashia, "Ashia's not talking, because she misses her dad." The teachers were sensitive to the possibility that Estella was linking

her experience with Ashia's. After discussing this together, Connie and Josh decided to look for ways to address Estella's desire to form a special bond with Ashia, but, at the same time, to engage the other children in conversations about how to maintain Ashia's status as a classmate available to all children. Rather than simply bringing up the issue during a large gathering, the teachers decided to plan several small-group conversations about the recurring conflict over possession of Ashia. They wanted to hear the children's ideas about sharing friends and to include the children's ideas for resolving such conflicts.

Connie invited a small group of six children to meet together in a quiet area away from the larger group. She selected children who had either spent a lot of time with Ashia or had verbalized concerns about not having enough time to play with her. Connie gave each child a clipboard with a pencil attached. She explained, "I thought that it might be a good idea for us to talk about our new friend, Ashia. These clipboards are for you to use during our conversation. Sometimes I know you like to draw your ideas or make lists of ideas, like I do. Do some of you remember what happened earlier today in the yard? I remember that Paloma and Jessica were sad because they wanted to spend time with Ashia. Estella was playing with Ashia and told them that they could not play with Ashia because she was still playing with her." Rachel and then Carlos added their own stories of not getting to play with Ashia when they wanted to. Paloma frowned and said, "It's not fair that only Estella holds her." Connie listened to the children and repeated each child's concern: "It sounds like there are a lot of you who want to hold and play with Ashia. How can we make sure that Ashia's time is shared with everyone?" Kelly suggested, "We can make more of her, so she can have real friends, too." Jessica's eyes lit up, and she shouted, Yes! And we can make shoes and socks, too, and more of her."

"These are great ideas," Connie said, "and I brought a book that might help us plan some ways to share Ashia. This story is about two boys who were friends, and they had a problem about how to share a pet toad. I'm thinking that this book might give us some ideas. Would you like me to read it?" The group readily agreed, and Connie recounted the story, after which she commented, "So that is what the boys decided to do. What new ideas do you have about what we might do to share Ashia? I'm going to write down your ideas here on this paper." Kelly suggested again, Make more." Estella turned to her and said emphatically, We can't cut Ashia in two, because she's a person!" The teacher Connie responded, "You bring up a good point, Estella. I'm not sure that's what Kelly meant." Before Kelly had a chance to respond, Carlos interjected, "She can't walk by herself, so she needs lots of us to help her walk around." Connie repeated Carlos' idea as she wrote it on the list and then said, "So, I'm wondering, from what Carlos suggested, one thing that we could do is divide the day into two parts: the morning and the afternoon. Then we could have morning helpers and afternoon helpers for Ashia." Paloma's eyes lit up as she said, "They could be on the job chart! So we can read who is the helper." Con-

nie wrote this down, saying, "Great idea, Paloma. That way, we would know who would be her helper in the morning and who would be her helper in the afternoon. What do the rest of you think?" All agreed to the idea about helpers, so Connie proceeded: "Okay, how about if some of you write Ashia's name on your clipboards? You can follow the letters I've written up here." Connie pointed to where she had written "Ashia" on the large sheet of paper and said the name of each letter as she pointed to it, "A-S-H-I-A. That way we have some names to use for the helper chart. I know some of you have enjoyed signing your own name when you come in, so you might want to help Ashia write her name when she arrives." Carlos watched as others copied the letters in Ashia's name onto their clipboards.

"I'm wondering about another idea, too," said Connie. "What if we take a clipboard and write "Ashia's helper" at the top? And then, if any of you would be interested in signing up to be Ashia's helpers, you could sign your name below. What do you think? Carlos, maybe we could use your clipboard." As the others agreed, Carlos pushed his clipboard toward Connie, who turned it so that Carlos could see her write the letters, again saying each letter as she wrote "Ashia's Helpers." She invited Carlos to be the first to sign. He scribbled a row of circles and then handed the pencil to Connie. Others followed, with some children's names being a simple scribble, others showing the first letter of the child's name followed by a line, and a few showing an attempt to write each letter of the child's name. Connie explained that she would put the list near the helper chart. Before *finishing, she suggested that the small group share the plan with the others during large-group time.*

Whether the activities are child-initiated or teacher-guided, children's use of materials in interest areas provide teachers with excellent opportunities to observe how they build concepts and skills and how they negotiate ideas with others. For example, in the preceding discussion, Connie was able to trace each child's ideas, solutions, and emerging concept of how to sign her or his name. Such moments of observed play and interactions also provide teachers with ideas on how to extend children's exploration and learning through future encounters with related materials that add novelty, challenge, and complexity in each domain.

Teacher-guided activities in large groups

Large groups provide another context for teacher-guided activities. The large group—typically a gathering of the entire class—works well for singing, acting out songs and stories, playing games, sharing experiences with each other, telling stories, building a sense of community, and organizing the daily schedule and activities. Storytelling is one of the more popular large-group experiences, one that has rich potential for adding to children's understanding about the world around them. Storytelling allows teachers, children, family members, as well as storytellers from the community to tap into and build children's knowledge and experiences in meaningful ways. Large-group time is also when teachers let the whole group of children know what new experiences will be available in the interest areas or what will happen in small groups that day. Large-group gather-

ings that occur at the end of day provide opportunities to review noteworthy happenings and to anticipate what will be available the next day. Teachers Connie and Josh used a large-group gathering to keep everyone current on Ashia's experiences in the classroom.

During a large-group gathering, the children who helped to make new cards for adding "Ashia's Helpers" to the job chart shared the new helper cards with the others. Then teacher Josh asked the children, "Remember how Ashia told us that she misses her father, who lives far away? I was wondering, since Ashia misses her father, maybe we could help her make a book that she could send him, with photos and stories about her experiences at school. I brought this book that has lots of empty pages and places for photographs or drawings. What do you think about keeping this book in our book and story area? That way, you can draw pictures or tell stories that we can add to the book." Niko offered, "And maybe we could take pictures of us and Ashia, too." Thomas chimed in: "So her Dad can see who we are, her new friends." A chorus of voices backed this idea. "Sounds like others really like your idea, Niko," continued teacher Josh. "We can use this clipboard for a sign-up sheet to have your photo taken with Ashia. That way, throughout the day, we can take some photos of you and Ashia doing lots of different things at school. I'll write "Sign-up for Ashia Photo" at the top of the paper. Watch to see the letters I use." As Josh wrote, he said each letter name aloud. "Okay, that's ready to go, so when you leave circle, you can find this sign-up sheet in the writing area.

If you need help writing your name, remember to flip through the name cards that have your photos on them. Once you find your name, if you want, you can look at your name as you write it."

The Curriculum-Planning Process

Planning preschool curriculum begins with teachers discovering, through careful listening and observing, each child's developmental progress in each domain. Observation is an essential teaching skill. When teachers mindfully observe, they discover how individual children make meaning within everyday moments of play and interactions, and how they can deepen their relationships with children.[35] Observing for the purpose of gathering evidence of individual children's learning means carefully watching and listening, with thought and reflection. In doing so, teachers find evidence of individual children engaged in making meaning. For example, through a note, a photo, or a sample of a child's work, teachers collect ongoing evidence that can be used periodically during the year when they complete the formal DRDP assessment. In the project in which children invited the persona doll Ashia to become part of their class, the teachers found that children revealed many ideas, concepts, and skills that could serve as evidence of children's developmental progress through the levels of the DRDP. Evidence related to concepts of print, number, language comprehension, self-identity, and problem solving was readily apparent. As teachers Connie and Josh reflected on the meaning of the evidence they had observed and gathered, they decided to offer the children an oppor-tunity to engage in a conversation about differences in skin color, a topic that arose in children's earlier conversations. Ashia's skin tone was a deep brown, her eyes were brown, and her hair was braided with extensions and beads. The teachers wondered whether a chance to make drawings of each other's faces might invite the children to explore, in a respectful, matter-of-fact way, the various skin tones, hair, and facial features of different individuals in the group.

At the large-group gathering, Connie read to the children a book entitled One Like Me, *which has a mirror built into the back cover. After reading the book to the group, Connie peered at herself in the mirror and described herself: "I see that I have wavy red hair and blue eyes, and that my skin is a color kind of like lightly browned toast." Some of the children giggled. Connie looked at teacher Josh, seated in the group, and continued, "And then there's teacher Josh. His hair is a different color than mine, a dark brown, with maybe a tiny bit of dark red. I'd say it is kind of brownish-blackish-reddish." Again, a few giggles. "And if you look closely, his eyes have a different shape from mine. His eyes are like ovals, and mine are also like ovals, but a little rounder. Can you see that?" Isabella, who along with the other children has turned to stare at teacher Josh, announced, "Him are my eyes." Teacher Connie responds, "That's right, Isabella. Both you and Josh have brown eyes. Your eyes are the same color as Josh's. When I look in the mirror and when I look at Josh, or at any of you, I can see how in some ways we look like each other and in some ways we look different. Teacher Josh's eyes are brown, and mine are blue. Josh and I both have short hair, but our eyes are different and our hair is different. How many of you have brown hair, like teacher Josh?" Almost everyone's hand shot up. Niko, seeing three-year-old Isabella raise her hand, declares, "Isabella, your hair is yellow, not brown." Isabella glances down at a strand of her hair and looks up smiling. "You're checking to see, aren't you, Isabella? And your hair is closer to yellow in color, what we call blonde. That's sort of what I was doing, looking at myself in the mirror, so that I could really see what color my eyes and hair are. Would you all like to use some mirrors to look closely at the features of your faces? If so, today, when you are playing, you will find some mirrors on the table in the art area. These are mirrors that stand up. Each mirror has two sides. This way, two friends can sit side by side and use one of the mirrors together to compare your faces, to see how your faces look the same or how they look different. Because some of you may want to draw what you see in the mirror, there is also a basket of pens, along with some paper. Teacher Josh will be there, too, to write down what you discover."*

In the basket on the art table, the teachers placed black pens with thin felt tips. They discovered in prior activities that these pens worked well when their objective was to prompt children to capture the detail in what they were examining. Additionally, they found that color choices were distracting. Before dismissing the group, Connie asked, "Let's look at the helper chart. Who is Ashia's helper this morning? Can you tell?" Clayton, seeing his name near the photo of Ashia,

thrust his arm into the air. Connie nodded, "That's right, Clayton, you're Ashia's helper. Clayton, can you bring Ashia to the art table so she can look in the mirror, too?"

As teachers observe children's play and interactions, children reveal evidence of their emerging skills and ideas. Such evidence, recorded as a written observation or a photo, is used in a child's portfolio to demonstrate developmental progress. As teachers observe children's play and interactions, they also discover ways to extend experiences in order to support children in building more complex and coherent ideas. Ideas for next steps in curriculum planning emerge as teachers reflect on how they might expand children's thinking, language, and interactions. From ongoing cycles of mindful observing, listening, documenting, and reflecting on what might come next, teachers not only gather evidence of children's progress in learning but also generate curriculum plans.

Observe, reflect, document

Observation means being present with children and attentive as they play and interact with others and the environment. This mindful presence is different from participating in children's play or direct-

The Reflective Curriculum Planning Process

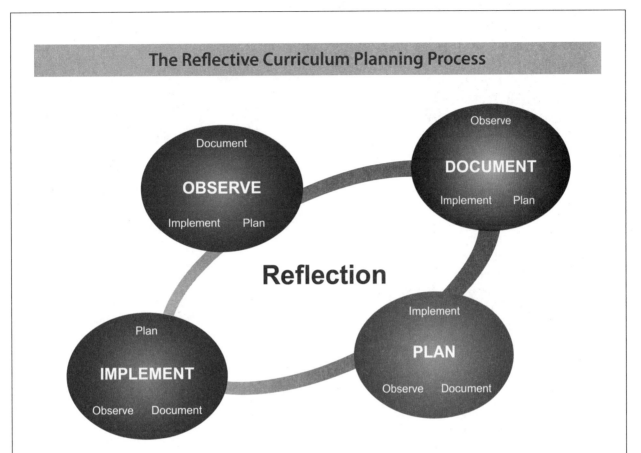

ing their play. Whether for one minute or five, a mindful and attentive presence means waiting to see what unfolds in order to gain a complete picture of children's play. A teacher who observes children as a first step in supporting learning discovers small scientists at work—they experiment, compare, make assumptions, form theories about what things are like or what they can do, test ideas, and, over time, build mastery of a wide range of concepts and skills. What follows are excerpts from Josh's notes as he watched the children use mirrors and explore concepts in the art area.

Paloma, Clayton, Estella, and Jessica sit around the table. Each child has her or his own mirror. At first, each explores her or his own image, showing little interest in looking at someone else's image. Jessica turns her face to the left and then to the right and zooms up close to the surface of the mirror. After repeating this action several times, she announces to the others, "I see two of me and two pairs of eyes." She then points in the mirror and counts, "One, two, three, four," and then she smiles before saying, "I have four eyes!'" After about six minutes of play, I [teacher Josh] mention, "Don't forget that the pens and paper are here in case you want to draw what you see." In response, Estella and Paloma reach for pens and paper. Estella looks in the mirror once, but then draws a face without looking in the mirror again. Paloma glances frequently at her image in the mirror, sometimes spending time making faces to change the image she sees. Clayton watches as Paloma draws. I propose, "Let's look in the mirror together, Clayton. What do you see?" Clayton shrugs his shoulders but gazes steadily at his image. "When you look at your face in the mirror, do you see anything that looks like a long circle, a shape called an oval?" I sketch a small oval in my notes and lay my notes near him to see. Clayton draws a long, slightly irregular oval on his sheet of paper. "Okay, look again in the mirror, Clayton. What else do you see?" Clayton puts his finger on his nose and says quietly, "My nose." "So, when you look at your nose, Clayton, do you see two long lines, one on each side? Or how about any small circles?" Clayton brings a finger to each nostril and then touches his reflection in the mirror. "Do you want to put those little circles on your drawing?" He draws two small circles on his oval. "Now where would you put two long lines? When you look in the mirror, do you see two long lines along the side of your nose?" Clayton looks at his drawing for about 30 seconds and then slowly moves the pencil in a long line up from the nostrils he has drawn, and then repeats this with a line parallel to the first.

Documentation means gathering and holding evidence of children's play and interests for future use. A common form of documentation in early childhood settings is a written note, often referred to as an observation anecdote. Anecdotal notes, along with other forms of documentation—photos, video recordings, and work samples—serve a dual purpose. First, they hold memories of a teacher's observations of children's expressions of feelings, thinking, and learning. Documentation can provide a useful guide as teachers determine what might be the next steps in day-to-day curriculum plan-

ning. Second, anecdotal notes and other evidence can be used to support a teacher's periodic assessment of a child's progress toward reaching competencies measured by the DRDP. In the small-group activity in which children were invited to draw their own faces, teacher Josh had several reasons for wanting to write down what had happened in a clear, vivid note. He wanted to capture children's ideas and thoughts in order to guide the next steps in planning this project. He also heard that, in what the children said and did, they were revealing evidence of how they were figuring things out or how they were applying an emerging concept or skill. In this way, the documentation—his notes, photos, and the children's drawings—supported curriculum planning. It also provided evidence for ongoing assessment of the children's developmental progress, which also informed curriculum planning.

Reflect, discuss, plan

As teachers reflect together on observational notes, photos, or samples of children's work, they discuss ideas for possible next steps in the curriculum—that is, ways to sustain and add complexity to children's learning. Documentation can also be used to engage the children's families in reflecting on the children's learning. Teachers might also decide to share the notes, photos, or work samples with the children, as a way to engage them in thinking about what the children might do next.

Josh told the children that he would save their drawings so that they could return to them another day and add some colors to them. When he and Connie met to review the documentation, they reflected on how the children were revealing their thoughts and ideas. Josh noted Estella's accurate use of the term "pair" and her proclamation of "four" as the quantity she saw in the mirror and suggested that a copy of this note be placed in her portfolio. They also decided to place a copy of Clayton's drawing, along with Josh's notes, in his portfolio, since Clayton previously had shown little interest in drawing. Josh and Connie studied the drawings to see if they could see any of the children's unique facial features. The teachers decided that their next plan would be to invite this same small group of children to an experience in which they would return to their drawings, but this time the available materials would include colored pencils selected to match the variety of hair, skin, and eye colors in this group of four children.

Documentation serves as a springboard for coming up with possibilities for exploring more deeply a topic that has engaged the interest of the children, the teachers, and the families. Further exploration might include, among other things, materials to add to interest areas, related books to read in either large- or small-group gatherings, or activities for small groups. With clear ideas or objectives in mind, teachers plan curriculum that includes strategies to enhance the learning of all children in a group, as well as strategies to support the learning of individual children. The experience of inviting the persona doll Ashia to join the group of children presented many opportunities for teachers to plan and implement curriculum prepared for the whole group and curriculum individualized for specific children.

In each case, the curriculum came out of a process of observing, listening, reflecting, documenting, discussing ideas, planning, and implementing, which, in turn, launched another cycle of observing and listening in order to find out what children did in response. In the example of offering colored pencils, teachers planned a follow-up experience to suggest new problems and new challenges that might add complexity to the children's ideas and understanding.

Implement

Once a plan is written, teachers implement it, but the planning continues even after an activity or experience is under way. As children encounter a teacher-prepared activity or initiate their own plan with the materials placed in an interest area, the teachers watch to find out how children respond to the materials they have prepared. In doing so, teachers observe, reflect, and document once again. Curriculum planning is a continuous cycle, as teachers watch to discover how children respond to the planned curriculum and how children show evidence of their developing skills and concepts during the planned learning encounters.

Several days after the first drawings were made using the mirrors, Connie invited this same group of children to a small-group activity. She kept the group small because she wanted to be available to guide each child in looking at her or his reflection and to try to figure out which colored pencil would work best to match actual skin, eye, or hair color. At the table, children found their original line drawings, along with a basket of flesh-colored pencils, which Josh and Connie had carefully selected to represent the spectrum of skin colors of children in the setting. "Remember when you drew your face? And remember how I asked you to let me keep your drawings so you could work on them later and, if you wanted, add some color to your drawings? Well, I collected an assortment of colored pencils and brought back the mirrors, so that you can look at yourselves again and decide what colors to use to make your skin color, eye color, and hair color. What do you think? Would you like to try finding the colors that match the colors in your face?" The children all nodded, but none reached for a pencil, so Connie added, "For example, here are the colors that I am guessing might be close to the color of my skin: a little light brown, perhaps a little of this pink, and maybe even a little of this light yellow. I need all three because I have freckled skin."

Paloma, who had brought Ashia to the table and set her in the chair next to her, announced, "Ashia's going to draw with me." Paloma immediately began to add another face next to the one she had drawn earlier. "This is me and Ashia." She then began to flip through the colored pencils. "Here the one for Ashia's hair." She picked out a charcoal black and added circles of hair to the face she had just drawn. "So, if that's for her hair, which one is the best match for her skin color?" asked Connie. "There are lots to

choose from here, many shades of browns and blacks, and each one has a different name. It's written on the side, so I can read you the name when you pick one out." Kelly reaches for a charcoal colored pencil and hands it to Paloma, saying, "She needs this one." Paloma had already picked out a deep brown tint and began to use it to color Ashia's face. She frowns at Kelly, saying, "Not that one, this is the one. I already picked it." She looks at Kelly and then adds, "Okay, she can be two pencils, like teacher Connie is. But this one," she continued, pointing to a light brown pencil, tucked under her arm, "is for her eyes, just like mine."

As with every phase in the planning cycle, teachers do well to approach this one with a sense of wonder, for they may be surprised and amazed by what children actually do as they engage with the materials or activity. To hold in memory significant parts of what they observe, teachers record notes, take a photo, or keep a work sample, labeling and noting the date on each one. They can review these documents later, along with parents and even with the children, as a way to assess the impact of the curriculum plans, to generate plans to further support children's learning, and to assess individual children's learning. For example, during such discussions, the following questions might be considered:

- Are children responding as we had predicted, or were there surprises?
- What do the children's responses tell us? How might we name the children's interests or intentions? What concepts and ideas are the children forming within their play?
- How might children who are learning English collaborate in small groups

with children who already speak English in order to learn from one another?

- How are the children showing evidence of progress related to the measures of the DRDP?

Partnering with families in curriculum planning

When teachers share with the children's families documentation of the children's experiences and learning, they invite the families to reflect together with teachers on children's learning and ideas for expanding the curriculum. Family members offer unique insights and provide important suggestions for curriculum development. They also help teachers understand their expectations, values, and beliefs that influence children's behavior and ideas.

During the small-group, face-drawing activity, Clayton was picking out pencils for his skin color when his mother arrived to pick him up. She knelt near the table as Connie read the name printed on the colored pencil that Clayton had selected. "This one says 'sienna brown.' What do you think, Clayton?" Connie asked, as she moved the tip of the pencil near his arm. "Is that your color?" Clayton smiled at his mother, "I'm sienna brown, mommy. Which one do you want to be?" A few minutes later, when Clayton was retrieving his things from his cubby, his mother confided in Connie how much she had enjoyed picking out her skin color with Clayton. She had been uncertain about how to talk with Clayton about skin color, because she was of European–American background and Clayton's father was African American, and most of the family members living nearby were Caucasian. They

discussed the possibility of doing an activity at the next parent meeting in which all the parents could explore the variety of flesh-toned colored pencils and even to blend different tints of homemade play dough that they could take home to enjoy with their children.

Discussions about projects—among teachers and with children's families—add much to the curriculum plans. Such discussions become a conduit for the exchange of resources and ideas, from home to school and from school to home. Curriculum projects that are planned together with families help to connect children's home and community experiences and their experiences at school.

Connections: A fertile ground for making meaning

The curriculum project involving the persona doll (Ashia) illustrates how teachers can help children connect with and learn about the world around them. Such project-oriented curriculum also gives children an opportunity to apply

emerging skills and concepts—what will become the foundation for language, literacy, science, history–social science, mathematics, physical development, health knowledge and skills, and the arts—within activities that are meaningful to them. When teachers plan curriculum to support children in constructing more complex ideas about experiences that genuinely interest them, young children build connections in their rapidly developing brains.

Young children's experiences at home, with their families, and in their communities are a powerful source of meaningful connections that support their learning. Curriculum for young children does not reside solely within the walls of the early childhood environment. Teachers and children's families work together to create curriculum. Teachers nurture in the children a desire to know more about the world around them, and they nurture in the children's family members a desire to join in as participants in developing ideas for curriculum. When a dynamic exchange of ideas and information occurs between home and school, a curriculum emerges that is tailored to the community and responsive to the history, interests, and values of the families and their cultures.

In response to conversations with children about where Ashia had lived prior to coming to the school, Connie and Josh decided to post a world map in the classroom. During large-group time, Josh put a sticky note to show where the school is and the community where Ashia and her mother now live. Then he put another sticky note on the spot where Ashia's father and grandmother live. This generated discussion about short distances and long distances between places.

When several children said they had relatives far away, Connie and Josh decided to invite families to be part of the experience and placed a note near the map, with a basket of sticky notes and a written request, asking the families to tell where some of their family members live.

Children bring much knowledge with them from their home and their community when they walk through the doors of a preschool program. For example, children may come to preschool with knowledge of many stories that come out of their family experiences. Their teachers may observe the children reenacting these stories in the dramatic play area or outdoors in the play yard. However, these stories remain unrecorded until teachers invite children to narrate them so that the teacher can put them in print. Once a child's story is put in print, the child comes to see himself as an author, one whose story can be read and re-read to others. Stories can generate a wealth of possibilities for teachers, family members, and children to partner together in documenting what goes on in their lives, both at home and at school. Whatever the topic under study in a project or investigation, story dictation can serve an important role. In planning the curriculum around Ashia (the persona doll), the teachers and family members might ask:

- Would the children be interested in seeing their family stories written down, just like they wrote down Ashia's story? And would such experiences help them increase their awareness of print in the world around them?
- What strategies or adaptations for family storytelling might engage a child who is nonverbal?
- For children who are learning English as their second language, might it be

easier to make the connection between the spoken word and print if the children could dictate their stories in their home language to family members or community volunteers?

- What topics may be interesting and engaging for children to dictate? What kinds of questions might be used to invite children who may have never dictated a story before, or whose home language is something other than English, to dictate a story? Might asking children about how their family helps them get ready for preschool encourage them to tell a story that has meaning for them? Or for a child who likes to draw pictures, might inviting her to describe what is going on in her drawing be a way to introduce her to the idea of dictating a story?

- How might the activity be adapted to accommodate children with disabilities or other special needs?

These questions may open doors to new topics for exploration by teachers, children, and their families. When children's learning is embedded in the context of their own lives, and when curriculum builds on and reflects the best of what children, families, and teachers bring in the way of interests and ideas, everything becomes more meaningful and understandable for children. Teachers and families also engage the children emotionally, generating an experience that builds thinking and reasoning while making learning pleasurable and a source of joy. The key is to discover which connections are meaningful for each child. Doing so requires that adults observe and listen to the ideas that engage the mind of each child. What adults discover prepares them to support young children in actively making meaning and constructing more complex ideas and skills while engaged in play, exploration, and interactions with others.

Endnotes

1. California Department of Education, *California Preschool Learning Foundations, Volume 3* (Sacramento: California Department of Education, 2012).

2. National Association for the Education of Young Children, *NAEYC Early Childhood Program Standards* (Washington, DC: NAEYC, 2008). http://www.naeyc.org/academy/standards/ (accessed November 30, 2008).

3. California Department of Education, *California Preschool Curriculum Framework, Volume 1* (Sacramento: California Department of Education, 2010).

4. California Department of Education, *Preschool English Learners: Principles and Practices to Promote Language, Literacy, and Learning,* 2nd ed. (Sacramento: California Department of Education, 2009).

5. National Center for Children in Poverty, "California: Demographics of Poor Children" (2010). http://www.nccp.org/profiles/state_profile.php?state=CA&id=7 (accessed January 4, 2011).

6. M. J. Guralnick, *Early Childhood Inclusion: Focus on Change* (Baltimore, MD: Paul H. Brookes Publishing Company, 2001).

7. California Department of Education, *Statewide Enrollment by Ethnicity 2009-10.* http://dq.cde.ca.gov/dataquest/EnrollEthState.asp?Level=State&TheYear=2009-10&cChoice=EnrollEth1&p=2 (accessed January 4, 2011).

8. Children Now, *California Report Card 2011: Setting the Agenda for Children.* http://www.childrennow.org/index.php/learn/reports_and_research/article/738 (accessed January 4, 2011).

9. Ed-Data, State of California Education Profile, 2009. http://www.ed-data.k12.ca.us/Navigation/fsTwoPanel.asp?bottom=%2Fprofile.asp%3Flevel%3D04%26reportNumber%3D16 (accessed January 2011).

10. Children Now, *California Report Card 2010: Setting the Agenda for Children.* http://www.childrennow.org/uploads/documents/reportcard_2010.pdf (accessed February 18, 2010).

11. Children Now, *California Report Card 2011: Setting the Agenda for Children,* p. 26. http://www.childrennow.org/index.php/learn/reports_and_research/article/738 (accessed January 4, 2011).

12. Children Now, *Children in Immigrant Families: A California Data Brief* (Oakland, CA: Children Now, 2007).

13. Children Now and Preschool California, *Kids Can't Wait to Learn: Achieving Voluntary Preschool For All in California* (Oakland, CA: Children Now and Preschool California, 2004).

14. California Department of Education, *Number of English Learners by Language, 2009-10.* http://data1.cde.ca.gov/dataquest/LEPbyLang1.asp?cYear=2009-10&cChoice=LepbyLang1&cTopic=LC&cLevel=State (accessed January 4, 2011).

15. California Department of Education, *Preschool English Learners: Principles and Practices to Promote Language, Literacy, and Learning,* 2nd ed. (Sacramento: California Department of Education, 2007).

16. National Center for Children in Poverty (NCCP), *California Early Childhood Profile* (New York: NCCP, 2009). http://www.nccp.org/profiles/pdf/profile_early_childhood_CA.pdf (accessed February 2010).

17. United States Census Bureau, *2006 American Community Survey: United States and States—R1704. Percent of Children Under 18 Years Below Poverty Level in the Past 12 Months.* http://factfinder.census.gov/servlet/GRTTable?_bm=y&-geo_id=D&-_box_head_nbr=R1704&-ds_name=ACS_2006_EST_G00_&-_lang=en&-redoLog=false&-format=D&-mt_name=ACS_2006_EST_G00_R1701_US30 (accessed October 25, 2010).

18. A. Douglas-Hall and M. Chau, *Basic Facts About Low-Income Children: Birth to Age 6* (New York: National Center for Children in Poverty, 2007).

19. Children Now, *California Report Card 2006–2007: The State of the State's Children.* http://www.childrennow.org/index.php/learn/reports_and_research/all (accessed July 14, 2008).
20. California Department of Education, *Special Education Enrollment by Age and Disability: Statewide Report* (Sacramento: California Department of Education, 2010). http://dq.cde.ca.gov/dataquest/SpecEd/SpecEd1.asp?cChoice=SpecEd1&cYear=2009-10&cLevel=State&cTopic=SpecEd&myTimeFrame=S&submit1=Submit&ReptCycle=December (accessed January 4, 2011).
21. Public Law 108-446; 118 Stat. 2647 (H.R. 1350). "Individuals with Disabilities Education Improvement Act of 2004."
22. J. Van Hoorn and others, *Play at the Center of the Curriculum,* 4th ed. (Upper Saddle Creek, NJ: Pearson Education, 2007).
23. E. F. Zigler, "Giving Intervention a Head Start: A Conversation with Edward Zigler" (*Educational Leadership* 65:8–14).
24. A. S. Epstein, *The Intentional Teacher: Choosing the Best Strategies for Young Children's Learning* (Washington, DC: National Association for the Education of Young Children, 2007).
25. California Department of Education, *Prekindergarten Learning and Development Guidelines* (Sacramento: California Department of Education, 2000).
26. California Department of Education, *Preschool English Learners: Principles and Practices to Promote Language, Literacy, and Learning,* 2nd ed. (Sacramento: California Department of Education, 2009), 43.
27. California Department of Education, *Prekindergarten Learning and Development Guidelines* (Sacramento: California Department of Education, 2000), 45.
28. J. E. Hale-Benson, *Black Children: Their Roots, Culture, and Learning Styles,* Rev. ed. (Baltimore, MD: Johns Hopkins University Press, 1986).
29. B. Y. Terrell and J. E. Hale, "Serving a Multicultural Population: Different Learning Styles," *American Journal of Speech-Language Pathology* 1 (1992): 5–8.
30. California Department of Education, *California Preschool Curriculum Framework, Volume 1* (Sacramento: California Department of Education, 2010), 178.
31. Ibid., 181.
32. Center for Applied Special Technology (CAST), "Universal Design for Learning." http://www.cast.org/udl (accessed October 26, 2010).
33. R. A. McWilliam, M. Wolery, and S. L. Odom, "Instructional Perspectives in Inclusive Preschool Classrooms," in *Early Childhood Inclusion: Focus on Change,* ed. M. J. Guralnick (Baltimore, MD: Paul H. Brookes Publishing Company, 2001).
34. California Department of Education, *Preschool English Learners: Principles and Practices to Promote Language, Literacy, and Learning,* 2nd ed. (Sacramento: California Department of Education, 2009).
35. J. R. Jablon, A. L. Dombro, and M. Dichtelmiller, *The Power of Observation,* 2nd ed. (Washington, DC: National Association for the Education of Young Children, 2007).

Bibliography

Bay Area Early Childhood Funders. *Play: It's the Way Young Children Learn.* 2007. http://earlychildhoodfunders.org/pdf/Play_pamphlet_eng.pdf (accessed November 18, 2010).

California Child Care Resource and Referral Network (CCCRRN). *2009 California Child Care Portfolio.* San Francisco, CA: California Child Care Resource and Referral Network, 2009.

California Department of Education. *Assessing Children with Disabilities Who Are English Learners: Guidance for the DRDP Access and the PS DRDP-R for Children with IEPs.* 2007. http://draccess.org/assessors/guidancefordrdp/ELGuidance.html (accessed November 18, 2010).

———. *California Preschool Curriculum Framework, Volume 1.* Sacramento: California Department of Education, 2010.

———. *California Preschool Learning Foundations, Volume 3.* Sacramento: California Department of Education, 2012.

———. *Inclusion Works! Creating Child Care Programs That Promote Belonging for Children with Special Needs.* Sacramento: California Department of Education, 2009.

———. *Number of English Learners by Language, 2008–09.* 2009. http://dq.cde.ca.gov/dataquest/LEPbyLang1.asp?cChoice=LepbyLang1&cYear=2008-09&cLevel=State&cTopic=LC&myTimeFrame=S&submit1=Submit (accessed October 18, 2010).

———. *Prekindergarten Learning and Development Guidelines.* Sacramento: California Department of Education, 2000.

———. *Preschool English Learners: Principles and Practices to Promote Language, Literacy, and Learning.* 2nd ed. Sacramento: California Department of Education, 2009.

———. *Students by Ethnicity, State of California, 2008–09.* 2009. http://www.ed-data.k12.ca.us/profile.asp?tab=1&level=04&ReportNumber=16&fyr=0809 (accessed October 18, 2010).

———. *A World Full of Language: Supporting Preschool English Learners.* DVD. Sacramento, CA: California Department of Education, 2007.

Center for Applied Special Technology (CAST). "Universal Design for Learning." 2007. http://www.cast.org/udl/ (accessed October 26, 2010).

Children Now. *California Report Card 2010: Setting the Agenda for Children.* 2010. http://www.childrennow.org/uploads/documents/reportcard_2010.pdf (accessed October 18, 2010).

———. *Children in Immigrant Families: A California Data Brief.* Oakland, CA: Children Now, 2007.

Children Now and Preschool California. *Kids Can't Wait to Learn: Achieving Voluntary Preschool for All in California.* Oakland, CA: Children Now and Preschool California, 2004.

Douglas-Hall, A., and M. Chau. *Basic Facts About Low-Income Children: Birth to Age 18.* New York: National Center for Children in Poverty, 2007.

Epstein, A. S. *The Intentional Teacher: Choosing the Best Strategies for Young Children's Learning.* Washington, DC: National Association for the Education of Young Children (NAEYC), 2007.

Garcia, O., J. A. Kleifgen, and L. Falchi. *From English Learners to Emergent Bilinguals. Equity Matters: Research Review 1.* New York: The Campaign for Educational Equity, 2008. http://www.equitycampaign.org/i/a/document/6468_ofelia-ELL_Final.pdf (accessed September 14, 2012).

Guralnick, M. J., ed. *Early Childhood Inclusion: Focus on Change.* Baltimore, MD: Paul H. Brookes Publishing Company, 2001.

Hale-Benson, J. E. *Black Children: Their Roots, Culture, and Learning Styles.* Rev. ed. Baltimore, MD: Johns Hopkins University Press, 1986.

Karoly, L. A., and others. *Prepared to Learn: The Nature and Quality of Early Care and Education for Preschool-Age Children in California.* Pittsburgh, PA: Rand, 2008.

McWilliam, R. A., M. Wolery, and S. L. Odom. "Instructional Perspectives in Inclusive Preschool Classrooms." In *Early Childhood Inclusion: Focus on Change*, edited by M. J. Guralnick. Baltimore, MD: Paul H. Brookes Publishing Company, 2001.

National Association for the Education of Young Children. *NAEYC Early Childhood Program Standards and Accreditation Criteria*. 2008. http://www.naeyc.org/academy/primary/standardsintro (accessed November 18, 2010).

National Center for Children in Poverty (NCCP). *California Early Childhood Profile*. 2009. http://www.nccp.org/profiles/pdf/profile_early_childhood_CA.pdf (accessed October 18, 2010).

National Center for Education Statistics. *The Condition of Education 2006*. 2006. http://nces.ed.gov/pubsearch/pubsinfo.asp?pubid=2006071 (accessed November 18, 2010).

———. *English Language Learner Students in U.S. Public Schools: 1994 and 2000* (issue brief). 2004. http://nces.ed.gov/pubsearch/pubsinfo.asp?pubid=2004035. (accessed November 18, 2010).

Passel, Jeffrey S., and D'Vera Cohn. *U.S. Populations Projections: 2005–2050*. Washington, DC: Pew Research Center, 2008. http://www.pewhispanic.org/2008/02/11/us-population-projections-2005-2050/ (accessed September 14, 2012).

Pew Hispanic Center. *Statistical Portrait of Hispanics in the United States, 2006*. Washington, DC: Pew Research, 2008.

United States Census Bureau. *2006 American Community Survey: United States and States—R1704. Percent of Children Under 18 Years Below Poverty Level in the Past 12 Months*. http://factfinder.census.gov/servlet/GRTTable?_bm=y&-geo_id=D&-_box_head_nbr=R1704&-ds_name=ACS_2006_EST_G00_&-_lang=en&-redoLog=false&-format=D&-mt_name=ACS_2006_EST_G00_R1701_US30 (accessed October 25, 2010).

Zigler, E. F. "Giving Intervention a Head Start: A Conversation with Edward Zigler." *Educational Leadership* 65 (2007): 8–14.

CHAPTER 2
History–Social Science

For many educators of young children, the terms *history* and *social sciences* conjure up images of children studying past presidents, learning about other countries, and exploring related topics during the primary school years. Yet a look at young children's emerging sense of identity, their growing interest in the larger social world in which they live, and their developing understanding of time and place shows that history and social sciences are relevant to them also. Young children are natural historians when they talk about their experiences and enjoy hearing family stories of "long ago." They are **intuitive** geographers when they recognize the route to the grocery store and create a map of the preschool room. Children are simple ecologists when they worry about a plant that is wilted or a bird's egg on a nature walk. They learn about democracy through their participation in shared decision making and taking turns on the playground. Their interactions with other children acquaint them with the diversity in culture, languages, backgrounds, and abilities in society. Young children are also everyday economists as they begin to understand how money, bartering, and exchange work in the world around them.

Preschoolers' understanding of history and social sciences naturally derives from their expanding knowledge of the world and their place in it. It also provides a foundation for the study of history, culture, geography, economics, **civics** and citizenship, **ecology**, and the global environment that begins in the primary grades and continues throughout life. Those topics are important because they provide a basis for understanding the responsibilities of citizens in a democratic society, the legacy of past generations who built society, the importance of caring for the natural world, and the rich diversity of other people. In preschool, they are introduced to these important issues through everyday activities such as caring for a plant, remembering a recent trip to the zoo, deciding as a group on a name for the class pet, creating a shoe store, engaging in imaginative play with adult roles, or sharing family traditions from home. In other words, young children learn about history and social sciences from personal experiences, as they are enlisted into a preschool curriculum, and also from their experiences at home.

A thoughtfully designed early childhood program includes many activities that contribute to children's understanding of history and social sciences.[1] Some activities are carefully planned by a teacher to help children learn about weather patterns, bartering for goods and services, responsibilities as a class member, adult occupations, and many other ideas and concepts. Other activities emerge from the opportunities created by children's spontaneous interests and a teacher's capacity to build these into teachable moments. Both kinds of activities are discussed in this curriculum framework. Taken together, they reflect the assumption that young children develop knowledge of history and the social sciences as they are encouraged to enact their understanding in everyday interactions with other children and adults.[2] This knowledge helps young children understand themselves in a wonderfully expanding world.

Guiding Principles

▶ **Build a cooperative, inclusive preschool community.**
Ensure that the preschool curriculum maximizes children's opportunities to work together in ways that require responsible conduct, fairness, and respect for others. Help children learn how to include diverse peers, including children of different genders, ages, abilities, family structures, and ethnic, linguistic, and cultural backgrounds. The term inclusive means more than simply "being together." Inclusion comes through in the ways the child is connected with other children, is an active participant, and "belongs"—has full, unconditional membership in the classroom community.[3]

▶ **Create activities that will actively engage children's social skills and understanding.**
Effective, meaningful activities will include rich conversation with adults and peers, shared projects involving exploration and discovery, and lots of play.

▶ **Affirm children's home cultures, experiences, and values.**
Provide plenty of opportunities for children to share stories and items from home, and welcome their family members to participate as they feel comfortable. In conversations with children, emphasize that each family does things differently and that diversity is valued in the preschool setting.

▶ **Encourage children's social curiosity.**
Build on preschool children's natural interest in their social world, and in the similarities and differences among the people in it. Acknowledge children's

awareness of differences while also expanding their understanding of these differences.

▶ **Model social behavior and attitudes with explanations.**
Model the ways you would like children to treat each other in the preschool setting, and explain why you do what you do. Show respect and concern for the rights and welfare of both adults and children in the preschool community.

▶ **Actively teach and practice the essential skills of democratic participation.**
Provide a preschool setting where children can learn and practice the skills they will need to be successful and contributing members of their communities. Emphasize the values of cooperation, consensus building, and respect for each child's perspective.

▶ **Encourage children to incorporate their knowledge of adult roles and occupations into their dramatic play.**
Use children's growing interest in their own and others' roles and responsibilities to help them learn about how various people contribute to a community.

▶ **Observe and converse with children during play in order to learn about their current understanding of time and history.**
Focus on children as they communicate about and act out past, present, and future experiences, as well as family stories and broader historical events. Use this information to shape future curriculum plans.

▶ **Help children deepen their own sense of place.**
Help children begin to understand and reflect on their sense of belonging in places and locations that are meaningful to them.

▶ **Nurture children's sense of wonder about nature.**
Observe preschool children's engagement with the natural world, and encourage their protective feelings toward it.

Environments and Materials

When planning an environment to support children's learning in history–social science, effective teachers consider the physical, curricular, and social elements. The *physical* environment and daily routine set the stage for children's inquiry and should include ample time for children's self-initiated work, different spaces for solitary play and for collaborative play, and engaging materials that children are encouraged to use creatively. The *curricular* plan needs to provide opportunities and adult support for both group learning and for informal discovery and skill development. The key to a positive *social* environment is a teacher who actively models curiosity, openness, and engagement and who is eager to explore the world together with children. An environment that supports children's learning in history and the social sciences has the following characteristics:

▶ **Extended projects that are centered on a topic in history or social science and emerge from children's interests and inquiries**

There are multiple opportunities for children to actively engage with subject matter (e.g., learning about group decision making or caring for the earth) in meaningful and familiar contexts. Adults prepare for individual investigations as well as small- and large-group explorations.

▶ **Reflective of diversity**

As opposed to a tourist approach, teachers and children participate in authentic experiences with culture. They routinely sing songs and read stories from different cultures. Adults engage children in meaningful conversations about daily life, highlighting diverse perspectives and experiences. Photographs, artwork, and music are representative of the children and families in the group, including children with disabilities. The dramatic play area is supplied with multicultural cooking tools, adaptive utensils, empty food containers, clothing, and other items reflective of the children's homes.

▶ **A balance between child choice and adult direction**

The daily routine supports both child-initiated play ("What's your plan for work time? Where will you play today?") and teacher-initiated learning experiences. Choice time offers children an opportunity to exercise creative freedom and decision making. Adults also initiate activities that support community participation and follow in order ("First we will sing songs as a group, and then we will have snack").

▶ **A variety of materials to support children's inquiry-based learning and practice in the skills of social science**

Open-ended materials (e.g., sand and water, blocks) encourage children's creative and divergent thinking. Paper, writing instruments, tallying tools, maps, charts, and other visual aids stimulate children to generate questions, collect information, summarize what they have learned, and form conclusions.

▶ **Materials that connect children to times and places**

Program materials include authentic objects (e.g., loom) and cultural artifacts (e.g., handwoven blanket) to encourage children's questions and active interest. Maps are displayed at the children's eye level.

▶ **Real experiences with nature and other environmental education materials**

Children have frequent access to an outdoor learning environment that is nature-oriented; ideally, it includes trees, plants, grasses, and other living things. The indoor learning environment is supplied with pictures, puzzles, toy animals, books, and other play materials to facilitate inquiry and

introduce children to less familiar **ecosystems**. The care of living creatures, such as preschool program pets, is also a part of the program curriculum.

▶ **Tools and practices for appreciating and caring for the earth and its resources**
Systems are in place to introduce the concept of "Reduce, Reuse, Recycle" ("It looks like you are all done with that piece of paper for your project. Let's put it in the recycling bin"). Materials are properly cared for, repurposed (e.g., paper is used on both sides), and shared across programs. Consumables are used as sparingly as possible.

▶ **Display of children's work and experiences**
Children's investigations are highlighted using photographs, child-created pictures and maps, dictation, and models. Displays are positioned at children's eye level.

▶ **Dramatic play props and materials that represent firsthand experience with social roles and occupations, as well as consumer actions**
The room provides an ample supply of clothes for dress-up, items from a variety of work settings, play money, and other real objects (e.g., a telephone) and print artifacts (e.g., a restaurant menu). The room intentionally incorporates play props for exploring themes in multiple learning areas (e.g., transportation in the block area).

▶ **High-quality children's books with content related to self, family, and community**
The preschool program introduces shared-book reading and discussions about book content to facilitate an understanding of human behavior and relationships. Books are selected and rotated based on emerging themes to

expand children's awareness of people, places, and time. Books reflect the background and experiences of children in the group, including those with special needs, as well as those that extend beyond familiar homes and communities.

▶ **Extension of learning into the local community to help children learn in the "here and now" of the world around them**
The program makes use of familiar contexts to permit successful explorations of self, family, and community, as children are able to draw from prior knowledge and experience. Plans are developed for fieldwork, such as visiting a local business or greeting the neighborhood postal worker, to expand learning beyond the classroom walls. If field trips are not practical, every effort is made to bring parts of the community into the setting via pictures, visitors, and props.

▶ **Family involvement in program planning**
The environment and its materials demonstrate a partnership with families and are inclusive of community goals and values.

Summary of the History–Social Science Foundations

Self and Society

The Self and Society foundations focus on young children's growing ability to see themselves within the context of society. *Culture and society* concerns preschoolers' growing interest in differences in culture, language, racial identity, abilities, and family traditions that are different from the child's own.[4] The preschool setting is a place where children explore differences and think about the messages they receive from society, the values they learn in their homes, and their own ideas about people. *Relationships* focuses on how young children develop skills in creating and maintaining close relationships, including recognizing the mutual responsibilities of relationships.[5] *Social roles and occupations* describes children's growing interest in and understanding of adult activities, including work and family roles.[6]

Becoming a Preschool Community Member (Civics)

The Preschool Community Member foundations are concerned with how young children become responsible and cooperative members of the preschool community.[7] *Skills for democratic participation* focuses on developing abilities to respect others' opinions and preferences, participate in group activities and decision making, and balance personal goals with the goals of others. *Responsible conduct* focuses on developing self-regulation of behavior in accord with group expectations and rules.[8] *Fairness and respect for other people* describes developing sensitivity to the feelings and needs of others through cooperation and helpfulness, and developing consideration of fairness

for all.[9] *Conflict resolution* focuses on young children's growing skill in managing conflict through bargaining and compromise.[10]

Sense of Time (History)

These foundations focus on developing understanding of past and future events and their association with the present.[11] *Understanding past events* describes children's developing ability to remember past events, the connection to other events of the past, and the connection to current experience. *Anticipating and planning future events* focuses on the ability to anticipate events in the near future and to make choices that prepare for future needs.[12] *Personal history* is concerned with young children's sense of their own growth and experiences. *Historical changes in people and the world* relates to children's efforts to create a mental timeline in which events of the past are properly sequenced, including family history.[13]

Sense of Place (Geography and Ecology)

These foundations focus on developing knowledge of the physical settings in which children live and how they compare with other locations.[14] *Navigating familiar locations* describes developing skills in understanding the characteristics and activities associated with familiar

locations (such as home and school), the routes between them, and broader features of the natural environment such as hills and streams and weather patterns. *Caring for the natural world* concerns preschoolers' expanding awareness of human–environment interaction, which is the basis for interest in taking care of plants and animals, knowledge of hazards such as pollution and litter, and an interest in natural environments that are different from their own.[15] *Understanding the physical world through drawings and maps* describes young children's growth in representing the physical world through their own drawings or by interpreting simple maps.[16]

Marketplace (Economics) Foundation

Preschoolers are curious and observant about the world of commerce, including the association between work and income, and purchasing. The single foundation, *Exchange*, describes young children's developing understanding of economic concepts, including the ideas of ownership, money exchanged for goods and services, value and cost, and bartering.[17]

Summary of the Strands and Substrands

The foundations of this section are organized according to the following strands and substrands:

Self and Society
Culture and Diversity
Relationships
Social Roles and Occupations

Becoming a Preschool Community Member (Civics)
Skills for Democratic Participation
Responsible Conduct
Fairness and Respect for Other People
Conflict Resolution

Sense of Time (History)
Understanding Past Events
Anticipating and Planning Future Events
Personal History
Historical Changes in People and the World

Sense of Place (Geography and Ecology)
Navigating Familiar Locations
Caring for the Natural World
Understanding the Physical World Through Drawings and Maps

Marketplace (Economics)
Exchange

Self and Society

An early childhood education setting acquaints young children with people who have different backgrounds, family practices, languages, cultural experiences, special needs, and abilities. In their relationships with teachers and peers, preschoolers perceive how others are similar to them and how they are different, and gradually they learn to regard these differences with interest and respect rather than wariness or doubt. This is especially likely if early childhood educators incorporate inclusive practices into the preschool environment. The relationships that young children develop with others in the preschool provide opportunities for understanding these differences in depth and in the context of the people whom the child knows well. One of the most valuable features of a thoughtfully designed early childhood program is helping young children to perceive the diversity of human characteristics as part of the richness of living and working with other people.

Young children are beginning to perceive themselves within the broader context of society in another way also. Their interest in adult social roles, occupations, and responsibilities motivates pretend play, excitement about visits to places such as a fire station or grocery store, and questions about work and its association with family roles and family income. Teachers can help young children explore these interests as children try to understand the variety of adult roles that may be open to them in the future.

In this section, specific strategies are discussed that support development in each of the following substrands:

1.0 Culture and Diversity
2.0 Relationships
3.0 Social Roles and Occupations

Research Highlight: Anti-Bias Curriculum Approach

High-quality early childhood programs support children in developing their physical, cognitive, social, and emotional potential. The settings encourage children to explore their own sense of self and to develop an awareness and appreciation of others. Such experiences are foundational to becoming positive and constructive members of society and the world.

Creating an inclusive community of learners—one in which all individuals feel comfortable, confident, and competent—requires that educators take an anti-bias approach to the planning, implementation, and evaluation of their program. Educators who embrace an anti-bias curriculum approach reflect on their own identity and experiences. They extend their knowledge of different cultures and communities through conversation and discussion with children, families, and colleagues. They also confront bias in the preschool setting (e.g., "Girls can't play here" or "His eyes are a funny shape") to send a message that all children should be respected and that one's words can hurt other people.

Instead of using a one-size-fits-all curriculum, anti-bias educators design environments and activities that reflect the real experiences of children's lives. Educators routinely partner with families and community members to further enhance the early childhood program. Throughout the day, the adults in the preschool setting engage children in developmentally appropriate conversations about similarities and differences, and promote justice and fairness for all by helping children think critically about teasing, bullying, and other hurtful behavior. Activities that promote anti-bias education are integrated throughout the daily routine, thereby avoiding a tourist approach. "The heart of anti-bias work is a vision of a world in which all children are able to blossom, and each child's particular abilities and gifts are able to flourish."[18] For more information on the anti-bias approach, refer to *Anti-Bias Education for Young Children and Ourselves,* by Louise Derman-Sparks and Julie Olsen Edwards.

1.0   Culture and Diversity

As preschoolers learn about themselves, they begin to appreciate the cultural, ethnic, racial, and linguistic characteristics that they share with family members. They also become interested in people with different backgrounds and practices to compare with their own. Although research shows that preschoolers tend to initially favor their own cultural, ethnic, or racial group, the early childhood education program offers opportunities to appreciate and value the cultural diversity of everybody in the group. Teachers can also help young children appreciate the broader range of cultures, languages, and practices in the world through stories, cultural artifacts, and conversation.

VIGNETTE

Ava and Wenqi relax in the reading area, leaning against the big pillows and looking at the new array of library books Ms. Zhang has arranged on the shelves. Attracted by the cover illustration of a child drawing with a stick in the sand, Ava begins paging through a book. Wenqi gestures to the characters as Ava turns a page. "Those look like the words in our books at home." "They're not words; they're just squiggles," replies Ava. "They ARE words," Wenqi insists, "My mama reads them. Ms. Zhang can read them, too."

Later, Wenqi shows Ms. Zhang the book and asks her to read it at story time. Ms. Zhang introduces it to the group by telling them, "This morning Wenqi noticed that I added some new library books to the reading area. Some of them have English words, and some of them, like this one, have Chinese words. This book is called At the Beach *by Huy Voun Lee. It is about a boy named Xiao Ming who goes to the beach with his mother. His mother teaches him how to write Chinese characters in the sand with a stick. I will read the Chinese words and the English words. They look and sound very different, but they tell us the same story."*

After Ms. Zhang finishes reading the story, she asks the class, "Do you want to write some of these Chinese words?" "Yes!" many children reply enthusiastically. Ms. Zhang writes on chart paper as she says the words: "人" (person; pronounced as ren), "大" (big; pronounced as da), "天" (sky; pronounced as tian). "I will put the At the Beach *book and these Chinese words on the writing table for you to use later."*

TEACHABLE MOMENT

> The bilingual teacher in this vignette has supplied the preschool reading area with books written in both of the home languages of the children in her class. She uses this story-time opportunity to introduce the idea that the same story can be told in different languages. Later, she can do the same with other books and can incorporate print in both languages into the program's displays and writing activities. For more information about strategies to support children who are English learners, see chapter 5 of the *California Preschool Curriculum Framework, Volume 1.*

VIGNETTE

Emma, Rakesha, and Annie all choose the dramatic play area as they make their plans for the day. Each of them has noticed the shiny new crowns their teachers have added to the dress-up clothes shelves since yesterday.

"Look at me. I'm a princess," says Annie as she twirls in front of the mirror with a crown on her head. "Me, too," adds Rakesha, choosing another of the crowns. "Mine has jewels."

Emma, who has light skin and light hair and often takes the lead in assigning dramatic play roles, looks at both girls and states emphatically, "No!" She turns to Rakesha, who has darker skin and darker hair, and says, "You can't be a princess because you don't look like one. You have to look like the one in the princess book."

Rakesha protests, "I can, too, be a princess! Everybody can be a princess."

The three girls continue to argue loudly about who can be a princess, and Ms. Denisha comes over to help them work out their disagreement. She sits down on the rug and motions to all three girls to sit down around her. She observes, "You girls look and sound pretty upset. What is the problem? Rakesha, why don't you tell us first what made you feel so upset?"

Rakesha repeats Emma's assertion that Rakesha can't be a princess. Emma and Annie both add details to the story of the argument. Ms. Denisha listens, asks questions, and restates the problem. She then tells them, "It really hurt Rakesha's feelings when you told her she couldn't be a princess. Rakesha was right. People with any skin and hair colors can be princesses and other special characters. We can find books about many kinds of princesses. Now, I will stay and help you think of some ideas for your play this morning."

TEACHABLE MOMENT

> This incident is an example of how young children bring ideas they have acquired in other settings (such as media images or home or neighborhood interactions) into their play

in the preschool setting. Teachers can often only guess about the specific source of children's ideas about social roles. However, they can play an important role in identifying and labeling as hurtful the judgments children sometimes express about others as well as about themselves. Ms. Denisha, the teacher in the preceding vignette, followed the kind of problem-solving process identified as a "best practice" for conflict situations. This conflict involved especially sensitive and fundamental issues, so she took extra time to listen carefully to the children's perspectives, correct a hurtful misconception, and support the children in more positive social interaction and cooperative play.

Sometimes a teacher may decide it would be helpful to follow up by mentioning to families, in general terms, that these kinds of issues are being explored in preschool play, and asking them to help affirm positive messages at home. She can also follow up by reading some relevant books at story time about how each person is different on the outside, yet similar on the inside, such as *Whoever You Are* by Mem Fox. In addition, teachers can supply the preschool setting with a wide variety of books and other images that portray people with a range of physical features in different roles, including roles with high social status.

VIGNETTE

Mr. Scott enters the block area, where Damon and Charlie are building towers with the large wooden blocks. Mr. Scott heard a loud crash and wants to make sure no one has been hurt. Charlie immediately tells him, "That was Damon's tower. He built it taller than you said we were supposed to, and it crashed down. It almost fell on me." Mr. Scott replies, "I'm glad no one got hurt."

Then he turns to Damon, who stands quietly with his eyes lowered. Mr. Scott says, "Damon, do you remember a few minutes ago when I asked you to build your block tower only as high as your shoulders? This was the reason. When block towers are this tall, they can really hurt someone if they fall. Would you like some help picking up these blocks?"

Damon continues to look down at the floor and says quietly, "No, sir."

"No, sir?'" repeats Charlie, in a puzzled tone of voice. "Why did you say that? Mr. Scott isn't a sir. That sounds stupid. He said he'd help you."

"Charlie," says Mr. Scott, "the way Damon spoke to me was not stupid. It told me that he had listened carefully to what I said. In some families, children do call their fathers and other men 'sir.' In your family, they may not. What do you call your dad?"

"Dad," replies Charlie.

"Well, Damon used a different way of talking with his dad. Remember the books I read to you at story time about all the different ways people say hello to each other in the world? This is just like that."

TEACHABLE MOMENT

In this situation, the two children who are building together come from two different family cultures. In Damon's family, a child in this kind of situation is expected to listen quietly to the adult's response and show respect, both by lowering his gaze while listening and by addressing the male adult as "Sir." In the preschool setting, he is behaving consistently with his home culture's expectations.

Charlie is clearly having trouble understanding Damon's response, which is very different from the casual give-and-take between adults and children that is the norm is his family. Mr. Scott explains to Charlie that families are different in the ways their members speak to each other. He describes the difference to Charlie simply, without using evaluative language. His words and manner convey to the boys acceptance of both interaction styles.

VIGNETTE

Daniel is already on the playground's tire swing when Isaiah approaches to ask if he can swing with him. "No," Daniel tells him. "Go away. My daddy says I can't play with you." "Why not?" asks Isaiah. Daniel answers, "'Cause you have two moms, and my daddy says that's bad. God doesn't like it. You've gotta have one mom and one dad." Isaiah responds, "That's mean. Two moms are just as good as one mom and one dad. I don't want to swing with you anyway!"

The next day at arrival time, one of Isaiah's parents tells the teacher what Isaiah said about the playground incident. This is not the first time Daniel has made similar comments about Isaiah's family being bad because he has two parents of the same sex. The parent understands that the comments stem from the family's strongly held religious beliefs, but she wants the teacher to do something. The teacher apologizes to her for not having observed and responded to the incident the previous day. The teacher also says she will talk to Daniel and to his parents about the hurtful effects of his speech and will check with Isaiah about the incident and assure him of her support at school. She decides to have a meeting with the children to talk about diverse family structures. She uses The Family Book by Todd Parr and All Families Are Different by Sol Gordon. She invites children to share about their own families, emphasizing similarities and differences.

TEACHABLE MOMENT

> Some of the most challenging interactions within a preschool community occur because each family is different. The families in a single program may come from different ethnic and cultural backgrounds, have different family structures, and hold divergent political and religious beliefs and values. Preschool children bring the characteristics and values of their families to the preschool setting in many ways. At times they can say or do things that are hurtful to others even though they do not fully understand the issues involved or the consequences of their speech and actions.
>
> Every child and family has a right to feel welcomed and included in the preschool setting. The teacher's role is to protect each child from words and actions that are hurtful and that devalue him or her. This does not require that the teacher personally agree with one perspective and disagree with another. However, an anti-bias educator affirms the universal value of respect for each family's culture, characteristics, and dignity. One message that is important for all children and their adult family members to hear in the preschool setting is "All families are different, and we respect everyone's family."

VIGNETTE

Circle time is beginning, and Nico, a child with physical disabilities, is settling into his usual seat with help from Ms. Elena, the preschool aide. Mara stands in front of them and asks, in a frustrated tone of voice, "Why does Nico always get to sit with you? It's not fair. I want to sit with you, too." Ms. Elena explains, "It's my job to help Nico with things that are hard for him to do by himself. Would you like to sit right next to us?"

TEACHABLE MOMENT

> Mara has noticed that Ms. Elena, an adult aide, assists Nico. Mara does not ask anything specific about Nico, but she perceives that it is unfair for Nico to have Ms. Elena's full attention during preschool. Ms. Elena addresses Mara's frustration by giving a simple, matter-of-fact explanation of her role and then welcoming Mara to join them. If Mara continues to show frustration or curiosity about Nico or Ms. Elena, Ms. Elena or the preschool teacher can follow up with more thorough explanations.

Interactions and Strategies

Practice a reflective approach to build awareness of self and others. Examine your own attitudes and values. How do these impact your caregiving style? As you work with others, stay mindful of potential bias and consistently practice perspective taking. Attend to personal cues of stress and frustration and self-regulation as needed. Use community and professional resources to build competence in reflective practice.

Maintain a healthy curiosity about the experiences of others. Ask authentic questions to build understanding. Consider the value of different caregiving practices and their purpose in supporting the development of the next generation of young children.

Partner with families in goal setting and program design. Make it a priority to learn individual family values. Listen attentively to each family's goals for their child's care and education. Show respect for each family's preferences for communicating. Seek knowledge and understanding when encountering differences in caregiving practices. Offer guidance that is sensitive to diversity, especially when negotiating conflicts. Request fam-

ily support as you implement or modify home practices for use in the preschool setting.

Prepare an active learning environment that incorporates the full spectrum of the human experience (e.g., diversity of cultures, ethnicities, gender, age, abilities, socioeconomic class, and family structure). Supply materials reflective of the diverse backgrounds and abilities of the children in your care. Include materials that encourage self-reflection and awareness of others, such as mirrors; dolls (e.g., different ethnicities, dolls in a wheelchair); toy people; multicultural crayons, pens, and paints; and so on. For additional ideas, read or consult *Anti-Bias Education for Young Children and Ourselves*, by Louise Derman-Sparks and Julie Olsen Edwards. Incorporate throughout the daily routine authentic experiences with language, utensils, foods, and music. Throughout the environment, display images and documentation that are inclusive of all children in the community of young learners.

Create an environment, both indoors and outdoors, that is inclusive of all children's abilities. Routinely evaluate the accessibility of the learning space. Make appropriate adaptations as required to ensure the successful participation of all children. For more information about resources for teachers of children with disabilities or other special needs, see appendix D of the *California Preschool Curriculum Framework, Volume 1*.

Address children's initial comments and inquiries about diversity with honest, direct communication ("I heard you talking about firefighters. Tell me more about what you know about firefighters"). Create an emotionally safe space for conversation and promote open communica-

tion by listening attentively to children's views and perspectives. Avoid judging or shaming children's initial questions or comments. Gently question children's limited views or perspectives by providing contrasting examples to help broaden their thinking ("My friend is a girl, and she is a firefighter"). Provide books and images that portray diversity in social roles and occupations.

Converse about similarities and differences. Children readily notice differences but generally need more support in attending to commonalities. Pose questions to extend children's initial observations and perspectives. For example, invite conversation in response to a question ("What do families do?"). Discuss the different tasks and routines of families, conversing about who does these things in each home. Model appropriate language and attitudes when talking about differences. Incorporate books such as *All the Colors of the Earth* by Sheila Hamanaka, *Whoever You Are* by Mem

Fox, or *A Cool Drink of Water* by Barbara Kerley to further understanding.

Sing songs and share stories in different languages. Invite family members to teach songs from their home culture during large-group activities. Create a community songbook that includes these songs. Engage in oral storytelling, teaching children key phrases in home languages and encouraging active participation from the community of families in your early childhood program. For more information about strategies to support children who are English learners, see chapter 5 of the *California Preschool Curriculum Framework, Volume 1.*

Plan meaningful celebrations with support of the children and families. Use information gathered from conversations with families to plan important events ("What traditions would you like to see included in our program?"). Ensure that celebrations are authentic by asking the community, children, and families for ideas about how they would like to plan and carry out events. Integrate family-inspired activities with existing daily routines.

Read and converse about books that accurately represent the lives and experiences of children. Examples include *In My Family/En mi familia* by Carmen Lomas Garza, *All the World/Todo el mundo* by Elizabeth Carton Scanlon, *My Very Own Room/Mi propio cuartito* by Amanda Irma Perez, *Gathering the Sun* by Alma Flor Ada, and *Going Home* by Eve Bunting. Promote discussion and encourage children to identify with the experiences of diverse story characters.

2.0   Relationships

Children learn about themselves and others through the relationships they develop with teachers and peers in preschool. In early childhood, there are significant advances in social skills with the growth of social and emotional understanding, and children grow in recognizing the mutual responsibilities and accommodations of relationships. Friendships become closer, more cooperative (which aids in conflict resolution), and often more exclusive as children increasingly value their friends. Teachers contribute to the development of these social skills through the close relationships they develop with the children in their care, their encouragement of shared activities with friends (and other peers), and their contribution to children's mutual understanding.

VIGNETTE

Jaime and Max are riding a tandem (two-seat) tricycle around the playground tricycle path, both grinning as they go around the curves. "Just a minute," Max tells Jaime. "I want to go over and get my jacket." "Okay," responds Jaime. "I'll save your seat."

As Max leaves, Sofia approaches Jaime and gestures to the empty second seat. "I want to ride with you," she tells him. "No, you can't. This is Max's place. I'm saving it for him," explains Jaime. "You can ride on that one," he suggests, gesturing to a tricycle nearby.

"That's not fair," protests Sofia. "I want to ride with you." "But I'm riding with Max," repeats Jaime. "We're friends." At that moment Max returns, wearing his jacket. "Okay, ready to go again," he tells his friend as he climbs back on. They zoom down the path as Sofia looks sadly after them.

Ms. Carla, monitoring the riding path area, approaches, squats down, and puts her arm around Sofia's shoulders. "It looks like you wanted to ride, too," she observes. Sofia tells her, "I want to ride with a friend."

Ms. Carla looks around the playground to see what other children are doing, hoping to find another child she thinks Sofia might enjoy joining in play. She notices Ana, also alone, hopping around the large circle of stepping stones. Knowing that the two girls have enjoyed conversation with each other indoors while building block structures, she comments, "I see your friend Ana enjoying the stepping stones. Shall we go over together and join her?" Sofia agrees, and Ms. Carla helps her to greet Ana in a friendly way and ask if Sofia can hop on the stepping stones with her. She leaves after the two girls begin to make up a story together about crocodiles that are in the water around the stepping stones and about how to avoid getting caught by them.

TEACHABLE MOMENT

▶ Ms. Carla knows the children in her preschool group. She respects special friendships of the kind that Jaime and Max have, while also being aware of children like Sofia, who need extra help finding compatible play partners and initiating interaction with them.

In this situation, she comforts and sympathizes with Sofia, understanding that Sofia's real desire is to play with someone, rather than simply to ride the tricycle. She bases her suggestion about joining Ana on her past observations of the children's interests and play styles and her judgment that they would probably enjoy playing together.[19] She also knows that Sofia needs support to initiate interaction, so she facilitates her entry into Ana's game and observes until the two girls seem to be playing companionably. She makes a note to herself to find other occasions during play and projects where she can nurture the children's relationship.

Interactions and Strategies

Develop quality, nurturing relationships with the children in your program. Make time to regularly connect with individual children throughout the daily routine. Observe children at play, noting personal styles, preferences in play and exploration, developmental levels, and special needs. Use this information to support children in child-initiated play and teacher-initiated instruction. For more information about resources for teachers of children with disabilities or other special needs, see appendix D of the *California Preschool Curriculum Framework, Volume 1.*

Model effective relationship skills as you interact with other adults and children. Communicate with care and respect. Make explicit your intent ("I am going to ask Ms. Wong if she and her class would like a turn with our new camera. I bet they would like to take

some pictures of their projects, and I like to help my friend!").

Prepare an early learning environment and daily routine that foster peer interaction. Supply the space with materials that encourage interaction. Plan the daily routine to include opportunities for children to work in pairs as well as small groups. As mentioned in the *California Preschool Curriculum Framework, Volume 1,* chapter 3, "Social–Emotional Development," choose well-balanced partnerships and groups with attention to individual

interests, energy, developmental stage, and emerging friendships.

Teach children positive interaction strategies during large-group meetings. Use visual aids, including posters and cue cards, to enhance children's understanding of pro-social behaviors. Break down social skills into simple steps and have children role- play—for example, "When you want to join others already playing a game, the first step is to move closer [points to picture of a child moving closer]. Next, watch how they are playing the game [points to picture of eyes]. Finally, ask to play [points to picture of a child interacting with the group]. Say or sign, 'Can I play?'" Provide children with a chance to practice with toy people or puppets. For specific ideas and strategies, refer to the teacher resources available from the Center on the Social and Emotional Foundations for Early Learning (CSEFEL); visit http://csefel.vanderbilt.edu/ for more information.

Provide all children with coaching and appropriate prompts as they maneuver through peer relationships. Observe the environment for children in need. Take advantage of teachable moments to remind children of skills previously introduced in large-group experiences. Offer words to support children's constructive behavior ("I can see you are waiting for a turn. Remember you can ask to ride the swing. Say or sign, 'I want a turn, please'"). For more information about strategies to support children who are English learners, see chapter 5 of the *California Preschool Curriculum Framework, Volume 1*.

Reinforce pro-social behavior and its impact on others. Draw attention to children's actions by using descriptive

language ("You gave Nolan a turn with the typewriter. He looks excited to get a chance to explore!").

Offer sensitive guidance as children experience challenges related to peer interactions and friendship. Communicate matter-of-factly about children's emotions and perspectives. Offer ideas for coping—"It looks like you are feeling sad that Van is playing with Riley. Sometimes friends play together, and sometimes they play with other friends. That can be frustrating. Maybe I could help you find someone who wants to play puzzles with you."

Facilitate positive social problem solving. Use open-ended questions and commentary to summarize the problem—"It sounds like Gwen wants to play with Jolie and Morgan, but Morgan, you just want to play with Gwen." Use active listening to encourage perspective taking ("Morgan, you are saying only two people can play princesses"). Ask for solutions— "What can we do? We have a problem." Offer suggestions as appropriate—"I wonder if there is another game you could all play together that has three princesses."

Read books that deal with the themes of friendship and relating to others. One example is *Jamaica and Brianna* by Juanita Havill. Help children prepare and confront challenges in relationships by offering indirect opportunities to explore friendship. Select books carefully to ensure they are representative of authentic experiences for the children in your care.

3.0   Social Roles and Occupations

Young children are fascinated by the world of adults. This is apparent in their careful observation of adult activities, reenactment of these activities in their play, questions about adult roles and occupations, and excitement about activities (e.g., visits to the fire station) that permit direct experience with adult occupations. An early childhood education program encourages this interest through activities such as creating a market or repair shop, providing artifacts of adult occupations in the dress-up area (such as a police officer's hat), and taking children to visit places where adults work.

VIGNETTE

Marcella knows exactly what she wants to do this morning when Mr. Paul greets her at the door. "I'm going to the block area," she indicates. She continues purposefully toward the shelves and takes down all of the long wooden blocks, piling them on the floor. She begins to build a pattern of horizontal and vertical blocks that looks like a series of window frames, and becomes frustrated when they fall over.

"We need some nails with the blocks," she tells Mr. Paul. "You can't make boards just stay together by themselves." As they converse about this idea, she tells him that her papa is working every day now, building the inside of a store. "Does he use nails when he builds?" asks Mr. Paul. "He has nails in his tool belt, she answers. "When we went there, he let me put it on. It was really heavy."

When Marcella's mother arrives to pick up Marcella from preschool, Mr. Paul relates the story and finds out that the project is in a local building that is being converted into two smaller stores. Marcella's papa and other carpenters have been hired to frame the interior walls and put up drywall.

Since the project site is in the school neighborhood, Mr. Paul arranges a walking field trip to visit it the following week. In preparation, the class makes a list of questions about the project. Mr. Paul checks out library books about carpentry and building projects to display on the shelves in the block area. One of them is called Let's Build a Clubhouse *by Marilyn Singer. He posts a set of blueprints and adds clipboards and pencils to a nearby shelf. He also brings out the carpentry prop box, which contains hard hats and plastic tools. He ensures that the books and images portray a variety of people, including women and people with disabilities, with active roles as architects, designers, and members of the building trades. During and after the field trip, he will observe what especially interests his class and decide what other elements might enrich this curriculum.*

TEACHABLE MOMENT

> In this situation, the teacher is attentive to a child's play and converses with her to find out what prompts her comments. He tries to match his curriculum to the interests of children in his class and takes this opportunity to address a new topic. This inquiry is specifically about a parent's job, but it could be expanded in many directions to explore work roles in the neighborhood, occupations of family members, and the skills and tools people use to do different kinds of work.

Interactions and Strategies

Design the early learning environment to encourage all children's active engagement in each area, regardless of gender, home language, or abilities. Invite participation in the block area, science area, art area, dramatic play area, and in all other designated learning areas of the program by carefully selecting materials for exploration based on observations of the group's individual children at play. Produce and post print (e.g., labels) in English and in the home languages of the preschool community. For more information about resources for teachers of children with disabilities or other special needs, see appendix D of the *California Preschool Curriculum Framework, Volume 1.* For more information about strategies to support children who are English learners, see chapter 5 of the *California Preschool Curriculum Framework, Volume 1.*

Provide children with play props for exploring occupations and work settings. Dress-up clothes, office supplies (e.g., computer keyboard, envelopes, stamps), and other tools (e.g., aprons, fire hoses, garden gloves) used in the workforce encourage children to imitate the actions of family members and other adults in their lives. Incorporate real objects when possible.

Get to know the workers in your setting. If your preschool program is housed within a larger school or community organization, visit the various workers on site to observe them in action. Have the children prepare a list of questions to ask them about their jobs. Draw a visual organizational chart showing each person's job name and where she or he works.

Convey respect for the roles of adults who work at home. In discussion, book selection, and visual documentation, include and represent the adults whose work is primarily within the family home. Tasks such as cooking, laundry, shopping, home maintenance, and baby care are essential to household functioning, and the family members who perform these tasks should be represented in the preschool setting.

Highlight the roles that elders play in family life and in society. Invite children's grandparents and older family members to visit the preschool setting, either as program volunteers or to share skills, hobbies, or stories with the group. Emphasize that children's grandparents are often in the paid workforce and in family caregiving roles. Read books that portray older adults positively, introduce photos and news stories involving older public figures, and emphasize the roles that elders have played in children's family histories.

Incorporate books, magazines, and other forms of print that include images and stories of different workers. Be sure to include people of different genders, abilities, and racial backgrounds. Display in conjunction with current program investigations.

Include the pursuit of further education among work options. Many young children have adult family members who are engaged in education or training programs—some of which constitute a full-time occupation. Discuss the importance of education and demonstrate respect for adults who balance parenting and study. Invite student parents to share their fields of study with the group. If possible, take a field trip to a setting where adults go to school.

Invite family members to share their work experiences, including those that may diverge from traditional gender roles. Help children prepare questions in advance about roles and responsibilities ("What do we want to know about being a cook?"). Provide photographs, pictures, and real objects to help children visualize work experiences.

Talk about future career goals. Ask children to share, in a large group, what jobs they hope to do when they grow up. Write a list of their ideas. Counter misconceptions directly ("Boys and girls can be teachers").

Visit community stores, businesses, and service providers to observe workers in action. Include opportunities to visit places and participate in activities that include people with physical disabilities or other special needs (e.g., dance troupe that includes dancers with special needs). Prepare them to ask questions during the visit. Record children's observations. Help them reflect on the purpose of the work and its impact on people's daily lives.

Bringing It All Together

"You always get to do the money," complains Emma. Beck announces, "No, Tommy, I'm the customer. I was here first." Ella and Maya argue about the pieces of a plastic hamburger: "You can't have it again. It's the only one . . . " These and similar interactions between children have been typical in the area ever since Ms. Berta added the "Restaurant" prop box to it.

Now Ms. Berta is struggling to figure out how to foster more cooperation among children playing in this dramatic play area. The restaurant theme is very popular, but children's play is currently dominated by arguments over who gets to use which items from the restaurant prop box. Each child seems to be trying, independently, to hoard the most items from the box.

Ms. Berta shares her dilemma with Ms. Galyna, the school's mentor teacher, who says she can come in for a quick visit during the next day's play time. She follows her visit with some suggestions that help Ms. Berta rethink the area's design for the following week.

On Monday, the children entering the area are greeted by a large restaurant sign. A waist-high shelf unit defines the front of the area. On top of it sit two toy cash registers, supplied with ample paper bills, plastic coins, receipt pads, and pencils. A clear plastic jar labeled "Tips" sits in between. On a hook, hang clip-on badges: Cook, Cashier, Server, and Customer. There are several of each. The shelves under the front counter hold stacks of paper drink cups and trays. The cooking pans and utensils are clearly displayed on the area's stove and sink shelves, as are multiples of food items and dishes in the refrigerator and cupboard. The eating table is set for customers.

Ms. Berta begins play time as a restaurant customer, placing her order, asking questions of the employees, and helping the other players think about what a cook, server, or cashier in a restaurant would do. She refers them to each other with their ideas and questions, and soon they are having restaurant conversations with her and with each other "in character."

Over the next two weeks, the group makes changes and additions to the restaurant. At a class meeting, the group votes to make it a pizza restaurant, and the teacher adds donated pizza rounds that children cover with drawn-on toppings. With Ms. Berta's help, interested children work in pairs to write and post menus. Several small groups of children remain intensely interested in the theme, and their play in the restaurant area becomes more elaborate and content-rich. With active teacher support and modeling, friends are able to constructively solve conflicts that occur.

The design of the early education environment can be crucial to encouraging positive interactions and relationships. In this example, the teacher, with mentoring, prepares a learning environment that leads to rich peer interactions focused on a play theme. She structures opportunities for children to work in pairs and small groups and to try out a variety of roles. The play theme appeals equally to boys and girls, and so it supports more social interactions between them than often occur in the dramatic play area. Children with special needs can be actively engaged in all the roles. It is also effective at including children who are English learners in a play scenario that can offer a variety of roles and can include some key vocabulary in their home language.

The teacher spends at least a few minutes each day playing a role in the restaurant, and sometimes invites a more socially or linguistically isolated child to join her to provide experience with peer-group entry skills. She intentionally interacts in ways that help children expand their collaborative play scripts as they try on a novel set of adult roles. Pretend play interactions such as these can be an important scaffold for children who are English learners and children with special needs to build language and social skills when they might otherwise feel more isolated.

Engaging Families

The following ideas may help families guide their children to expand their understanding of family culture, relationships, work, and roles in the home and in the broader world:

✔ Encourage families to tell stories and sing songs to their child about their home culture. Children benefit from learning about the things that are important to their families. They develop a sense of pride in their heritage, including customs, history, and talents of family members.

✔ Remind families that they are the child's most influential models. The attitudes of families toward people with different cultural and racial backgrounds, abilities, and personal characteristics will shape their children's attitudes. Encourage them to draw their child's attention to the positive ways they interact and cooperate with others in their community.

✔ Support families to help their child develop strong, warm relationships with adults and children among their family and friends. Children need opportunities to practice their positive social skills with people they love and trust. Coach them in how to talk and play with others in polite and friendly ways.

✔ Suggest ways that family members can talk with their child about the daily work they do. The tasks adults do at home, at a job, in the community, or in school are important for children to be aware of as "work." They are beginning to learn about the different ways people contribute to their families and communities. Family members and other adults can help shape their ideas about future possibilities open to them.

Questions for Reflection

1. What are some of your own biases and "blind spots" about people whose racial or cultural backgrounds are very different from yours?

2. What could you add to your early education environment that would help children learn to appreciate the diverse characteristics of people different from themselves?

3. In what ways could you partner with the families in your preschool program to support attitudes of acceptance and inclusion?

4. What specifically could you do to support children from diverse linguistic and cultural backgrounds to engage with peers who may not share that home language or culture? In what ways could you facilitate interaction between typically developing children and children with special needs?

5. In what ways do you see your style of interacting with children reflected in the ways they interact with each other in the preschool setting?

6. What could you add to your curriculum and interactions to help children become more aware of the roles and occupations open to them as adults?

Becoming a Preschool Community Member (Civics)

An early childhood program is a wonderful setting for learning how to get along with others and for understanding and respecting differences between people. It is also an important setting for learning about oneself as a responsible member of the group. In an early childhood education setting, young children are enlisted into responsible citizenship for the first time outside of the family, encouraged to think of themselves as sharing responsibility for keeping the room orderly, cooperating with teachers and peers, knowing what to do during group routines (e.g., circle time), cleaning up after group activities, participating in group decisions, supporting and complying with the rules of the learning community, and acting as citizens of the preschool.

This early experience in elementary civics is challenging for young children because it requires that children balance their own desires and goals with those of others. For this reason, many of the skills of preschool community membership take time to develop as young children gradually acquire the social understanding, self-regulatory capabilities, and motivation to compromise, bargain, negotiate, take turns, and act in other ways that respect the needs and interests of their partners.

Many formal and informal activities of an early childhood education setting contribute to developing the skills of preschool community membership. These include group decision making that may occur during circle time (including voicing opinions, voting on a shared deci-sion, and accepting the judgment of the majority); resolving peer conflict and finding a fair solution; understanding the viewpoints of another with whom one disagrees; respecting differences in culture, race, or ethnicity; sharing stories about acting responsibly or helpfully and the guidance that older children can provide younger children or children with less positive experiences about being a preschool community citizen. In this section, specific strategies are discussed that support development in each of the following substrands:

1.0 Skills for Democratic Participation
2.0 Responsible Conduct
3.0 Fairness and Respect for Other People
4.0 Conflict Resolution

1.0   Skills for Democratic Participation

An early childhood program is the first social setting outside the home in which young children can learn, understand, and practice the skills of democratic participation. These skills are learned by doing. The opportunity to be a responsible member of the group, to share in group decision making, to express an opinion and listen respectfully to others' views, and to accept the majority decision but also respect the feelings of the minority—these are skills that most preschoolers are ready to learn because of advances in their social and emotional understanding. Even so, young children may be challenged to cooperate with a group decision that they do not share, and teachers can be helpful as they model democratic practices in the preschool setting, encourage children's positive participation in group activities, and acknowledge the disappointment that can arise from not always getting one's way.

VIGNETTE

The children gather with Ms. Yana in a circle on the rug for their morning meeting. After they join in singing their greeting song, Ms. Yana shares some news while holding a round fishbowl with a blue beta fish in it. "Ms. Katrina, who works in our school office, has given us this fish for our preschool room. She has given us the fishbowl and fish food, too." Many children are excited and want to ask questions and tell stories about fish. Ms. Yana reminds them of the class rule they agreed on: "One person at a time. Please wait for your turn," she says. Several children indicate that they have ideas to share. Ms. Yana calls each by name in turn, and several children in the group remind others of their rule to listen quietly during others' turns. During their meeting, they discuss ways to keep the fish safe and healthy, and Ms. Yana lists on chart paper the ideas they suggest. Their list includes: Feed it every day; don't drop things into the fishbowl; make sure the water is clean; don't give it too much food; and several other ideas.

Lev adds, "Hey, our fish needs a name." Ms. Yana puts up a new piece of chart paper and asks each child around the circle for a naming idea, which she writes on the list. "Now that we have everyone's ideas, we can vote on a name. It looks like we have five to choose from. Listen as I read and point to our whole list of names. Think carefully about which one you would like to give our fish, and then raise your hand when you hear or see your favorite fish name."

They complete the process of voting, and Ms. Yana records the numbers on the chart. Several of the older children identify "7" as the highest number on the list. "Yes, seven people voted for the name 'Stripey,' so that will be our fish's name. I will make a nametag for the fishbowl during work time."

TEACHABLE MOMENT

▶ This anecdote describes a class meeting with older preschool children who have had experience with class meetings throughout the year. The class has established rules together, and some children want to make sure that everyone follows them—typical behavior at this age. They have participated in simple voting before, but they still need the teacher's specific instructions and reminders about how the process works. With practice, most children can participate successfully in a brief, well-structured group meeting that focuses on a topic of interest to them. A voting exercise also provides a manageable experience of active participation for children who are English learners. For more information about strategies to support children who are English learners, see chapter 5 of the *California Preschool Curriculum Framework, Volume 1.*

Interactions and Strategies

Share control of the preschool environment with children. An environment that prepares children to become members of a democratic society fosters mutual respect and focuses on how children feel, act, and interact with others. Rather than primarily asserting their authority and giving orders, teachers sensitively attend to children's ideas and offer developmentally appropriate guidance to enable children's successful, shared engagement in the early learning environment ("It seems that you all want to play with the new blocks. How can we make sure that everyone gets a turn?"). Assigning class jobs is another way of sharing control. Having a responsibility helps children to have a different perspective.

Promote a sense of connection and community by using terms such as "we" and "our" when speaking with children and adults: "We all clean up at the end of play time." "Our garden needs water to grow. Who will help water it?" "Our friends need help solving their problem. What can we do to help?" This intentional language choice communicates shared responsibility for both the people and things in the preschool setting. Encourage shared goals by planning for shared work and events. As children participate in group activities, both small and large, they see themselves as active members of a community with an important role in its success—"Let's bounce the balls on the parachute together. We need everyone's help to keep the balls in the middle of the parachute."

Incorporate class meetings into the daily routine of older preschool children. Community meetings offer children an opportunity to practice communicating in groups by sharing their own ideas as well as carefully attending to the ideas of their peers. Set aside time each day for children to gather as a group for problem solving, project planning, and collaborative learning. Class meetings should be brief, lasting no more than 10 minutes. Teachers set the tone for participation in group meetings by creating a predictable structure for the event. They may consistently begin with a greeting song before introducing new materials for the week ("This week we have watercolor paints in the art area. Does anyone know how to use watercolors?"), opening up a discussion about a program problem ("A lot of our friends have been worried about not getting a turn with the new bikes. What ideas do you have for solving our problem?"), or inviting the children to share an important learning experience ("Taylor found out something about magnets. Let's listen to what she has to tell us").

Support freedom of thought and speech in individual investigations, as well as in planned group experiences. Free speech is an important foundation of democracy. Children can practice expressing their own ideas, thoughts, and feelings as they create unique art, build with blocks, develop their own ideas about scientific phenomena, and dictate their stories. Teachers should listen attentively to children's ideas and mediate conflicting viewpoints and perspectives ("You think the balloon will get bigger, and Taiga thinks it will stay the same size. You have different ideas"). Such intentional efforts facilitate a communication-friendly environment that promotes critical thinking and the sharing of differing ideas and perspectives.

Generate community rules and expectations to protect the rights of each individual and to create a community of trust and security. Begin with a group discussion about how rules keep order and ensure fairness for all. Extend the conversation to include rules of the community (e.g., circle time rules). With an understanding of rules and expectations, invite the children to create rules for the indoor and outdoor settings.

Engage children in community brainstorming and problem solving. As children share their thoughts for program planning and problem solving, they develop their ability to communicate ideas and influence group decisions. Engage children in brief discussions both individually ("Sasha, what role will you play in the doctor's office?") and in small and large groups, documenting their ideas and using charts to organize suggestions for action ("Lili, I'm asking all of our friends what we would like to have in our pretend restaurant. Do you have ideas for me to write down?").

Make group decisions when appropriate. Voting, a cherished right and privilege of democracy, introduces children to accepting the majority's judgment while still respecting the minority view. Teachers should first set up voting activities that permit each child to have his or her own way. ("Which topping will you have on your biscuit? Butter or jam?") Graph votes to document individual and group decisions ("Four friends will have butter, and 10 friends will have jam"). With experience, children can vote using the majority rule. Make decisions about what to name a program pet, what type of restaurant to add to the dramatic play area, or what game to play at large-group time ("Some of our friends wanted to play 'Red Light, Green Light,' but more of our friends wanted to play 'Simon Says,' so today we will play 'Simon Says'"). When children have strong differing points of view, build consensus through discussion and negotiation.[a]

Acknowledge emotions related to group brainstorming and decision making. Young children struggle with impulse control as it relates to group wants and needs and may express strong reactions to what they perceive to be disappointing decisions. Teachers who describe what they see, putting language to the child's response and the experienced outcome, help children make sense of democracy in action—"You really wanted to name the fish 'Blue' but more friends wanted to name the fish 'Stripey.' It's frustrating when the group makes a decision we don't like."

Model citizenship skills. Adults who form positive relationships with children, characterized by mutual respect and care, encourage children to replicate such sensitive and attentive interactions with their peers. For example, a teacher, working with a child to fold a paper airplane, suggests asking the other children for help when they become stuck in the process—"I can't remember what comes next. Maybe we could ask our friends if they have ideas about making paper airplanes." Teachers

also reinforce citizenship skills as they model pro-social behavior in their relationships with other adults—"I'm going to offer these extra crickets to Mr. Sanchez. I know his group likes insects, too."

Use guidance to redirect children to more appropriate actions and behavior. Set predictable and consistent limits based on agreed upon community rules. Encourage children to reflect on their actions and recall expectations for behavior—"You look angry. Yesterday we created a list of rules, and we all agreed to be gentle with our friends. We said, 'no hitting' [pointing to rule chart]. What can we do?" Offer more specific support as needed—"You can tell Rosa, 'I'm not done. I want the binoculars back.'"

Reinforce behavior. Teachers who draw attention to the positive actions of children build a foundation for respecting and protecting the rights of others ("Bruna, you're helping Vicente and Marcos build their castle. And you are each taking turns adding pieces to the top. You are all making sure each friend gets a turn").

Create an inclusive environment that values and encourages the participation of children from all cultural and linguistic backgrounds as well as children with special needs. Children need adult guidance in order to develop respect for individual and group differences. Teachers who model respect encourage children's positive, inclusive behavior. Adults can further promote the active participation of all members of the preschool community by intentionally including multicultural, anti-bias literature, displays, materials, and goods that represent the linguistic and cultural backgrounds of the community. Adults can also adapt materials and activities, when necessary, to foster inclusion of children with special needs. For

---

a. Specific strategies to assist children who do not easily accept group decision making can be found in "Resources for Teachers of Children with Disabilities or Other Special Needs," appendix D of the *California Preschool Curriculum Framework, Volume 1.* Or visit http://csefel.vanderbilt.edu/, the Web site of the Center on the Social and Emotional Foundations for Early Learning (CSEFEL). Additionally, teachers should consult with family members and specialists (i.e., mental health consultants and early childhood special education specialists) about positive behavioral supports that will facilitate inclusion of children with emotional and behavioral challenges in group settings.

example, use a variety of voting methods (e.g., buttons, stickers) to ensure all children's active participation. By representing and including all children, teachers promote children's positive self-concept and affirm the value of diversity. For more information about strategies to support children who are English learners, see chapter 5 of the *California Preschool Curriculum Framework, Volume 1*. For more information about resources for teachers of children with disabilities or other special needs, see appendix D of the *California Preschool Curriculum Framework, Volume 1*.

2.0 Responsible Conduct

Young children enjoy being helpful. Their self-esteem is enhanced by assisting others and by being regarded by adults as responsible group members. As preschoolers develop greater self-regulatory skills, and as their memory for preschool setting expectations and rules grows, they become more capable of responsible conduct in the early childhood education setting. Teachers contribute to the growth of responsible conduct when they ensure that group expectations for behavior are developmentally appropriate, the schedule and environment are organized to enhance children's self-regulation, and when they help children understand and enact appropriate behavioral expectations.

VIGNETTE

On Monday morning, Will, Peter, and Emma choose the art area as their first stop for the day. As they begin to gather the materials they need for their projects, they are upset by the condition of the art area. "Ms. Mary, the art area is messy! The glue sticks don't work, and the ribbons, buttons, and paper are gone. Yucky sticky scissors, too!" they report to her with dismay. She joins them to survey the area.

Ms. Mary commiserates with the children. "I'm so sorry it looks this way. While I was home sick last week, our teacher helpers had so much to do, and they didn't know how we store the things in our classroom. We always keep our art shelves neat and clean. What shall we do now to fix the art area?"

The children, who are used to their active role in helping maintain the classroom environment, begin to talk about the things that need to be done. As they do so, Ms. Mary brings over trays and suggests that they place the dry glue sticks, sticky scissors, and empty collage material bins on them. She then asks them to look around again and tell her all the things that need to be done as she writes a list. As she supplies soapy sponges, they volunteer to help clean up messy shelves and art tools while she resupplies materials from the cupboards. After a few minutes of group work, Ms. Mary looks around and says, "Thank you all for your hard work. This already looks better. Work goes so much faster when we do it together."

TEACHABLE MOMENT

In this anecdote, the teacher affirms the children's frustration about the disarray in the art area. While providing an explanation but not blaming others, she quickly guides them into problem solving and cooperative work to help correct the situation. This reinforces their sense of group responsibility and ownership of the preschool environment. Her follow-up comments reaffirm the value of group collaboration in addressing a problem.

Interactions and Strategies

Set the tone for responsible conduct by creating a high-quality learning environment and thoughtfully scheduled daily routine. Make the space aesthetically pleasing and designate learning areas to guide children's constructive, self-initiated play. Choose developmentally appropriate materials organized for exploration to ensure successful learning experiences for all children. Plan a predictable daily routine that promotes self-regulation; limits transitions, and offers a balance of active and quiet activities, individual and group experiences.

Create community rules with children's input. Converse with children about the purpose of rules and their impact on our day-to-day lives—"What rules do you have at home?" "What would happen if we didn't follow rules?" Invite children to share ideas for caring for the room and one another. Summarize and post these rules at the children's eye level.

Model the behaviors you expect. Children imitate the behavior of others, especially that of the trustworthy adults important to them. For this reason, adults must make sure to follow all community rules and expectations; having adults not adhering to group standards confuses children. Be consistent. Communicate the purpose of your actions—"I am helping Owen put away these train tracks so our other friends have more room to play."

Help children remember and meet community generated rules and expectations by providing both visual and auditory cues and prompts. Display posters with pictures illustrating steps for positive action throughout the environment ("Gentle hands, Emilia. See [pointing to the rule poster], our rule is 'be gentle'"). Use picture cards in different contexts with children to help them recall and apply appropriate social norms ("Look. Wait." [Child looks and points at a picture of child waiting for a turn.] "Yes, it's time to wait. It will be your turn to wash hands next"). Coach children and provide prompts to prepare them for success ("I can tell you are excited for our walk to the park. Remember, we hold hands together on our walk. Ask Liam, 'Can I hold your hand?'"). When commenting on appropriate behavior, link the behavior to the rule or expectation ("Wow, you handed her the block so carefully. Way to use gentle hands!"). For more information about resources for teachers of children with disabilities or other special needs, see appendix D of the California *Preschool Curriculum Framework, Volume 1.* For more information about strategies to support children who are English learners, see chapter 5 of the *California Preschool Curriculum Framework, Volume 1.*

Plan opportunities to further explore and converse about community rules during small- or large-group meetings. Connect rules to everyday experiences ("What if you wanted to ride the bike, but a friend was already using it? What is our preschool rule?"). Rules can be context-specific (e.g., home and school). Help children differentiate social norms and behavioral expectations across settings ("At school, the rule is we all put away our toys when we are finished playing").

Redirect children's actions toward more appropriate behavior by using positive descriptions of what you expect children to do. Rather than limiting children's forward movement with "No," "Stop," or "Don't . . . ," state expectations for action in clear, short statements ("Walk inside." "Keep the cornmeal in the tub."

"Feet stay on the ground"). Give reminders as children work to internalize rules of conduct. Enforce developmentally appropriate consequences connected to the behavior as needed ("It looks like it is too hard to keep our blocks low right now. Let's find a new activity. We can try again later").

Facilitate problem solving. Help children plan for the future by asking open-ended questions and offering supportive comments ("What could you do next time a friend takes your truck? . . . Yes, you could say no. What if they don't listen to you? . . . Pushing could hurt, and our rule is 'be gentle.' You could get a teacher to help, though. Come find me next time a friend won't listen to your words").

Reinforce responsible conduct by using descriptive language. Acknowledge children's actions by reporting what you see ("You sat quietly at large-group time without any help. And you raised a quiet hand to share your idea!"). Emphasize the positive impact of a child's actions on others— "When you gave Kamau a turn with the dinosaur puzzle, it made him happy! That is being friendly."

Utilize books to build on the children's ability to empathize and extend care to others. Stories can promote positive values such as cooperation, generosity, kindness, compassion, and interdependence. Read stories and engage children in conversation about the content. Help them extend ideals described in text and illustrations into their own lives and social experiences.

Assign tasks for community care, such as watering plants, feeding program pets, or helping to prepare snack, to help children practice responsibility. Rotate jobs and make developmentally appropriate adaptations to include all children's active participation. For more information about resources for teachers of children with disabilities or other special needs, see appendix D of the *California Preschool Curriculum Framework, Volume 1.*

3.0 Fairness and Respect for Other People

"That's not fair!" expresses a preschooler's concern for fairness, and the child's growing sensitivity to others' feelings also contributes to this concern. Efforts to act fairly can be manifested in turn-taking, sharing, cooperation, and understanding how preschool program rules help to maintain fairness. During the preschool years, children gradually become more capable of balancing their own interests with those of other children and of respecting another's desires and goals. Teachers contribute to these achievements as they explain rules (and the reasons for them) that emphasize fair conduct, the need to cooperate with the interests of others, and using words to help children understand another's emotions, viewpoints, and goals. It is also important to assist children when they think that fair equals the same. Sometimes what is fair is doing what is needed for each child. There are times that a child may need an adult's help to do something (e.g., hold the jar steady) and another child is asked to do it without an adult's help.

VIGNETTE

Three children spin around on the playground tire swing, two of them laughing and talking as they go. "Faster, faster," Mariana and Isabel tell Mr. Kevin, who is pushing the swing. "No, slow down," counters Juana. "My head is feeling too dizzy." Mr. Kevin stops the swing from spinning and says, "It sounds like we have a disagreement about how fast to swing." "We want fast! We want fast!" chant the two girls.

Mr. Kevin leans in to speak calmly to all three girls. "I know it's fun for you to twirl fast, but it makes Juana feel sick. What shall we do to make sure she can have a good time on the tire swing, too?" They all think for a minute. "I know," responds Isabel." "We can have a turn for kids who want to ride fast and then a turn for kids who want to ride slow." Mr. Kevin turns to Juana. "How does that sound to you?" Juana nods her agreement. Mr. Kevin repeats the plan and then tells the girls, "You figured out a fair way for everyone to have fun on the swing."

TEACHABLE MOMENT

In this situation, the teacher was attentive to the experience of all three children and stopped the game when one expressed discomfort. His words helped the two friends consider the well-being of the third, as well as affirming her right to have her needs respected. He can extend this learning to the rest of the class by recounting the experience with the girls during the next large-group gathering and emphasizing their successful problem-solving process.

Interactions and Strategies

Maintain a culturally inclusive environment. Encourage friendships among all children in the preschool community. Be mindful of the social expectations of children's home cultures. Build strong relationships with families and ask authentic questions to gain insight into family norms and values.

Model respect and care in everyday interactions. Attend to children's cues ("It looks like you are feeling frustrated. I'm concerned. What's wrong?"). Listen attentively to children's ideas and feelings. Paraphrase and restate the feelings they express to ensure your own understanding of each child's individual perspective and experience ("Oh, you wanted to play with Jiyou, but she's playing with Valerie right now").

Use language that promotes concern and care for the community. Using descriptions such as "our class," "our room," and "our program" encourages a sense of responsibility for the care and well-being of one another.

Converse about the "whys" of fairness and respect. Some program resources are limited; therefore, help children consider the importance of sharing. Provoke a large-group discussion about "why we share." Promote children's self-reflection to further their understanding of the feelings involved in such situations ("What does it feel like when a friend tells us we can't play with a toy?" "Why might the friend not want to share her toy?" "What could she do to help solve the problem?"). Some children might use equipment in such a way (or need adaptations) that might not be seen as "fair." Use these situations to talk about differences and fairness.

Teach social skills, such as patience and generosity, by using social stories and role-play experiences. Introduce perspective-taking activities in pairs, small, or large groups to further children's ability to treat others with sensitivity and care. Plan small group or partner activities during which children can practice these skills.

Coach children during their interactions with peers. Build perspective by describing another person's feelings and needs and offer suggestions for appropriate responses: "She looks upset that you grabbed the paper airplane without asking. Hand it back and then let's ask Beatrice if you can have a turn with it. You could say, 'Beatrice, can I hold the airplane you made?'"

Intervene and address negative interactions immediately. Create an environment where all children feel safe and secure. Take immediate action when someone is being mistreated. Seek information from both the initiator and the child being targeted. Provide guidance to both children. Offer effective coping strategies ("Get a teacher") and additional pro-social instruction for relating to one another ("I don't like that. Please stop"). If you see patterns beginning to emerge, you may need to provide more focused teaching of social skills; ideas are available through the CSEFEL Web site (http://csefel.vanderbilt.edu/).

Use storybooks to enhance children's understanding of ways to express feelings and build peer relationships. Select books, such as *If Everybody Did* by Jo Ann Stover, *My Mouth Is a Volcano* by Julia Cook, or *Jamaica and Brianna* by Anne Sibley O'Brien, to match emerging challenges with fairness and respect in the preschool community. Encourage children to reflect on the text and illustrations ("What do you think Jamaica is feeling now? What does the illustration show us?"). Invite them to share personal experiences that match story content ("Have you ever felt mad at a friend? What did you do? How did you solve the problem? Was it fair?").

4.0   Conflict Resolution

Conflict with peers and teachers is inevitable in an early childhood education setting, and it offers opportunities for learning about conflict resolution. Young children are becoming more capable of understanding others' views and goals, coordinating them with the child's own desires, and devising strategies for mutual accommodation. Although distress, aggression, and adult mediation are common outcomes of peer conflict, so also are bargaining, negotiation, compromise, and other approaches that reflect growth in social and emotional understanding and in self-regulation. Teachers contribute to these achievements as they put children's feelings into words, encourage children to think of solutions to their own problems, and model skills of compromise and negotiation.

VIGNETTE

Four children play in the block area, building a complex array of roads and garages for the small metal cars that teachers have just introduced into the area. "Hey, that one is mine!" shouts Peter, who has quickly gathered all but one of the shiny red cars close to his legs. Abdul tightens his grip on the red car he holds and looks at Peter. Nolan also notices that Peter has most of the red cars. He tells him, "Peter, that's not fair. We get some, too." Peter still refuses to let go of any of "his" cars, and tells the others that he got them first. Owen, who is still working on the road, looks cautiously at the others as he builds, listening to their conversation.

Nolan looks at the rest of the cars in a pile on the floor and tells Peter he needs to share the good ones. When Peter refuses, Nolan finds Ms. Deborah, who accompanies him back to the block area, where she gathers the children around her on the rug and uses questions to prompt them to describe what has happened and their feelings about it. "You were all working on the road together, but now I hear that everyone is upset and worried about who is going to use which cars on it, especially the new red ones," she summarizes. "I'm glad you came and asked me to help you figure it out."

Then Ms. Deborah asks, "What are your ideas for solving this problem?" She makes sure that each of them has a chance to contribute to the conversation, rather than allowing it to be dominated by the two most verbally assertive children. When they cannot agree on which idea to try first, she suggests a plan that combines the ideas from several children. As they get back to work, each with a couple of cars, she selects a car that no one else has chosen and runs it toward the road while asking the builders about the next step in their road design.

TEACHABLE MOMENT

> This is a fairly complex conflict-resolution situation, involving several players, as is common in preschool dramatic play and block play areas. The teacher has the children describe the situation, which she did not observe, including the children's emotional cues she did observe, and pauses the action while involving everyone in a problem-solving conversation. She is especially deliberate about representing the interests of the less verbal children. She is aware that the issues may resurface, particularly if children did not fully process the emotions they were experiencing, so after the incident is resolved for the moment, she remains in the block area to support this group's play and interaction for as long as she can.

Interactions and Strategies

Prevent conflicts by limiting program transitions and minimizing waiting time. Overly competitive games can work against community caring and collaborative learning and should be avoided. Plan group projects with a shared goal that requires children to work together.

Model cooperation and care for others. Be mindful of your interactions with the other adults and children in the preschool setting. How do the children perceive your efforts to resolve disagree-

ments among staff members? How do you respond to differences of opinion with children's family members? How do you handle disagreements between children? Children will naturally imitate adults. Be consistent in implementing a sensitive, positive approach with others.

Provide children with a calm presence in conflict situations. Begin by stopping any harmful actions, stepping in between the children in conflict. Gently hold onto any object in dispute to help children focus on the problem at hand. Take an unhurried and neutral approach to resolving conflicts. Give all children involved a chance to identify their feelings, then have them generate ideas for solutions. As they are supported to approach the conflict in a consistent way, they will begin to work through the steps on their own with minimal support from the teacher.

Use descriptive language to help children make sense of conflict. Verbalize your observations of the children's physical actions in response to conflict—"Your fists are really tight, Lucas. Ellie, you're holding on tight to the blue shovel." Encourage the children to identify and label their emotions. Offer tentative interpretations of the children's emotional state as additional support ("You both look angry").

Prompt children with open-ended questions and statements. Ask each child to share their version of the incident ("What happened, Taiga?"). Offer appropriate ways for the children to express their wants and needs—"Oh, you don't like it when Cara moves over your road. You can tell her to go around." Attend to the needs of children who have difficulty expressing themselves verbally. Offer them effective tools for communicating with others.

Involve children in the problem-solving process. Facilitate rather than direct the solution process. Ask children to share ideas for resolving the problem. Include all children involved in the conflict. Patiently wait for them to agree upon a solution—"So you are saying you don't like that idea. What ideas do you have for solving the problem? . . . What do you think Kelsey? Do you like Megan's idea of taking turns?" Once a decision has been made, offer follow-up support as needed—"Okay, I will come back in five minutes when it is Kelsey's turn to wear the dress."

Create problem-solving kits. Prepare sets of visual cue cards (e.g., picture of children finding more, taking turns, waiting). Keep problem-solving kits easily accessible and stationed throughout the early learning environment. Introduce their use to children during a large-group meeting. Remind children of this resource as conflicts arise ("Let's grab a solution kit to help us think of ways to solve our problem"). For details about solution kits, refer to the CSEFEL teacher resources available at http://csefel.vanderbilt.edu/.

Read books related to social conflict. Help children connect previous experience with storybook content. Invite them to think of ways the characters could solve their problem.

Use "persona dolls" or puppets and social stories to promote skill development and perspective taking. Choose an area in which the children are currently challenged in their social interactions. Prepare a puppet show or social story based on the problem. Introduce the characters and the conflict between the characters. Encourage the children to support the characters in their resolution of the conflict. Create a list of pro-social options. Demonstrate the positive resolution of the conflict by using the puppets.

Bringing It All Together

The children gather for circle time, and after the group's gathering song, Ms. Anya begins dramatically. "Today I am going to tell you a story about something that just happened in our room.

At the beginning of playtime today, two of our friends, Julia and Javier told me their plan was to work with the medical kits in the house area. They were going to use the stethoscopes, bandages, and all the other medical tools to take care of the babies. I told them I would plan to visit later to see if their patients were feeling better.

A few minutes later, Julia and Javier hurried over to tell me that all the babies were missing. They had looked all over the clinic, and had found no babies! Where do you think they looked?"

The children in the group call out their ideas about all the places the children could have looked. Ms. Anya continues, "You are right. They looked in all those places. No babies. So what did they do next?" Many children around the circle who are now recalling the incident call out, "They asked us to help!" "That's right," affirms Ms. Anya. "They know what good problem solvers you are and how good you are at teamwork, so they asked you. Pretty soon you gave them lots of helpful suggestions of places to look. And did they find the babies?" "Yes!" the children call out. "And where were the baby dolls, Julia and Javier?" "They were out on the porch!" the children respond, laughing.

Ms. Anya concludes the story by repeating, "Yes, you are right. The dolls were out on the porch drying after yesterday's bath. Thank you all for helping us solve the mystery of the missing baby dolls."

This anecdote illustrates one technique a teacher has chosen to help build a sense of community among her preschool class members. Children love to hear stories about themselves, especially stories they can all help to tell. With practice, an attentive teacher can learn to recount and elaborate on everyday preschool experiences in ways that help a group of children remember them positively and draw from them important lessons about their own pro-social behavior. A good story can do far more than merely entertain. See the "Research Highlight" below.

Research Highlight

Young children's memories of past experiences are important, but their recall is sometimes scattered and incomplete. Adults often discover that young children do not remember the details of an event that the adult would expect (such as which team won the ballgame, or the ducks encountered on a nature walk), but instead they recall the funny sound of someone's voice, a piece of paper picked up along the way, or the snack after returning home. Likewise, the way people tell about past experiences varies across cultural groups. When an adult takes the time, however, to reminisce about the event with the child, researchers have found that young children remember more and their memories are better organized as a result. Adults are particularly helpful when they talk about the child's past experiences in an *elaborative* manner.[20] Elaborative speech expands on the details of what happened, asks the child *wh-* questions (such as *what* happened next? *Why* did she say that? *Who* was that person?), and provides clarifying feedback, such as confirming the child's accurate recall but questioning mistakes in memory. Elaborative speech also supports alternative styles of storytelling that may not be familiar to the adult, thus supporting the skills of memory and storytelling among children from diverse cultures and linguistic backgrounds. Young children are just beginning to develop the skills of remembering, and reminiscing about past experiences with an adult who is elaborative provides children with enhanced memory for these experiences and help in recalling them.

Engaging Families

The following ideas may engage families in helping their children learn and practice the foundational skills of positive community participation.

✔ Suggest that adults find household projects to work on with their child. Everyday chores, like folding laundry and putting away groceries, can provide opportunities to work together and to give children an experience of contributing to the household.

✔ Remind adults to notice and recognize times when their child is being cooperative and responsible. Comment positively about what you notice and appreciate. Having the approval of their special people is important to preschool children. It motivates them to behave responsibly in the future.

✔ Encourage adults to talk with their child about respect and fairness. When children disagree with siblings or others during play, remind them that their way of solving the problem should be fair to everyone involved. Point out to them rules and laws you follow that help protect people's rights, especially the rights of people who are not as strong or powerful as others. This can explain why some things are not "the same" and are still fair.

✔ Work with adult family members as they establish some simple, age-appropriate rules to be followed at home and help children understand that there is a reason for each rule. "We need to be quiet when other people in the house are sleeping" conveys the message that you behave in ways that respect others' needs for sleep and, thus, contribute to their welfare. Talk with family members of children with special needs to identify triggers of uncooperative behavior and strategies for calming, establishing rules and so on.

Questions for Reflection

1. What techniques and activities do you use to build a sense of community among the children and adults in your preschool setting?

2. What process do you use to create expectations or rules for responsible behavior in your preschool setting? What differences do you observe in rule-following behavior when children participate in setting class rules?

3. How do you partner with children's families to teach the values of respect, fairness, and cooperation that are important in family and community life?

4. What do you do to encourage and support children in seeking assistance from peers and in collaborating to achieve their play-project goals?

5. How does your program work to help children who are English learners build a sense of being part of the preschool community and overcome possible feelings of being outsiders?

6. How can you introduce the concepts of fairness and respect for everyone into the preschool curriculum activities?

7. In what ways do you set a good example for children to follow as they learn skills for being members of a community?

Sense of Time (History)

One of our unique human characteristics is the ability to think of ourselves in relation to past events and to anticipate the future. The ability to see oneself in time enables us to derive lessons from past experiences, understand how we are affected by historical events, and plan for the immediate future (such as preparing a meal) or the long-term (such as obtaining an education). The ability to see oneself in time is also the basis for perceiving one's own growth and development, and the expectation of future changes in one's life.

The preschool years are a period of major advances in young children's understanding of past, present, and future events and how they are interconnected. Yet their ability to understand these interconnections is limited and fragile. Young preschoolers have a strong interest in past events but perceive them as islands in time" that are not well connected to other past events. As they learn more about events of the past, and with the help of adults, children develop a mental timeline in which these events can be placed and related to each other. This is a process that begins during the preschool years and will continue throughout childhood and adolescence.

A thoughtfully designed early childhood program includes many activities that help young children develop a sense of the past and future. The activities may include conversations about a child's memorable experiences, discussions of a group activity that occurred yesterday, stories about historical events, circle-time activities in anticipation of a field trip tomorrow, and picture boards with the daily schedule in which special events can be distinguished from what normally happens. In these and other ways, teachers help young children construct their own mental timelines.

Sample Developmental Sequence: Sense of Time

As children mature, they are better able to relate past and future events to their current experience. As they do so, they are developing an expanded and more detailed mental timetable that they can use for remembering the past and anticipating the future.

Beginning level: Children can talk about events in the immediate past and ask questions about activities in the near future, but they need an adult's help to understand events in detail that are not part of immediate experience.

Next level: Children remember past events easily, enjoy hearing stories about "long ago," and anticipate events in the near future, but are often confused about when these events occur in relation to each other (for example, Grandpa was a boy "long ago," but is this the same "long ago" when the dinosaurs lived?). Children also enjoy talking about their experiences of the recent past.

Next level: Children demonstrate greater skill in relating past events to one another (Grandpa was a boy "long ago," and that was before your mom was born), knowing how past events affect the present (Maria is happy today because Daddy arrived home yesterday from a long trip), and planning in simple ways for future activities.

Mature or proficient level: Children are now capable of distinguishing events that happened "long ago" from those of the more recent past, and distinguishing events in the near future from those much later in the future. Their mental timeline is more detailed and accurate. In addition, children enjoy telling more complex autobiographical stories about their own experiences, reflecting the importance of their personal past to who they are today.

In this section, specific strategies are discussed that support development in each of the following substrands:

1.0 Understanding Past Events
2.0 Anticipating and Planning Future Events
3.0 Personal History
4.0 Historical Changes in People and the World

1.0   Understanding Past Events

Young children enjoy talking about their own experiences and hearing stories about past events. They are also slowly developing an ability to understand when past events occurred in relation to one another (such as realizing that their birthday was celebrated after they started going to preschool) and how past events are connected to current experience. By conversing with young children about events of the past, asking questions and making connections between past and current experience, teachers can help children begin to construct a mental timeline of past experiences. They can also use visual aids, stories, and other tools to communicate about events of the recent past and "long ago."

VIGNETTE

At outdoor play time, Mateo hurries over to a large tree limb lying at the edge of the playground. "Look what happened!" he exclaims. "Yeah," agrees Luis, who had joined him, "the wind did it. It crashed down our big tree, too, right into the street. Some guys are coming to saw it up." Luis pauses. "My grandma said that tree was really old." Ms. Sofia, who has followed them to the area, joins the conversation. "Your grandma told me about that when she came with you this morning. It's a big surprise when a tree that was there just yesterday suddenly isn't there anymore today, especially when it had been growing there for a long, long time. Things like that can happen fast. What do you think will be different when you get home this afternoon?"

TEACHABLE MOMENT

The teacher observes their intense interest in the fallen playground limb and listens attentively to Luis' narrative description of the fallen tree at home. When she joins the boys' conversation, she uses time words and phrases, including *yesterday, today, this afternoon, suddenly, fast,* and *a long, long time.* She can tell by listening that the event made an emotional impression on Luis, and she affirms that it was a big surprise. With her question, she encourages him to think about how the change will feel. See the "Sample Developmental Sequence: Sense of Time" on page 87 for more information.

VIGNETTE

As circle time begins, the teacher says, "Right before we went home yesterday, we sang our 'Slippery Fish' song. This morning I noticed that Jonah and Hailey were singing the song in the reading area and were using these shark and whale finger puppets to act it out. I could tell they were really enjoying singing that story, so I found more puppets for them to use." She holds up a small fish, a bigger fish, and an octopus finger puppet as the children name them. She asks them if they would all like to sing the song again and then asks them to recall the sequence of the sea animals in the song. As they call out or sign the animal names, she arranges them on the floor in the middle of the circle. As she points, they name each one, and then the group sings the song, performing the gestures. Afterwards, she tells them that the basket of finger puppets will be in the reading area tomorrow for them to use.

TEACHABLE MOMENT

► This teacher is attuned to children's activities during play time and modifies her circle time plan to build on an interest she has observed. She chooses to revisit a song they have enjoyed the day before and retrieves props from a cupboard—the finger puppets—to help focus the group's attention on the sequence of sea animals in the song. She uses playful repetition during the group activity to reinforce the concept of sequence and the words *first, next,* and *last* as she arranges and then points to the animal puppets. She encourages the children to use gestures or signs and follows up by telling the children where they can find the puppets the following day.

Interactions and Strategies

Use predictable routines to facilitate children's sense of time. Incorporate visual and auditory aids to promote understanding and use them in conversation with children—"Yes, before we went outside we played inside (pointing at a picture on the daily routine chart), went to circle time, and then had snack. We are very busy at school."

Incorporate time words into conversation. Intentional use of words like *before, after,* and *yesterday* supports the development of a child's sense of time

sequence. Calendar activities, such as Calendar Time during class meetings, provide labels for concepts such as first, last, next, and later ("Last Friday was Orrin's birthday, this Thursday is Maya's birthday, and next Friday is Wenqi's birthday. We have a lot of birthdays this month!"). See the "Sample Developmental Sequence: Sense of Time" on page 87 for more information.

Create opportunities to converse with children about meaningful experiences and build connections between current and past events. Encourage small-group conversation during mealtime ("What was the first thing you did at work time?").

Invite community reflection during large-group time ("What did we do before we came inside?"). Initiate one-on-one conversation during child-initiated play—"You started this project yesterday during outside time. What did you use to build the bottom of your fort? . . . What will you add today?"

Listen attentively to children's narrative descriptions. Regularly invite children to share past and current personal experiences. Extend and expand on a child's initial statement with descriptive language—"Yes, last week we did go on a special field trip to the post office. We had to walk very safely. We will have to be safe again today when we go on our neighborhood bird walk." Make use of reflective comments and open-ended questions—"I liked seeing the scrub jays and hearing their calls. What things did you like best about our bird walk?"

Communicate with awareness about children's narrative style, noting preferences for time sequences, emotional cues, and other practices that influence the formation of mental "scripts." Adults may recall experiences differently than children; they may attend to different details of the event and bring a deeper understanding of sequence and time. Listen attentively to children's descriptions of past events. Take note of what parts of the occasion were most important to the child. Ask open-ended questions to extend the conversation ("What happened after you went to the park?"). Add your own observations to elaborate and expand on children's initial

recollections ("I am usually ready for a rest after a long day of playing, too"). Pay attention to the pace of the child's communication. Avoid rushing the conversation; pause and wait for details. See the "Research Highlight" on page 83.

Document and display children's work at their eye level to encourage recall and reflection. Invite children to talk about their learning experiences one-on-one ("Tell me about this drawing of the robot you made. How many days ago did you make it?") as well as with peers during large-group experiences—"During our class meeting, Kaylah is going to share with us what she made with recyclables on Monday." Take pictures of projects that extend over time and converse about the exploration process. Write down the children's words as they describe their work—"When we started our paper mache project last week, we first had a wire shape. Then it took several days to add the wet strips of paper. Now that it is dry, we can start painting our paper mache animal."

Sing songs, recite poetry, and read books that involve sequencing. Popular stories, shared in book format or by oral storytelling, like *The Very Hungry Caterpillar* by Eric Carle, *We're Going on a Bear Hunt* by Michael Rosen, or *The Three Billy Goats Gruff* offer children a predictable sequence of events to recall and discuss—"What happened first?" "Then what happened?" "How did the story end?" Songs that include a progression in activity, such as the Peanut Butter and Jelly song, offer a similar experience.

2.0   Anticipating and Planning Future Events

"What happens next?" is in the mind (and are the words) of young children as they try to anticipate events, such as what will happen tomorrow. They can anticipate events because they understand the predictable routines of their lives, such as the daily schedule of the preschool, or what usually happens after they wake up in the morning. During the preschool years, children become more skilled at planning for these routine events and even anticipating unusual events, such as a family visit that will happen soon. Teachers can contribute to the development of these future-oriented skills by helping young children understand the regular routines of daily life, conversing with them about unusual events to come (such as a visit to the fire station), and helping them plan (such as talking about dressing more warmly when the weather turns colder).

VIGNETTE

Beata and Simon are painting at the easels when Ms. Neva begins reminding children in each interest area that it is time to begin finishing their work before cleanup time. As she approaches the easels, Simon tells her, "Mira! I painted three pictures before cleanup time."

TEACHABLE MOMENT

> In this preschool program, the teacher has established a predictable daily routine, and Simon knows that cleanup time always follows playtime. His teacher gives the children a reminder ahead of time so they can predict the transition to cleanup time.

VIGNETTE

The children in Mr. Ricardo's group have just returned from winter break. During circle time, Mr. Ricardo tells them, "We're going to start a cooking project. We'll make three different kinds of bread on three different days this month." He points to a date on the calendar, and says, "On this day, Kristen's father is going to bake corn bread with us." "Oh, I've had corn bread before. It's soft," says Sara. "It's yellow," adds Maya. "It'll be fun to see whether our corn bread is like the kinds you have had," Mr. Ricardo says.

Next, he points to another date and says, "After that, on this day, Mei's mom will make scallion pancakes with us." "Oh, I love scallion pancakes! I've had them in a Chinese restaurant," says Ben. Mr. Ricardo responds enthusiastically, "I have never had them before. I can't wait to taste them! Our last bread will be tortillas. Yaritza's grandma will help us make them on this day," he adds, pointing to a calendar date at the end of the month. Several children share that they eat tortillas at home. "We'll take photos of all three breads and you can draw your own pictures, too. We'll also write down the recipes to make a Bread Book."

Mr. Ricardo then asks children to think about what kinds of cooking tools they may need for the bread project, and he starts making a list on large paper he has posted, repeating each item someone suggests as he adds its name and a simple drawing of it to the group's list (e.g., bowl, spoon, pan). "We have made a good start today. We will do more planning tomorrow so we will be ready to make cornbread, our first bread, on Friday," he summarizes, pointing to Friday on the calendar.

TEACHABLE MOMENT

This vignette describes a teacher-planned group meeting designed, in part, to involve children in advance planning and preparation for activities. The teacher has organized a large project that will take place on a sequence of future dates. He uses a calendar to illustrate the time that will pass between cooking days. He also engages children in anticipating what they will need to gather ahead of time to be ready to work with their guest cooks.

VIGNETTE

"My birthday is just two more days," Jordan tells Ms. Trisha excitedly. She responds with enthusiasm and suggests that they look at the class birthday calendar together. He finds his photo and name on a calendar square, and she shows him the square for today and notes how close together the two are. He begins looking for his friends' photos on the calendar and asking how soon their birthdays are. Ms. Trisha converses with him about how many days make it seem like a short or a long time, and about how it feels to be waiting.

TEACHABLE MOMENT

This situation illustrates the emotional challenges of anticipating and waiting for future events, and how teachers can begin to introduce time concepts. It shows how difficult it is for young children to understand how their experience of time relates to the calendars, timers, clocks, and other tools adults used to represent it.

Interactions and Strategies

Maintain a consistent daily routine so children can anticipate, predict, and follow through with program expectations. A picture schedule may be used to help children visualize and understand the sequence of events, as well as get ready for program transitions ("It's almost circle time, Everett. Let's pull off your picture and get your chair for circle time").

Converse with children about upcoming events. Invite children to share their plans for the weekend—"I know Grandma is picking you up today for your weekend together. What will you do at her house?" Prepare children for any change in program routine—"Today we have a special visitor. Yana's father will come to talk to us about his job at the grocery store during small group time. Instead of sitting at your tables, we will meet at our circle time rug."

Comment on behaviors that anticipate future events. Describe steps for participating in a daily routine—"Before we go to snack, we wash our hands") or explain a child's response to an expected experience—"I think Hailey is feeling excited about her dad coming for a visit. She's missed him while he's been away." Explain your actions that look ahead to a future event—"I am putting our outdoor water toys away. It is almost winter, and it will be too cold to use them until the weather warms up again in the spring." See the "Research Highlight" on this page.

Promote planning as children engage in child-initiated projects. Begin a play period with a brief planning time. Ask children to share their idea for play. Using comments and open-ended questions, encourage children to provide details about their play plans. Help children anticipate problems and support their ideas for solutions—"So, you plan to play with the droppers and test tubes in the science area. Yesterday you ran out of baking soda for your experiment. What can you do today to make sure you have enough baking soda to go with your vinegar?"

Involve children in program planning. To prepare for change in curriculum, invite children to share their current knowledge of a subject and then ask for ideas for supplying the learning environment—"What do you know about airports?" "What will we need to build an airport in our room?" Plan meaningful celebrations by asking children to suggest elements from their home celebrations that could be translated for the group setting. See the "Research Highlight" on this page.

Introduce time-keeping tools to help children monitor the passage of time— "I'm looking at our timer. We have to wait three more minutes until it will be your turn on the tire swing." A paper chain can be used to help children count the number of days before an exciting event—"We have two more rings on our chain. That means two more days until our Día de los Muertos celebration. I know Tia Liz has been baking bread at home." Mark special days on the program calendar. Keep the calendar accessible and use child-friendly pictures and symbols (e.g., a photograph of a child on a calendar square to denote his birthday).

Talk with children using time words— "Tomorrow morning we will have more time to play with our hamster. She needs to rest now. I know a whole day can seem like a long time to wait."

Research Highlight

Planning for a future activity requires anticipating what one might need, and preschoolers are developing skill in this kind of "mental time travel." In one study, three-, four-, and five-year-olds were shown photographs of several natural settings and were encouraged to imagine that they were in those environments (such as imagining walking across a sunny desert, or walking across a rocky stream).[21] Children were then asked to choose what they would need for that activity from among three items. After hearing the story about the desert, for example, children were asked to choose a bar of soap, a mirror, or a pair of sunglasses. Most of the children at each age chose the correct item (e.g., the sunglasses for the desert), but their skill improved with age, and older children were much more capable of explaining their choice with reference to a future need (e.g., "The sun will be shining").

3.0   Personal History

A sense of time also includes understanding one's personal history. For young preschoolers, the awareness that they are changing appears in their pride in displaying their developing accomplishments, knowledge, and skills. Older preschoolers may explicitly contrast what they can do now with the fact that they could not do this when they were younger. In addition, children are beginning to create an **autobiographical** **memory** of their personal experiences that they enjoy sharing with others. Teachers contribute to this developing sense of personal history by recognizing children's accomplishments, sharing their pleasure in their expanding competencies, and discussing with children the experiences that are significant and memorable to them. See the "Research Highlight" on page 83.

VIGNETTE

Today is Annie's fifth birthday, and her mother has sent an envelope of photos of Annie at different ages for her to share at circle time. Annie is excited to show them to Ms. Jen, who takes time to sit down at a table with her to look at them. Ms. Jen comments on each one Annie takes out, asking questions and encouraging her to reminisce about what the photo shows her doing. She then suggests that they line up all six photos on the table in sequence, starting with the one that shows Annie as a newborn baby and ending with a recent family celebration.

TEACHABLE MOMENT

Ms. Jen acknowledges Annie's excitement about the birthday photos and takes time to converse with her about them. Her questions and comments help Annie to recall more details. She uses them to prompt her and then informally assess Annie's sequencing abilities.

VIGNETTE

Two children look around the room to find their teacher. "Mr. H, look what we made!" Mr. H walks over to where they have finished constructing a long tunnel using cardboard tubes and masking tape and are now rolling marbles through it. "You finished your experiment, and now you're testing it," he observes enthusiastically. "Is it working the way you had wanted it to?" As the children decide to prop it up on blocks to carry the marbles down faster, Mr. H stays with them, and he and they converse about the long time they worked on it, the challenge of getting the masking tape to hold together the tubes, and the fact that they now are both very good at using masking tape themselves and at helping younger children and children with motor difficulties learn how to use it.

TEACHABLE MOMENT

> In this interaction, Mr. H expresses enthusiasm about the children's accomplishment, reviewing with them the steps of their project and acknowledging how challenging the task was. He reminds them of how much their skills have grown and lets them know that he has noticed them helping other children learn the same skills.

VIGNETTE

For today's circle time, Ms. Robin has prepared a two-column chart with the headings: "When I was a baby, I couldn't . . ." and "Now I can . . ." She reads the first phrase and asks the group to think of things they were not able to do as babies. As children share their ideas, including, "I couldn't walk; I couldn't ride a trike, I couldn't eat apples . . ." she lists them in the first column. When they finish, she reads all the ideas aloud to the group.

Ms. Robin then points to the phrase, "Now I can . . ." and again asks for children's ideas. After they finish sharing, she reads aloud the second list. As she points to each list, she comments to the group enthusiastically, "Look how many things you couldn't do when you were a baby! Look how many things you can do now! You've grown so much!"

TEACHABLE MOMENT

> This example presents a more structured way to involve the entire group in contrasting their current abilities with their abilities at earlier ages. They will not, of course, be able to remember their own lives as babies, but will be able to share ideas based on family stories and on their current experiences of the babies in their lives. The activity can also be done individually or in a small-group setting.

Interactions and Strategies

Share memories. Engage children in conversation about their own current work and recent accomplishments—"You did it! You filled in all the pieces of the puzzle." Communicate observations of children's abilities of over time—"You wrote the letter A. You've been working hard on writing this year."

Ask questions to increase children's recollections of events. Use open-ended

questions to invite language-rich conversation and prompt children's recall of specific details—"Tell me more about your family reunion. It sounds like you had a lot of aunts and uncles there. Did you eat something special at the party?"

Encourage children to express their feelings and reactions to experiences. Ask children to share their personal reactions as they pursue new challenges, face frustration, and experience success—"It took a long time to climb that ladder. How did it feel?" Use descriptive statements to paraphrase their response—"So you were feeling scared at first, but then you felt better after you climbed back down." Such conversation supports the development of self-awareness.

Document children's work over time and create individual portfolios for each child. Include photographs, **anecdotal notes,** samples of writing and artwork, and other pieces of work. Organize materials in chronological order to illustrate changes and the passage of time. Share with children and families ("I remember when you first started preschool you rode the small yellow bikes. Now [pointing at a picture] you are big enough to pedal the large bikes.").

Acknowledge birthdays. With sensitivity to family preferences, plan a simple activity such as highlighting the date on the calendar or singing a preferred song of the child. Use language focused on developing children's understanding of change—"You were three, and today you are four years old!" Where possible, invite families to participate—"Meera's grandmother is here with her today to share some family photos of her growing up these last four years and to sing her favorite song in Arabic."

Provide activities that invite personal reflection. Use old photographs, clothes, and personal data (e.g., length at birth) to help children think about personal change—"You were 21 inches long when you were born. Let's use a tape measure to see how big you are now . . . Wow! You are 40 inches tall! You've grown so much!" Ask questions to invite appropriate comparisons—"What was something you couldn't do when you were a baby, but is easy now?"

Make use of children's stories that explore growth and individual change. Stories like *Leo the Late Bloomer* by Robert Kraus, *Peter's Chair* by Ezra Jack Keats, or *The Growing Story* by Ruth Krauss can be used to further children's understanding of personal change over time. Engage children in conversation about their experiences of growth—"Peter outgrew his chair. He was too big. Is there something you had when you were little that you are too big for now?"

4.0 Historical Changes in People and the World

Young children enjoy learning about events of "long ago" and displaying their knowledge of dinosaurs or other historical knowledge. They also enjoy hearing stories of their family history. Their understanding of time is reflected in their ability to distinguish events of the recent past from those of "long ago," but they are confused over when different histori-cal and family events occurred in relation to each other. Teachers can aid children's developing historical understanding by sharing their enthusiasm for the events of "long ago" that provoke their interest, and discussing with them the family stories that tell of the past experiences of their family members.

VIGNETTE

The teacher notices that several children are standing by the tall sunflowers that the class had started from seeds last spring. She joins them, asking if they remember planting the seeds. After listening to their comments, she adds, "Yes, that does seem like a long time ago. It was before we said good-bye for the summer. Now we are back at school in the fall, and look how much our sunflowers have grown and changed. They are taller than most of us, and their seeds are almost ready to roast and eat or to save for planting time next spring."

TEACHABLE MOMENT

This teacher uses the children's interest in the sunflowers to begin a conversation about seeds growing into plants, reminding them of both the beginning and end of the cycle, as well as its relationship to the seasons of the year.

VIGNETTE

Adelia's aunt has come to the group's circle time to tell stories about her town's holiday fiesta. She has brought a colorful dancing skirt and shawl for the children to see. Adelia adds, "We only do that kind of dancing at special parties. You need the right kind of music." Her aunt explains that, when she was growing up, many people played musical instruments and danced often. The teacher converses with the group about how sometimes the way people do things changes over time. "Remember, when Lan's mom came to talk to us about Chinese New Year? She said that a long time ago, when she was small, some of the most important things children could get were new clothes. What about now?" One child raises his hand, and the teacher asks him to speak: "People can get new clothes more often, not just during the New Year." The teacher makes a "mental note" to find more books at the library about holiday traditions.

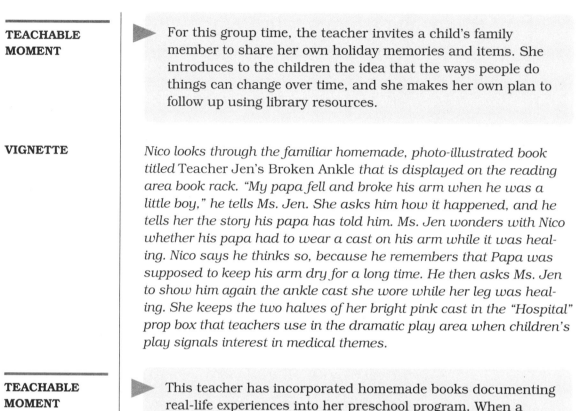

TEACHABLE MOMENT

For this group time, the teacher invites a child's family member to share her own holiday memories and items. She introduces to the children the idea that the ways people do things can change over time, and she makes her own plan to follow up using library resources.

VIGNETTE

Nico looks through the familiar homemade, photo-illustrated book titled Teacher Jen's Broken Ankle *that is displayed on the reading area book rack. "My papa fell and broke his arm when he was a little boy," he tells Ms. Jen. She asks him how it happened, and he tells her the story his papa has told him. Ms. Jen wonders with Nico whether his papa had to wear a cast on his arm while it was healing. Nico says he thinks so, because he remembers that Papa was supposed to keep his arm dry for a long time. He then asks Ms. Jen to show him again the ankle cast she wore while her leg was healing. She keeps the two halves of her bright pink cast in the "Hospital" prop box that teachers use in the dramatic play area when children's play signals interest in medical themes.*

TEACHABLE MOMENT

This teacher has incorporated homemade books documenting real-life experiences into her preschool program. When a book reminds the child of a family story, she listens and encourages him to think about more of his story's details. She extends the interaction using an authentic prop that Nico remembers.

Interactions and Strategies

Utilize familiar resources, such as parents, grandparents, family members, close friends and community members, to share their own childhood experiences. Encourage them to share photographs of themselves when they were the children's age. Prepare questions to facilitate the conversation: What games did they like to play? What was something that was hard to do then, but is easy now?

Read children's stories about different places and times to expand children's perspective. Converse about concrete comparison experiences—"How do the homes in the book differ from the homes we live in?" "Do you have clothes like the children in our story?" "What are they eating in the story?" "Do we still eat it?"

Expose children to the arts. Sing traditional songs from a variety of cultures, both familiar and unfamiliar to the children. Listen to music and introduce art from different eras. Invite conversation about children's initial impressions and observations.

Observe changes in animals, plants, and the outdoors. Record children's

remarks over time and compare notes—"Yes, Harley the Hamster was small in September. I'll write down she is now five blocks long." Take photographs and create a chart to illustrate change—"This is our seasons poster. Let's add the pictures we took of our neighborhood in spring . . . See how the trees have new green leaves? In winter our trees looked so empty." Converse about change—"What did you notice about our bean sprouts . . . Yes, they've grown quite tall with sun, water, and time." Provide children with documentation tools to keep details of their observations over time.

Celebrate special events in a meaningful and authentic way. Avoid "tourist curriculum" by maintaining a consistent daily routine and incorporating celebratory events into regularly scheduled activities. Seek ideas from families and community members; incorporate them into the experience (e.g., "Today at large group, Andrew's mother is going to teach us how to move like lions and dragons").

Children should be an integral part of the planning process. Brainstorm ideas together and then put children's ideas into action. Keep activities simple and understated. Introduce key concepts related to celebrations, holidays, and rituals in concrete terms—"During Chinese New Year, some people decorate their homes, cook special food, and exchange gifts." For additional ideas and information, refer to *Celebrate! An Anti-Bias Guide to Enjoying Holidays in Early Childhood Programs* by Julie Bisson. For more information, see the "Research Highlight: Anti-Bias Curriculum Approach" on page 51.

Record significant events on a large calendar to create a program history. Refer back to the calendar and previous events as opportunities arise—"Last month we went on a field trip to the grocery store. This month we have planned a trip to the library."

Provide children with hands-on experiences with concrete artifacts and historical objects (e.g., toys, utensils, tools). Allow children to explore and experiment. Facilitate conversation about how the object was used and compare with current tools—"We have three kinds of egg beaters: a hand egg beater, an egg beater with a crank, and an electric egg beater. Which one do you think will work the fastest? Which one is the hardest work for your body?" Document the conversation and display with the objects.

Bringing It All Together

The preschool year is almost over, and Ms. Nguyen has finished compiling the portfolios for the children in her group. She will review and discuss them with family members at year-end parent conferences, and then families will be able to take them home. First, though, she has brought them to share with children during a small-group time.

"These are special books," Ms. Nguyen tells the small group of children around the table. "There is one for each of you, and it is all about you. Let's see if we can figure out together which is whose." She holds up the first one, with a photo and large printed name on its cover. "That's me!" exclaims Lamar, and Ms. Nguyen hands him the book. "We'll need to turn the pages gently so none of them will rip," she reminds the group. The other children identify their books, and then they all spend a few minutes paging through them, looking at their photos, artwork, dictated stories, writing and drawing samples, and other items put aside in their folders during the preschool year. While handing the book over to Griselda, Ms. Nguyen opens up the last few pages with Griselda's drawings and the dictated English sentences beneath the drawings, and says "Look, how much more English you can say now than before!"

"Look! That's me carrying back that bag of apples we bought at the store," Tyree shares. As the children look and comment, Ms. Nguyen reminisces with them about the shared experiences their portfolios document, like their walk to the grocery store and the signs children made afterward while setting up their own store in the dramatic play area. She has saved these signs and other contributions made

by children and has noted the date on the back of each one. She encourages them to converse with each other, as well as with her, about the memories their portfolio pages evoke.

The practice of making portfolios to document children's activities and growth over the course of the year contributes to their understanding of the passage of time. It also affirms for families how capable their children are becoming as they grow. Ms. Nguyen's group viewed a sample portfolio early in the year, and she explained that they could choose to save some of their work to add to their own special book. Throughout the year, the teacher has labeled and filed samples of each child's work, including art, writing, dictated stories, and teacher-recorded anecdotes

about projects and milestones she has observed. At times, she has asked a child if a specific item should be saved for his special book In addition, she and family volunteers have documented with photos some of the significant group experiences and projects of the year, and the program has printed copies for families. A portfolio takes planning, but it is a significant gift of personal history for both children and their families.

Engaging Families

The following ideas may engage families in helping their children begin to understand the concept of time and the passage of time in their own lives.

✔ Share ways to establish some dependable family rituals and routines. Children enjoy being able to anticipate predictable elements of each day, week, and season. Daily rituals can include a bedtime story or song or a special morning good-bye routine. Friday night pizza or a Saturday morning family walk can be weekly markers. Holiday rituals and traditions that include children can be anticipated and then remembered over time.

✔ Remind families to discuss family plans and events with children before they occur. Find some choices that children can make at home, such as choosing before bedtime which clothes to wear to school the next day or which color cup to use for drinking milk. Inform children of upcoming changes in advance. Knowing about a parent's planned absence, a weekend family gathering, or a move to a new apartment can help children cope with change.

✔ Share with family adults the importance of recounting past shared events with their children. Suggest that they use storytelling to help children remember the sequence and details of both everyday and special experiences. Emphasize the importance of including details and using descriptive words that will both increase children's vocabularies and help them expand their own capacities for organizing memories. Encourage them to make interactive storytelling a regular part of their times together.

✔ Suggest that families find a special place for items that document children's growth. This can be a scrapbook or album, a box, or a drawer. Include photos taken at different ages, artwork or dictated stories from preschool, a first stuffed animal, birthday cards, or other keepsakes. These are tangible reminders of a child's own personal history.

✔ Encourage adult family members to tell children stories about their family's history. Hearing stories about the past experiences of people close to them brings to life the idea that people grow and change over time and that everyone has a personal story. Hearing the childhood memories of adult family members is especially memorable to children.

Questions for Reflection

1. What kinds of comments and questions can you use when children share stories about their personal experiences with you?

2. How can you partner with children's family members to make the preschool environment reflective of their diverse family stories?

3. In what ways can you ensure that your preschool setting's daily routine is accessible and understandable to all of its children?

4. What can you do to make concrete documentation of each child's growth manageable for teachers and meaningful to children and families?

Sense of Place (Geography and Ecology)

ach person has a sense of the places to which they belong: home, workplace, school, and other locations that are familiar and meaningful. Young children experience this sense of place strongly because familiar locations are associated with important people who constitute the child's environment of relationships. Locations are important because of the people with whom they are associated: home with family members, preschool with teachers and peers.

Preschoolers also experience a sense of place because of the sensory experiences associated with each location: the familiar smells, sounds, and sometimes temperatures and tastes combine with familiar scenes to create for young children a sense of belonging.

Developing a sense of place also derives from how young children interact with aspects of that physical location. Preschool children relate with their environments as they work with materials; rearrange tables, chairs, and other furniture; create maps to familiar locations; travel regularly from one setting to another; and work in other ways with their environments. Young children also interact with their environments as they learn to care for them. Young children's natural interest in living things engages their interest in caring for plants and animals, concern for the effects of pollution and litter on the natural environment, and later, taking an active role in putting away trash and recycling used items.

These interests present many opportunities to the early childhood educator. Young children can be engaged in activities that encourage their understanding of the environments in which they live, whether they involve creating drawings and maps of familiar locations, talking about how to care for the natural world, discussing the different environments in which people live worldwide, or taking a trip to a marshland or a farm. In this section, specific strategies are discussed that support development in each of the following substrands:

1.0 Navigating Familiar Locations
2.0 Caring for the Natural World
3.0 Understanding the Physical World Through Drawings and Maps

Sample Developmental Sequence: Sense of Place

With each year, children better understand the settings where they live and learn, the routes between these places, and the natural environment in which they are located. As they do so, children also become interested in places that are unfamiliar and different.

Beginning level: Children use their knowledge of familiar places, like home and school, to confidently find the people and things they need. They can become confused or distressed if these settings change abruptly, such as if a room is redecorated at home.

Next level: Children are aware of a broader variety of physical settings, such as the places where familiar people live and work.

Children also recognize the routes between well-known locations and may use simple drawings to describe them.

Next level: Children's broadening understanding of the environment includes an appreciation of landscapes like hills and streams, weather patterns, and other features of the environment. Children also become more skilled at understanding the relative distances between familiar locations.

Mature or proficient level: Children's understanding of their own environment leads to expanding interest in unfamiliar locations and the people and activities associated with them. This can lead to an interest in maps and globes to understand "faraway" places.

1.0   Navigating Familiar Locations

The earliest "sense of place" that develops for young children is their personal experience of familiar locations, such as their home, preschool, and the routes connecting them to each other. Younger children identify familiar locations by the people and activities associated with each one and the routes between them, while older preschoolers have a wider view of the world in which differences in the physical ecology (e.g., hills and streams), weather, and common activities are better understood. Teachers can contribute to this developing understanding in their efforts to help young children understand their familiar locations in relation to the other places that people live and work, and by helping children better comprehend the physical world in which they live through activities such as nature walks.

VIGNETTE

Michael sits down with his peers and Mr. Sean at the snack table. "There was a huge dump truck going down my street today," he tells everyone. Mr. Sean asks him what was in the truck. "Rocks and big sidewalk pieces," replies Michael. "I know that," adds Rio. "It's by my house. Papa says they're digging up the street for water pipes." Several other children nod and agree that they know where that is and they have gone by it, too. Mr. Sean tells the children that the construction site they are talking about is just around the corner and down one block from their preschool. "Would you like to take a walk together to watch them work?" he asks. "It sounds like a big and exciting construction project is happening in our neighborhood."

TEACHABLE MOMENT

These children have noticed something exciting that is happening to the landscape of their preschool neighborhood. Mr. Sean notes their interest and joins the conversation, pinpointing the geographical location of the construction site. He makes plans to follow up on their interest by arranging a walk to watch the work being done. Mr. Sean considers how all children can participate in the visit to the work site.

Interactions and Strategies

Supply open-ended materials in the indoor and outdoor early learning environment to promote exploration of spatial relationships. Blocks, plastic or wooden animals and people, and transportation vehicles offer children opportunities to construct pretend homes and habitats as well as larger cities and worlds. Provide additional loose parts to designate bodies of water (e.g., an empty container filled with water or pieces of blue felt) and land formations (e.g., small cardboard boxes).

Describe your own actions as you travel between locations—"I am going to walk to the office to make a copy of our project. I will have to walk through the Toddler Yard to get there." "I go across a bridge each day when I drive to work."

Play games about how to get from here to there. Challenge children to see how many different ways (e.g., walking, skipping, crawling, and so on) they can move from one location to another ("Today let's see how we can get from the door to the swing set? . . . Instead of walking, let's try hopping across the yard"). Incorporate children with mobility challenges utilizing their adaptive equipment (e.g., wheelchair, walker, "skateboard"). For more information about resources for teachers of children with disabilities or other special needs, see appendix D of the *California Preschool Curriculum Framework, Volume 1.*

Engage children in conversation about how they travel to and from preschool each day. Plan a discussion during a large-group gathering. Create a list of the many forms of transportation. Pictures of different types of transportation may

Traveling around the world.

encourage all children's participation and can be mounted for the discussion. Extend the conversation to include what children observe while on their way to preschool. Compare with the route home. Is it the same or different? Talk about travel time.

Take walks through familiar locations and neighboring areas. Make a list of the things the children notice, rephrasing the children's language to elaborate on their ideas—"I can hear the creek, too! We must be getting very close to the water now." Invite children to record their observations during the walk using drawings and photographs. Repeat the same walks to build children's familiarity with and knowledge about significant landmarks. See the "Sample Developmental Sequence: Sense of Place" on page 104 for more information.

Converse about the here and now as well as encouraging later reflection. Discuss the walking surfaces children encounter—"How does the surface feel when we walk on the grass or touch it with our hands?" "How is it different from the gravel?" Help children recall important landmarks from recent outings— "Which building did we notice first on our walk?"

Locate and explore local landmarks.
Research and introduce bodies of water and landforms in your region. Visit sites when possible or share photographs of them. Compare and contrast the characteristics of each attraction—"What do you notice about these two pictures? . . . Yes, one is the Golden Gate Bridge, and the other is the bridge near our preschool. How are they the same? How are they different?" Extend the learning into the home by encouraging family outings to local destinations.

Promote children's understanding of weather and its impact on their day-to-day experiences. Use small- and large-group activities to reflect on clothing choices for the seasons. Help children attend to the impact of weather on living things and outdoor spaces—"How does weather change our environment?" Comment on weather and its influence on the daily routine—"I hear thunder and lightning. We will stay inside today until the weather clears." "It's a windy day, perfect for flying the kites we made last week!"

Comment on weather patterns and invite children to share their observations. Record patterns over time on poster board and post documentation at the children's eye level. Take dictation as children comment on weather. Elaborate on their descriptions—"Adelia says 'It's hot and sticky.' It is hot, and with a lot of gray rain clouds over our heads it feels humid. The extra moisture in the air makes us feel 'sticky.'" Take photographs of the appearance of familiar landmarks (e.g., trees) over time to show a continuum of change in weather through the seasons and its influence on the natural world.

Read aloud books and engage children in storytelling related to navigating familiar locations and daily routines. *Corduroy Lost and Found* by B. G. Hennessy, *Rosie's Walk* by Pat Hutchins, and *Jesse Bear, What Will You Wear?* by Nancy White Carlstrom are treasured children's books that depict characters encountering and responding to the physical features of their world.

2.0   Caring for the Natural World

Young children have a strong interest in the natural world because of their direct experience with growing things—a flower or plant, a kitten or puppy—that they care for. A plant or pet may be a young child's first experience of providing nurturance to one who is dependent on others' care (just as the child depends on the care of others). Teachers contribute to this awareness by guiding children's understanding of the connection between their feeding and watering and the growth they observe in a plant or class pet. They also encourage young children's understanding of caring for the natural world through their guidance about the hazards of pollution and litter. Teachers can also help preschoolers learn about natural

ecologies that are very different from their own, whether arctic, jungle, or other regions of the world.

VIGNETTE	*As the preschool group prepares to go outside, Ms. Toni comments, "Yesterday I noticed something different about the trees along our playground fence. This is the season we call autumn, and in autumn, the trees begin changing. Let's observe them while we are playing outside today, and we'll talk about them when we come back in."*
TEACHABLE MOMENT	▶ This simply stated observation by Ms. Toni draws children's attention to something they see every day but may not have intentionally observed. Mentioning it just as the children are going outside will focus their attention on the trees for long enough so that most children will notice the changing colors of the leaves. Having introduced the concept ahead of time will enrich the follow-up indoor discussion and story time about trees that she has planned.
VIGNETTE	*"I like this place," shares Maya as she looks around the small reading area. "What do you like about it?" asks Ms. Nicole. "I like the green. It's like un bosque." Yes, agrees Ms. Nicole. The green plants do make it seem like a forest."*

TEACHABLE MOMENT

▶ Plants in the preschool environment have a positive effect on children's mood and behavior. They can make an otherwise institutional space feel welcoming and homelike. Green, growing plants are an especially important element to include indoors when a playground does not provide much green space outdoors. Working together to water and care for a variety of indoor plants in the early childhood setting can be incorporated into the group's weekly routine.

Interactions and Strategies

Use children's current knowledge to plan effective curriculum. Attend to children's spontaneous inquiry and provide them with the materials and tools needed to expand their understanding of a particular topic or phenomena—"Hmm . . . you are wondering if our pet walking stick has eyes. Let's get a magnifying glass from our science kit and find out."

Set aside time for outdoor explorations each day. The natural world supports all areas of learning, but the program's outdoor environment is especially appropriate for children's dramatic play, gross-motor activity, and scientific inquiry. Children need plenty of time to investigate, repeat actions, and attempt new tasks. Plan the daily schedule to include at least 30–40 minutes of outdoor play every day. Encourage weather-appropriate clothing so that children may explore the outdoor spaces year-round.

Provide children with sensory experiences, especially those with sand and water. Create a generously sized sandbox in the outdoor environment with access to water for children's experiments. Indoors, offer children a sensory table for similar, small-scale investigation. Supply children with tools for exploration (e.g.,

magnifying lenses, small shovels, buckets, clear containers, drawing tools).

Integrate living things into the indoor learning environment. Choose program pets carefully with thought to the amount of care and attention they will require. Provide a clean, comfortable habitat. Post the name of the animal and information about its care at the children's eye level. Encourage the children to participate in its care as appropriate. Incorporate child-safe, nontoxic plants throughout the program. Choose plants with different shapes, colors, and textures. For additional ideas, refer to *Designs for Living and Learning* by Curtis and Carter or *Natural Playscapes* by Rusty Keeler.

Observe life in its natural setting. In addition to making observations in the outdoor learning environment, plan frequent nature walks through surrounding neighborhoods. Offer children tools to focus their observations (e.g., paper towel tubes, binoculars, paper, pencils, cameras). Talk with children about how to be good observers (e.g., sitting quietly and giving an animal space to feel safe in its natural habitat).

Model respect and care for the natural world. Be careful to leave wildflowers, branches from trees, and insects and other creatures alone—"I see a caterpillar walking across the sidewalk. Let's all move around so we do not hurt it."

Use descriptive language to converse about the earth and its features. Encourage children to reflect on the colors, shapes, textures, smells, and size of elements in their natural world. Extend the discussion by sharing your own observations—"This plant has rough leaves, but this plant has smooth ones."

Compare and contrast living and non-living things. Invite children to observe different objects and living things in indoors and outdoors. Ask them if each is living or not living. Encourage deeper analysis by asking, "How can you tell?" For more ideas on this topic, refer to chapter 3, "Science."

Teach young children easy ways to conserve the earth's resources. Create an accessible recycling center for the program—"It looks like we have some scraps from our paper-cutting activity. I will put them in our recycling bin so they can be made into new pieces of paper." Repair toys and books where possible instead of purchasing new ones—"I think we can glue this traffic sign back together. Let's try it. If it works, we won't have to buy a new one." Reuse materials in different ways. Read *Not a Box* by Antoinette Portis to children and encourage them to think of creative ways to use recyclable materials. See the "Research Highlight" on page 111.

Grow a garden in the program's outdoor space. Use small plant boxes or

build a large planting bed. Plant seeds as well as seedlings. Document the garden's growth over time with photographs. Encourage children's observations and record them in a garden journal. Discuss why some things grow and why others may not.

Eat fresh produce at snack time and obtain food directly from a local gardener, farmers market, or food vendor when possible. Take time to converse with the children about where the produce came from and how it was grown.

Use books to extend children's investigations of the earth and its attributes. Some explorations of the natural world may not be possible in the early learning environment or accessible to children in the program. Books allow children an alternative way to explore small- and large-scale phenomena (e.g., volcanoes). Display concept books close to related ongoing investigations in classroom areas.

Research Highlight

Caring for the natural world gradually develops as young children begin to understand how human activity affects animals, plants, and the natural environment. One research team created a measure of environmental understanding to assess how much preschool children knew about everyday practices that affect the environment.[22] In this measure, preschool children were told about two different types of children and were asked which they most resembled. In one item, for example, they heard "Some children like to leave the water running when they brush their teeth" and "Other children always turn the water off while brushing their teeth," and they were asked to indicate which kind of child they were like. The measure was given to children ranging in age from 40 to 73 months. The research team found that scores for environmental awareness increased with age, and scores were also associated with parents' reports of how often children participated in environmentally relevant activities in the home, such as recycling.

3.0 Understanding the Physical World Through Drawings and Maps

One way of understanding the physical world is by describing it through a drawing or a map of a familiar location. Older preschoolers may spontaneously create a map of the directions to an imagined treasure or a real discovery. It is more difficult for young children to use a map drawn by another to identify a location, although preschoolers make significant advances in doing so with adult guidance. Teachers contribute to these achievements by encouraging young children to represent their physical environments through drawings and maps and prompting use of them to find locations or to explore.

VIGNETTE

"This is the castle for the princess and her friends," explains Grace to Tanya as she describes her unit block structure. "Here's the bedroom over here, and the tower over there."

Ms. Julia, sitting in the block area to observe children's play, responds, "It looks like a very long way from the bedroom to the tower. Do the princess and her friends ever get lost in the castle?" "Well . . . sometimes they do," replies Grace. "I wonder if we could draw something to help them find their way," suggests Ms. Julia. "Like a map!" exclaims Tanya to Grace.

Ms. Julia offers to bring the clipboards, equipped with paper and pencils, from the art area. She takes one and begins describing her drawing plan. "First I'm going to draw a square for the bedroom in this corner . . . " The girls begin by imitating her technique and soon are exchanging ideas with each other as they draw their versions of the castle. When they are finished, Ms. Julia asks questions about the parts of their castle maps and offers to label them. When the maps are finished, labeled, and signed, Ms. Julia asks the girls' permission to display them on the block area wall.

TEACHABLE MOMENT

▶ This experience with map making occurred in a constructive play setting, which often provides similar opportunities. The children needed some support and guidance from an adult, but then they were able to create their own maps. Labeling and displaying the child-drawn maps identifies them as important work and may inspire other children to pair map making with their constructive play. Some children may need physical assistance in creating maps; they could share ideas for a peer to draw.

Interactions and Strategies

Engage children in a conversation about maps—"What are they? What do they do?" Expand on children's ideas about the purpose and use of maps. Share that maps are smaller pictures of streets and roads, the places we live in, and the world.

Supply the learning environment with a variety of blocks and other open-ended materials to support the symbolic representation of the world the children see and experience each day. Provide traffic signs, train tracks, road pieces, and other materials that may be used to create roadways, landmarks, and buildings.

Incorporate maps in dramatic play experiences. Supply prop boxes and learning areas with maps that match emerging play themes. For example, if the children express an interest in camping, include trail maps, maps of different campsites, and other local attractions. Peers can assist children with special needs to participate in the creation of maps of their physical environment through drawings based on mutual observations.

Provide children with map-making tools in both the indoor and outdoor preschool settings. Include paper, drawing tools, glue sticks, tape, scissors, and other art supplies.

Capitalize on children's initiative in exploring maps. Comment on their observations and work—"Oh, you're drawing a picture of the tire swing on the playground, and that is the sandbox next to it. It looks like you are making a map." Expand on their initial view by drawing

attention to additional features of the space—"I know we have a tree in between the tire swing and the sandbox. Will you add that to your map?" See the "Sample Developmental Sequence: Sense of Place" on page 104 for more information.

Utilize maps while planning and attending group outings, in preparation for safety exercises (e.g., fire drills), and as children join the program or move to a new home. Introduce maps prior to the event. While on an outing, check the map to highlight past, current, and upcoming locations—"First we crossed this street. Now we are at the fountain. Keep alert now for the sign that says [shows picture to children of sign] 'Train Station.'"

Play board games that use trails and pathways. In children's board games, the game pieces follow a specific path that includes "landmarks" throughout each player's journey.

Make a map of the early learning environment. Begin the project first with blocks and other three-dimensional materials. Help children attend to different barriers and furnishings—"Let's make a map of our classroom in the block area. What blocks could we use to represent our couch? What's next to the couch? A shelf . . . hmm, could we use this block to be the shelf?" Next create a map on paper—"Let's draw a picture of our blocks. This will be our paper map of the classroom."

Invite children to use their imagination and create maps to go along with familiar stories. Choose stories where the main characters are going on an adventure ("How would Max get to the where the wild things live?"). Help children recall the land and water features the characters would encounter on their journey.

View locations from different physical perspectives. Make opportunities for children to explore familiar settings from different perspectives. Encourage reflection using open-ended questions— "What does our yard look like when we are in the sandbox?" "How is it different when we look down from our climbing structure?" Take pictures of other local attractions from different heights—"I took

this picture of our city when I went on a hike in the hills. What do you see in the picture?"

Prepare a treasure hunt. Provide child-friendly maps and clues for their search. Have children work in pairs or small groups to support collaborative learning and facilitate perspective taking—"What do you think, Jorge? Where do you think the blue bear might be hiding? . . . Your idea is that the bear is where the blue mark is on our map. Let's test your idea. Let's go to the tree with the blue mark."

Document work over time. Display children's map-making projects in the early learning environment at their eye level. Maintain records of children's work to illustrate a change in spatial awareness and attention to detail—"When you first started drawing maps, you used lines and 'x' marks. Now you have pictures of different landmarks like the bridge and the lake. It is clear how we had to go over the bridge to get to the lake."

Bringing It All Together

At circle time, Mr. Kyle reminds the children that last week many of them were burying treasures in the sandbox for their friends to find. "Since that seemed like such a good idea, I thought it might be fun to have a bigger treasure hunt."

"Yeah," agree the children. "X marks the spot," adds one.

"Before you came to school this morning," Mr. Kyle continues, "I hid our teddy bears (plastic counting bears) all around the playground. To help you find them, I drew a map." Mr. Kyle unrolls a large piece of mural paper in the center of the circle. He gives the children a little time to look at it, listening to their comments to assess whether they are able to identify his representations of playground landmarks.

"What do you think?" Does this look like our playground? "Can you spot some familiar things on the map?" The children begin pointing to the various line drawings and naming playground features: slide, balance beam, tree, sandbox. Mr. Kyle then points to some of the colored "X" marks he has made on the map. "Each X marks a spot where bears are hidden. When we go outside, I will put the map on the picnic table so you can look for the X marks and remember where to hunt for bears.

Checking for understanding, Mr. Kyle asks, "Andy, where do you see an X for bears?" "By the slide," responds Andy. "I see one at the bottom of the big tree," adds Jana. After several more children have added their observations to the conversation, Mr. Kyle says, "I can see that you really know how to use this map. Let's meet at the door to get ready to go on a bear hunt."

Using a printed map is a skill beyond the capacities of most preschool children. A simple hand-drawn map of a very familiar location, such as the indoor or outdoor preschool setting, can be a good way to develop this skill with older preschool children. Keeping it simple and talking about its features together as a "rehearsal" for its use will increase children's success. To accommodate children with varying skill levels and children with visual or motor challenges, consider having children explore the area in small groups instead of individually. For more information about resources for teachers of children with disabilities or other special needs, see appendix D of the California *Preschool Curriculum Framework, Volume 1.*

Engaging Families

The following ideas may help families to increase their children's familiarity and engagement with the world around them.

✔ Suggest that they look for maps in places where their family goes. Draw a child's attention to maps posted at the bus stop, in a big store or shopping mall, a museum, or elevator or emergency exit in public buildings. Point to the "You are here" dot and trace with your finger where you are going.

✔ Suggest taking different routes when going to familiar places. Make a game of taking a different route to a park, preschool, a friend's house, or a store. Try narrating the trip, saying things like, "Now we are turning the corner, and then we will go over the bridge and across the street."

✔ Encourage families to talk about nature (i.e., weather, seasons, plants, animals, and so on) with their child. Use different weather words to describe the temperature, wind, cloud patterns, and precipitation. Children can become more aware of the information their senses are taking in if they have descriptive language for it. Saying, "The wind is cold and gusty today" makes the experience more graphic.

✔ Encourage families to have conversations about ways they can help the earth (reduce waste, conserve natural resources, compost, and so on). Suggest giving a preschool child a role in recycling items used at home, including paper, food containers, and boxes. Encourage children to think about other ways their family can help practice conservation of the environment.

✔ Suggest that adult family members share with their child elements of the natural world they especially enjoy. Hearing Mom say that spring is her favorite season or that Grandma loves listening to birds sing can help children reflect on their own personal favorites in the outdoors. Children will often come to value the things that the important adults in their lives value.

Questions for Reflection

1. What are the features you think preschool children would include in a description of your program's indoor environment and outdoor physical environment?

2. Which program practices can you change to indicate to the children that it is important to take good care of the natural world?

3. What simple activities can you incorporate into your curriculum to increase children's familiarity with their preschool neighborhood?

4. Which children's books do you already read aloud that could be used as starting points for conversations and activities about aspects of the natural world like weather, seasons, and living things?

Marketplace (Economics)

Young children's interest in adult roles and occupations extends to the economy. Preschoolers know that adults have jobs, and they observe that money is used to purchase items and services, but the connections between work, money, and purchasing are unclear to them. This does not stop them, however, from enacting these processes in their pretend play and showing great interest in the economic transactions they observe (such as a trip to the bank with a parent). Moreover, young children are also active as consumers, seeking to persuade their families to purchase toys or access to activities that they desire, sometimes hear-

ing adult concerns about cost or affordability in response. On occasion, they also learn about economic differences between people and families, such as when a parent is unemployed or when families are living in poverty. All of these activities convince them that the economy, while little understood by them, is important.

A carefully designed early childhood education setting provides many opportunities for young children to explore these ideas through play, conversation, and the creation of economic items to buy, sell, or exchange.

In this section, specific strategies are discussed that support development in the substrand of Exchange.

1.0 Exchange

Young children have a remarkable intuitive grasp of basic aspects of economic exchange. They understand the concept of ownership. They recognize that obtaining something requires giving something in exchange (often money). With time, they also appreciate that goods and services vary in cost and that the more people want something, the more can be sold. Teachers contribute to this growing understanding by providing young children with opportunities to explore economic exchange through pretend stores and services, talking about money and its uses, and enlisting children's understanding of the economic activities of the adults in their lives.

VIGNETTE

For this week, Ms. Laura and Mr. Luan have transformed a corner of the dramatic play area into a shoe store. They observed children's interest in the many dress-up shoes in the area and heard conversations about shoe sizes, styles, prices, and parent spending on shoes. Setting up a store seemed like a good way to help children explore these economic concepts in more depth.

A set of shelves displays open shoeboxes. Chairs for customers and rulers for measuring feet fill the area. At the entrance is a table with a cash register, play money, pencils, and receipt pads. Notepaper and masking tape are available for making signs and price tags.

The first children to enter the store take on roles of seller and buyer. "Hey, I can't find the shoes I like," says Alicia. "Where are the sparkly red ones?" Zara replies, "Maybe they already got bought. My mommy really gets mad when that happens to her." As the morning progresses, many children visit the store and a teacher tries to be present and engaged in some of the conversations that develop. Children's behavior and comments clearly reflect their own family experiences. They bring "children" whose feet are growing "too fast," tell the cashier they have enough money this time only for school shoes—not party shoes, and they want to trade one pair of shoes for another. Mr. Luan helps interested children write sale signs and install them and stick price tags onto shoeboxes. He encourages some boys, who have not yet entered the store to come in and discover that there are lots of shoes for them, too.

TEACHABLE MOMENT

▶ Providing a variety of marketplace opportunities in a preschool setting's dramatic play areas is a valuable way to encourage children to explore their ideas about economic exchange. It is important for teachers to not only provide the play props but to facilitate the play when they can. This can be done by entering into the play as a "customer," complete with customer comments and questions, and by engaging in related conversations with children as they play various roles. Teacher–child conversation about children's home and community experiences with the larger marketplace, including their considerable exposure to media messages, can also be very helpful.

Interactions and Strategies

Introduce economic concepts (e.g., production, exchange, consumption) through children's books. Some books that highlight such concepts are *Alexander, Who Used to Be Rich Last Sunday* by Judith Viorst, *A Chair for My Mother* by Vera B. Williams, *The Great Pet Sale* by Mick Inkpen, and *Sheep in a Jeep* by Nancy Shaw. Help children focus on themes such as the following: What did the characters want? What did they really need?

Provide open-ended materials to support children's spontaneous investigations of business and the economy. Supply the learning environment with play money, paper pads for receipts, stamps, and cash registers. Introduce ways such materials may add to children's play—"I hear you are building a shoe store. I wonder if you might need a cash register to hold the money your customers give you for the shoes? We have one in our prop box in the house area."

Offer dramatic play experiences that allow children to explore economic concepts. For example, prepare a pre-

tend restaurant in the dramatic play area. Use your observations of children's play to plan meaningful play opportunities. Incorporate realistic play props (e.g., dress-up clothes, office supplies, cash registers). Supply poster boards for making business signs. Display photographs of a variety of people at work and consuming goods. Avoid any images that perpetuate stereotypes.

Explore alongside children, expanding on their initiative—"You want more [pretend] money. Simon and I are play-

ing house, and our sink is broken. I can give you money for fixing our sink. I will pay you twenty dollars," Introduce the vocabulary of the marketplace into play experiences.

Draw attention to trends of consumption in the preschool setting—"We used a lot of glue this week. We will need to order more soon. I wonder if we can think of ways to save some glue until our new glue is delivered." Extend learning into the home. Invite families to create a collage of items their family purchases regularly—What do they consume now? What do they want to consume in the future?

Converse about wants and needs. Speak with children about individual wants—"It sounds like you really wanted that school bus toy. We only had two, so you found a fire truck." Use books to further illustrate these concepts, such as *Those Shoes* by Maribeth Boelts. Talk about choices in consumption—"Did you like your choice of a fire truck?" Additionally, in large groups brainstorm materials needed for the emerging investigations. Introduce economic alternatives—"We do not have enough money to buy new baby beds for our baby hospital. What can we use instead? . . . Yes, we could make beds with shoe boxes from the art area."

Allow children to make economic decisions. As a group, make a purchase for the community. Pose a choice between two options. Encourage the children to discuss the reasons for their choice. Help them distinguish between something the program wants and something the program needs.

Explore all forms of exchange. Reflect on times when children traded one object for another. Document the children's recollections. Use play money as you participate in children's dramatic play—"Thank you for packing my groceries. Here is money for the things I bought." Plan an outing where children can observe the exchange of real money—"Today we will walk to the market to buy strawberries for snack."

Visit local businesses. Prompt children to ask store owners or managers where the goods in their businesses come from and how the goods are transported from one place to another. Document the outing, including information shared by store owners. Display photographs and dictation alongside ongoing explorations of economics in the classroom to inspire and support children's play—"Remember when we visited the smoothie store near preschool? Worker Tiffany showed us how to make a smoothie and collect money from the customer."

Create an opportunity for children to make their own product. Plan, prepare, and implement a Market Day for families. Ask for children's ideas about what to sell at their market. Offer limited choices to ensure a reasonable plan—"Should we sell muffins or breads in our market?" Encourage each child's active participation as they make signs, advertise their product, and bake goods. Donate the money to a local charity and share how the money will help someone else purchase needed goods.

Bringing It All Together

Ms. Jen settles into the reading chair to begin large group story time. She holds a tall empty jar, a small cloth bag, and a book.

"Today I brought something with me to help me tell a story," she begins. Then she holds up the small drawstring bag and shakes it. "Money!" call out the children. "Yes, it is money. My little bag is full of coins: nickels, dimes and quarters," she says, pulling out one of each. "This book is all about a family who collects coins and saves them in a jar that looks a lot like this one. It's called A Chair for My Mother, and Vera B. Williams is the author. She wrote the words. She is also the illustrator, which means she painted the pictures."

As Ms. Jen reads the book, she stops frequently to converse with children about what is happening in the story. "The mother in this story works as a server in a restaurant. That's how she earns money to buy the things her family needs." After reading the page that describes the "tips" that Mother brings home and puts into the jar, Ms. Jen asks the group if anyone they know gets tips at work. After explaining the idea, she pours the coins from her small bag into the tall jar she has brought as a story prop.

When she reads the pages about the family's moving day, when all their relatives and neighbors brought things they needed to replace the ones lost in the fire, Ms. Jen talks about how people don't always buy all the things they have. Sometimes people receive gifts and things that others share with them.

As each economic concept is introduced in the book, Ms. Jen pauses to draw attention to it, while maintaining the flow of the story. At the end, she holds up the jar of coins and asks the group how long they think it took for Josephine's family to collect enough coins to buy the chair. She responds to their comments, listening as they share their own related ideas. She concludes by telling them that the book will be in the reading area tomorrow for them to enjoy again.

Reading stories that incorporate economic ideas and events is an effective way to put them in a real-life context for children. This particular book addresses everything from earning wages to losing material possessions in a fire, experiencing the generosity of friends and neighbors, planning and saving for a large purchase, and sharing good and bad economic times as a family. The teacher structures an interactive reading experience to introduce ideas that she can revisit with children later in play and projects.

Engaging Families

The following ideas may support families as they help their children learn about family wants and needs and the roles that money and broader economic conditions play in family life.

✔ Encourage families to talk with their child about the connection between cost and decisions to buy items and services. Children can learn how to look for the price signs at the grocery store and compare numbers. Family adults can talk about how they decide which item to buy.

✔ Assure families that it is fine to have conversations about "wants" and "needs." Preschool children often feel their strong desire to buy a toy or food treat as a need. Hearing about how their families decide what is most important to buy (e.g., food for dinner) and whether to buy other things family members want (e.g., sparkly red party shoes) will influence their later ability to make responsible financial decisions.

✔ Suggest that families show their child some alternative ways to acquire things the family needs or wants, as well as ways to help meet the needs of others. For example, they or someone in their family, neighborhood, or religious community may give haircuts, do free repairs, share garden vegetables, provide child care, or make clothing for others. It is important for children to know that people barter, trade, and share, and that not all good things cost money.

✔ Encourage families to begin to share with preschool children their own values about money. If some of their financial decisions are based on values children can understand, such as the importance of sharing a portion of income with extended family members who need it or giving money or goods to their religious community, converse with children about those values.

✔ Prepare yourselves, as early care and education professionals, to play an active role in supporting families facing personal economic crises. Educate yourselves about available community services and, when possible, help families to obtain access to them. Expect that children whose families are experiencing economic hardship will need extra nurturing and stability in their preschool environment.

Questions for Reflection

1. What kinds of child conversation about money-related topics do you most often hear in your preschool setting? In what ways do these reflect the economic circumstances of the children's families?

2. How can you use resources in your preschool neighborhood, including stores, restaurants, service providers, and work sites, to introduce children to different aspects of their community's economic life?

3. What can you incorporate into your preschool curriculum that will convey messages about economic justice and values appropriate to your program's context?

4. What vocabulary words can you use with children to help them better understand the economic world of their community?

5. Are there additional ways you can be supportive to the families in your program who are experiencing particularly difficult financial circumstances?

Concluding Thoughts

The knowledge and skills in history and social science that preschoolers acquire in an early education setting provide a foundation for their understanding of themselves and the world in which they live. Adults benefit from the perspective of history (of society, families, and one's personal past). People are connected deeply to the physical settings and natural ecologies in which they live. People learn about themselves and others by comparison with people who differ in culture, language, ethnicity, traditions, and abilities. Human lives are shaped by the economy and its influence on people's roles as workers, consumers, and investors. Citizens participate with others in the political process and in building their communities. As preschoolers learn about these topics through instruction, enactment, and play, they are introduced to issues that will remain important to them for years to come.

Map of the Foundations

Domain ——————▶ ## History–Social Science

Strand ——————▶ ### Sense of Time (History)

Substrand ——▶ **2.0 Anticipating and Planning Future Events**

At around 48 months of age	At around 60 months of age	◀—— **Age**
Foundation ▶ **2.1** Anticipate events in familiar situations in the near future, with adult assistance.	**2.1** Distinguish when future events will happen, plan for them, and make choices (with adult assistance) that anticipate future needs.	

Examples ▶ **Examples**	**Examples**
• When the teacher points to the art photo in the picture schedule, the child begins to prepare (putting on an apron, moving paper to the easel). • When asked what he is going to do tomorrow, indicates that he will have breakfast and then come to school. • Tells an adult, "When we go outside, I need a plastic bag on my cast so it won't get muddy." • Tells other children that she and her papa go outside to look at the stars when it gets dark, right after they eat dinner. • Knows, with the help of a picture schedule, that snack time at preschool always follows circle time. • Excitedly tells the teacher, "We're going to the airport to pick up my uncle from Taiwan next week!" but has no idea how soon next week will be. • At planning time, a child who is nonverbal uses a communication board with pictures to indicate where he will play first. • When asked for an idea about what the group will need to bring on a lunchtime picnic, suggests a blanket.	• As the group gets ready to go on a trip to the fire station, asks the teacher whether they should bring the firefighter's hat from the dress-up area. • Tells a friend that she has to give away toys to make room for her grandparents from India, who will be coming to live with her. • Because of a special event, the day's schedule is changed. Several children express concern that snack time will be skipped. • Communicates to a friend, "Next time we go to the zoo, I will have my electric wheelchair, so I can keep up with you." • Tells teacher, "I get to visit my cousins on Saturday. Mommy says that's after two more sleeps!" • Encourages friend to put on his shoes and jacket fast so they will have more time to dig in the sandbox together. • When the nurse enters, a child tells her friend that it is time for a tube feeding and that she will come back to play in 10 minutes. • Knowing that park time is at 10:00 every day, brings jacket from cubby and asks, "Is it 10:00 yet?"

Teacher Resources

Bisson, J. *Celebrate! An Anti-Bias Guide to Enjoying Holidays in Early Childhood Programs.* St. Paul, MN: Redleaf Press, 2002.

Bredekamp, S. "Resolving Contradictions Between Cultural Practices," in *A World of Difference: Readings on Teaching Young Children in a Diverse Society.* Edited by C. Copple. Washington, DC: National Association for the Education of Young Children, 2003.

The Center on the Social and Emotional Foundations for Early Learning (CSEFEL). http://csefel.vanderbilt.edu/. Promotes the social–emotional development and school readiness of young children from birth to age five.

Curtis, D., and M. Carter. *Designs for Living and Learning: Transforming Early Childhood Environments.* St. Paul, MN: Redleaf Press, 2003.

Derman-Sparks, L., and J. O. Edwards. *Anti-Bias Education for Young Children and Ourselves.* Washington, DC: National Association for the Education of Young Children, 2010.

Deviney, J., and others. *Inspiring Spaces for Young Children.* Silver Spring, MD: Gryphon House, 2010.

Edwards, C. P. "Thinking About Friendship: Fostering and Extending Young Children's Understanding," in *Connecting: Friendship in the Lives of Young Children and Their Teachers.* Edited by D. P. Wolf and B. Neugebauer. Redmond, WA: Exchange Press, 2004.

Edwards, C. P., and P. G. Ramsey. *Promoting Social and Moral Development in Young Children: Creative Approaches for the Classroom.* New York: Teachers College Press, 1986.

Epstein, A. S. *The Intentional Teacher: Choosing the Best Strategies for Young Children's Learning.* Washington, DC: National Association for the Education of Young Children, 2007.

———. *Me, You, Us: Social–Emotional Learning in Preschool.* Ypsilanti, MI: HighScope Press, 2009.

Hohmann, M., and D. P. Weikar. *Educating Young Children.* 2nd ed. Ypsilanti, MI: HighScope Press, 2002.

Hopkins, S., ed. *Hearing Everyone's Voice: Educating Young Children for Peace and Democratic Community.* Redmond, WA: Child Care Information Exchange, 1999.

Katz, L. G., and D. E. McClellan. *Fostering Children's Social Competence: The Teacher's Role.* Washington, DC: National Association for the Education of Young Children, 1997.

Keeler, R. *Natural Playscapes: Creating Outdoor Play Environments for the Soul.* Redmond, WA: Exchange Press, 2008.

Mindes, G. "Social Studies in Today's Early Childhood Curricula." *Beyond the Journal: Young Children on the Web* 60, no. 5 (2005): 12–18.

———. *Teaching Young Children Social Studies.* Lanham, MD: Rowland and Littlefield Education, 2006.

National Arbor Day Foundation/Dimensions Educational Research Foundation. http://www.arborday.org/explore/. Provides training materials and resources for creating nature-focused outdoor play spaces for children.

National Council for the Social Studies (NCSS) teaching resources. http://www.social-studies.org/resources.

Project Learning Tree. http://www.plt.org/. Provides resources that encourage children to enjoy hands-on experiences with trees and nature.

Seefeldt, C., and A. Galper. *Active Experiences for Active Children: Social Studies.* 2nd ed. Columbus, OH: Pearson, 2006.

Seefeldt, C., and others. *Social Studies for the Preschool/Primary Child.* 8th ed. Boston, MA: Merrill, 2010.

Endnotes

1. G. Mindes, *Teaching Young Children Social Studies* (Lanham, MD: Rowland and Littlefield Education, 2006); C. Seefeldt and others, *Social Studies for the Preschool/Primary Child,* 8th ed. (Boston, MA: Merrill, 2010); C. Seefeldt and A. Galper, *Active Experiences for Active Children: Social Studies,* 2nd ed. (Columbus, OH: Pearson, 2006); A. S. Epstein, *Me, You, Us: Social–Emotional Learning in Preschool* (Ypsilanti, MI: HighScope Press, 2009).

2. G. Mindes, "Social Studies in Today's Early Childhood Curricula," *Beyond the Journal: Young Children on the Web* 60, no. 5 (2005): 12–18.

3. California Department of Education, *Inclusion Works! Creating Child Care Programs That Promote Belonging for Children with Special Needs* (Sacramento: CDE, 2009), 2.

4. F. E. Aboud, *Children and Prejudice* (New York: Blackwell, 1988); F. E. Aboud, "The Formation of In-Group Favoritism and Out-Group Prejudice in Young Children: Are They Distinct Attitudes?" *Developmental Psychology* 39 (2003): 48–60; F. E. Aboud, "A Social–Cognitive Developmental Theory of Prejudice," in *Handbook of Race, Racism, and the Developing Child,* ed. S. M. Quintana and C. McKown (New York: Wiley, 2008), 55–71; O. A. Barbarin and E. Odom, "Promoting Social Acceptance and Respect for Cultural Diversity in Young Children: Learning from Developmental Research," in *Handbook of Child Development and Early Education: Research to Practice,* ed. O. A. Barbarin and B. H. Wasik (New York: Guilford Press, 2009), 247–65; R. S. Bigler and L. S. Liben, "Developmental Intergroup Theory: Explaining and Reducing Children's Social Stereotyping and Prejudice," *Current Directions in Psychological Science* 16, no. 3 (2007): 162–66; P. A. Katz, "Racists or Tolerant Multiculturalists? How Do They Begin?," *American Psychologist* 58, no. 11 (2003): 807–909; S. M. Quintana, "Children's Developmental Understanding of Ethnicity and Race," *Applied and Preventive Psychology* 7, no. 1 (1998): 27–45; S. M. Quintana, "Racial and Ethnic Identity: Developmental Perspectives and Research," *Journal of Counseling Psychology* 54, no. 3 (2007): 259–70; S. M. Quintana, "Racial Perspective Taking Ability: Developmental, Theoretical, and Empirical Trends," in *Handbook of Race, Racism, and the Developing Child,* ed. S. M. Quintana and C. McKown (New York: Wiley, 2008), 16–36.

5. J. G. Parker and J. M. Gottman, "Social and Emotional Development in a Relational Context: Friendship Interaction from Early Childhood to Adolescence," in *Peer Relations in Child Development,* ed. T. J. Berndt and G. W. Ladd (New York: Wiley, 1989), 95–132; K. H. Rubin, W. M. Bukowski, and J. G. Parker, "Peer Interactions, Relationships, and Groups," in *Handbook of Child Psychology: Social, Emotional, and Personality Development,* vol. 3, 6th ed., ed. W. Damon and R. M. Lerner, vol. ed. N. Eisenberg (New York: Wiley, 2006), 571–645; K. H. Rubin and others, "Peer Relationships in Childhood," in *Developmental Science: An Advanced Textbook,* 5th ed., ed. M. H. Bornstein and M. E. Lamb (Mahwah, NJ: Erlbaum, 2005), 469–512; L. J. Berlin, J. Cassidy, and K. Appleyard, "The Influence of Early Attachments on Other Relationships," in *Handbook of Attachment: Theory, Research, and Clinical Applications,* 2nd ed., ed. J. Cassidy and P. R. Shaver (New York: Guilford Press, 2008), 333–47; J. Dunn, *Young Children's Close Relationships: Beyond Attachment* (Newbury Park, CA: Sage Publications, 1993); W. W. Hartup, "The Company They Keep: Friendships and Their Developmental Significance," *Child Development* 67, no. 1 (1996): 1–13; C. Howes and S. Spieker,

"Attachment Relationships in the Context of Multiple Caregivers," in *Handbook of Attachment: Theory, Research, and Clinical Applications*, 2nd ed., ed. J. Cassidy and P. R. Shaver (New York: Guilford Press, 2008), 317–32; National Research Council and Institute of Medicine, Committee on Integrating the Science of Early Childhood Development, *From Neurons to Neighborhoods: The Science of Early Childhood Development*, ed. J. P. Shonkoff and D. A. Phillips (Washington, DC: National Academies Press, 2000).

6. C. P. Edwards and P. G. Ramsey, *Promoting Social and Moral Development in Young Children: Creative Approaches for the Classroom* (New York: Teachers College Press, 1986).

7. Ibid.; R. A. Thompson, "The Development of the Person: Social Understanding, Relationships, Self, Conscience," in *Handbook of Child Psychology: vol. 3. Social, Emotional, and Personality Development*, 6th ed., ed. W. Damon and R. M. Lerner, vol. ed. N. Eisenberg (New York: Wiley, 2006), 24–98; R. A. Thompson, R. Goodvin, and S. Meyer, "Social Development: Psychological Understanding, Self Understanding, and Relationships," in *Handbook of Preschool Mental Health: Development, Disorders, and Treatment*, ed. J. Luby (New York: Guilford Press, 2006), 3–22; R. A. Thompson and M. Goodman, "Development of Self, Relationships, and Socioemotional Competence: Foundations for Early School Success," in *Handbook of Child Development and Early Education: Research to Practice*, ed. O. A. Barbarin and B. H. Wasik (New York: Guilford Press, 2009), 147–71; R. A. Thompson and H. A. Raikes, "The Social and Emotional Foundations of School Readiness," *Social and Emotional Health in Early Childhood: Building Bridges Between Services and Systems*, ed. D. F. Perry, R. F. Kaufmann, and J. Knitzer (Baltimore, MD: Paul H. Brookes, 2007), 13–35.

8. G. Kochanska and R. A. Thompson, "The Emergence and Development of Conscience in Toddlerhood and Early Childhood," in *Parenting and Children's Internalization of Values*, ed. J. Grusec and L. Kuczynski (New York: Wiley, 1997), 53–77; R. A. Thompson, S. Meyer, and M. McGinley, "Understanding Values in Relationship: The Development of Conscience," in *Handbook of Moral Development*, ed. M. Killen and J. Smetana (Mahwah, NJ: Erlbaum, 2006), 267–97.

9. R. A. Thompson and K. Lagatutta, "Feeling and Understanding: Early Emotional Development," in *The Blackwell Handbook of Early Childhood Development*, ed. K. McCartney and D. Phillips (Oxford, UK: Blackwell Publishers, 2006), 317–37; R. A. Thompson, "Empathy and Its Origins in Early Development," in *Intersubjective Communication and Emotion in Early Ontogeny: A Source Book*, ed. S. Braten (New York: Cambridge University Press, 1998), 144–57; J. G. Smetana, "Preschool Children's Conceptions of Moral and Social Rules," *Child Development* 52, no. 4 (1981): 1333–36; J. G. Smetana, "Preschool Children's Conceptions of Transgressions: The Effects of Varying Moral and Conventional Domain-Related Attributes," *Developmental Psychology* 21, no. 1 (1985): 18–29.

10. R. A. Fabes and N. Eisenberg, "Young Children's Coping with Interpersonal Anger," *Child Development* 63, no. 1 (1992): 116–28.

11. W. J. Friedman, "The Development of Children's Memory for the Time of Past Events," *Child Development* 62, no. 1 (1991): 139–55; W. J. Friedman, "Children's Time Memory: The Development of a Differentiated Past," *Cognitive Development* 7, no. 2 (1992): 171–87; W. J. Friedman, A. G. Gardner, and N. R. E. Zubin, "Children's Comparisons of the Recency of Two Events from the Past Year," *Child Development* 66, no. 4 (1995): 970–83; W. J. Friedman, and S. Kemp, "The Effects of Elapsed Time and Retrieval on Young Children's Judgments of the Temporal Distances of Past Events," *Cognitive Development* 13, no. 3 (1998): 335–67; W. J. Friedman, "The Development of a Differ-

entiated Sense of the Past and the Future, in *Advances in Child Development and Behavior* 31, ed. R. V. Kail (San Diego, CA: Academic [Elsevier], 2003), 229–69; W. J. Friedman, "Developmental and Cognitive Perspectives on Humans' Sense of the Times of Past and Future Events," *Learning and Motivation* 36, no. 2 (2005): 145–58.

12. C. M. Atance, "Future Thinking in Young Children," *Current Directions in Psychological Science* 17, no. 4 (2008): 295–98; C. M. Atance and L. K. Jackson, "The Development and Coherence of Future-Oriented Behaviors During the Preschool Years," *Journal of Experimental Child Psychology* 102, no. 4 (2009): 379–91; C. M. Atance and A. N. Meltzoff, "My Future Self: Young Children's Ability to Anticipate and Explain Future States," *Cognitive Development* 20, no. 3 (2005): 341–61; C. M. Atance and D. K. O'Neill, "The Emergence of Episodic Future Thinking in Humans," *Learning and Motivation* 36, no. 2 (2005): 126–44; J. A. Hudson, L. R. Shapiro, and B. B. Sosa, "Planning in the Real World: Preschool Children's Scripts and Plans for Familiar Events," *Child Development* 66 (1995): 984–98.

13. K. C. Barton and L. S. Levstik, "Back When God Was Around and Everything: Elementary Children's Understanding of Historical Time," *American Educational Research Journal* 33 (1996): 419–54; L. S. Levstik and K. C. Barton, "'They Still Use Some of Their Past': Historical Salience in Elementary Children's Chronological Thinking," *Journal of Curriculum Studies* 28 (1996): 531–76.

14. S. Catling, "What Do Five-Year-Olds Know of the World? Geographical Understanding and Play in Young Children's Early Learning," *Geography* 91, no. 2 (2006): 55–74.

15. R. Luov, *Last Child in the Woods: Saving Our Children from Nature-Deficit Disorder* (Chapel Hill, NC: Algonquin Books, 2005); S. Cohen and D. Horm-Wingerd, "Children and the Environment: Ecological Awareness Among Preschool Children," *Environment and Behavior* 25, no. 1 (1993): 103–

20; L. M. Musser and K. E. Diamond, "The Children's Attitudes Toward the Environment Scale for Preschool Children," *Journal of Environmental Education* 30, no. 2 (1999): 23–30.

16. L. S. Liben, "Spatial Development in Childhood: Where Are We Now?" in *Blackwell Handbook of Childhood Cognitive Development,* ed. U. Goswami (Oxford, UK: Blackwell Publishers, 2002), 326–48; L. S. Liben, "Education for Spatial Thinking," in *Handbook of Child Psychology: Child Psychology in Practice,* vol. 4, 6th ed., series ed. W. Damon and R. M. Lerner, vol. ed. K. A. Renninger and I. E. Sigel (New York: Wiley, 2006), 197–247; National Research Council, *Learning to Think Spatially: GIS as a Support System in the K-12 Curriculum* (Washington, DC: National Academies Press, 2006); N. Newcombe and J. Huttenlocher, *Making Space* (Cambridge, MA: MIT Press, 2000).

17. A. E. Berti and A. S. Bombi, *The Child's Construction of Economics* (Cambridge, UK: Cambridge University Press, 1988); V. Burris, "Stages in the Development of Economic Concepts," *Human Relations* 36, no. 9 (1983): 791–812; M. C. Schug, "Children's Understanding of Economics," *The Elementary School Journal* 87, no. 5 (1987): 506–18; R. S. Siegler and D. R. Thompson, "'Hey, Would You Like a Nice Cold Cup of Lemonade on This Hot Day?': Children's Understanding of Economic Causation," *Developmental Psychology* 34, no. 1 (1998): 146–60; D. R. Thompson and R. S. Siegler, "Buy Low, Sell High: The Development of an Informal Theory of Economics," *Child Development* 71, no. 3 (2000): 660–77.

18. L. Derman-Sparks and J. O. Edwards, *Anti-Bias Education for Young Children and Ourselves* (Washington, DC: National Association for the Education of Young Children, 2010), 2.

19. C. P. Edwards, "Thinking About Friendship: Fostering and Extending Young Children's Understanding," in *Connecting: Friendship in the Lives of Young Children and Their Teachers,* ed. D. P. Wolf and B.

Neugebauer (Redmond, WA: Exchange Press, 2004), 28–33.

20. R. Fivush, "Owning Experience: Developing Subjective Perspective in Autobiographical Narratives," in *The Self in Time*, ed. C. Moore and K. Lemmon (Mahwah, NJ: Erlbaum, 2001), 35–52; K. Nelson and R. Fivush, "The Emergence of Autobiographical Memory: A Social–Cultural Developmental Theory," *Psychological Review* 111, no. 2 (2004): 486–511.

21. W. J. Friedman, "Developmental and Cognitive Perspectives on Humans' Sense of the Times of Past and Future Events," *Learning and Motivation* 36, no. 2 (2005): 145–58; C. M. Atance, and L. K. Jackson, "The Development and Coherence of Future-Oriented Behaviors During the Preschool Years," *Journal of Experimental Child Psychology* 102, no. 4 (2009): 379–91.

Bibliography

Aboud, F. E. *Children and Prejudice.* New York: Blackwell, 1988.

———. "The Formation of In-Group Favoritism and Out-Group Prejudice in Young Children: Are They Distinct Attitudes?" *Developmental Psychology* 39 (2003): 48–60.

———. "A Social–Cognitive Developmental Theory of Prejudice." *In Handbook of Race, Racism, and the Developing Child,* edited by S. M. Quintana and C. McKown. New York: Wiley, 2008.

Atance, C. M. "Future Thinking in Young Children." *Current Directions in Psychological Science* 17, no. 4 (2008): 295–98.

Atance, C. M., and L. K. Jackson. "The Development of Coherence of Future-Oriented Behaviors During the Preschool Years." *Journal of Experimental Child Psychology* 102, no. 4 (2009): 379–91.

Atance, C. M., and A. N. Meltzoff. "My Future Self: Young Children's Ability to Anticipate and Explain Future States." *Cognitive Development* 20, no. 3 (2005): 341–61.

Atance, C. M., and D. K. O'Neill. "The Emergence of Episodic Future Thinking in Humans." *Learning and Motivation* 36, no. 2 (2005): 126–44.

Aukrust, V. G., and C. E. Snow. "Narratives and Explanations During Mealtime Conversations in Norway and the U.S." *Language in Society* 27, no. 2 (1998): 221–46.

Banks, J. A. *Cultural Diversity and Education: Foundations, Curriculum, and Teaching.* 5th ed. Boston, MA: Pearson/Allyn and Bacon, 2006.

Barbarin, O. A., and E. Odom. "Promoting Social Acceptance and Respect for Cultural Diversity in Young Children: Learning from Developmental Research. In *Handbook of Child Development and Early Education: Research to Practice,* edited by O. A. Barbarin and B. H. Wasik. New York: Guilford Press, 2009.

Barton, K. C., and L. S. Levstik. "Back When God Was Around and Everything: Elementary Children's Understanding of Historical Time." *American Educational Research Journal* 33 (1996): 419–54.

Bennett, M., and F. Sani. "Children's Subjective Identification with Social Groups." In *Intergroup Attitudes and Relations in Childhood Through Adulthood,* edited by S. R. Levy and M. Killen. Oxford, UK: Oxford University Press, 2008.

Benson, J. B. "The Development of Planning: It's About Time." In *The Developmental Psychology of Planning: Why, How, and When Do We Plan?,* edited by S. L. Friedman and E. K. Scholnick. Mahwah, NJ: Erlbaum Publishers, 1997.

Berlin, L. J., J. Cassidy, and K. Appleyard. "The Influence of Early Attachments on Other Relationships." In *Handbook of Attachment: Theory, Research, and Clinical Applications,* 2nd ed., edited by J. Cassidy and P. R. Shaver. New York: Guilford Press, 2008.

Berti, A. E., and A. S. Bombi. *The Child's Construction of Economics.* Cambridge, UK: Cambridge University Press, 1988.

———. "The Development of the Concept of Money and Its Value: A Longitudinal Study." *Child Development* 52, no. 4 (1981): 1179–82.

Bigler, R. S., and L. S. Liben. "Developmental Intergroup Theory: Explaining and Reducing Children's Social Stereotyping and Prejudice." *Current Directions in Psychological Science* 16, no. 3 (2007): 162–66.

Bowman, B. T., and E. K. Moore. *School Readiness and Social–Emotional Development: Perspectives on Cultural Diversity.* Washington, DC: National Black Child Development Institute, 2006.

Bredekamp, S. "Resolving Contradictions Between Cultural Practices." In *A World of Difference: Readings on Teaching Young Children in a Diverse Society,* edited by C. Copple. Washington, DC: National Association for the Education of Young Children, 2003.

Bronson, M. B. *Self-Regulation in Early Childhood: Nature and Nurture.* New York: Guilford Press, 2000.

Brown, C. S., and R. S. Bigler. "Children's Perceptions of Discrimination: A Developmental Model." *Child Development* 76, no. 3 (2005): 533–53.

Burris, V. "Stages in the Development of Economic Concepts." *Human Relations* 36, no. 9 (1983): 791–812.

Busby, J., and T. Suddendorf. "Recalling Yesterday and Predicting Tomorrow." *Cognitive Development* 20, no. 3 (2005): 362–72.

California Department of Education. *Inclusion Works! Creating Child Care Programs That Promote Belonging for Children with Special Needs.* Sacramento: California Department of Education (CDE), 2009.

Carta, J. J., and others. *Project Slide: Skills for Learning Independence in Developmentally Appropriate Environments.* Longmont, CO: Sopris West Educational Services, 2000.

Catling, S. "What Do Five-Year-Olds Know of the World? Geographical Understanding and Play in Young Children's Early Learning." *Geography* 91, no. 2 (2006): 55–74.

Cohen, S., and D. Horm-Wingerd. "Children and the Environment: Ecological Awareness Among Preschool Children." *Environment and Behavior* 25, no. 1 (1993): 103–20.

Copple, C., and S. Bredekamp, eds. *Developmentally Appropriate Practice in Early Childhood Programs Serving Children from Birth Through Age 8.* 3rd ed. Washington, DC: National Association for the Education of Young Children, 2009.

Denham, S. "The Emotional Basis of Learning and Development in Early Childhood Education." In *Handbook of Research on the Education of Young Children,* 2nd ed., edited by B. Spodek and O. N. Saracho. Mahwah, NJ: Erlbaum, 2006.

———. *Emotional Development in Young Children.* New York: Guilford Press, 1998.

Derman-Sparks, L., and J. O. Edwards. *Anti-Bias Education for Young Children and Ourselves.* Washington, DC: National Association for the Education of Young Children, 2010.

Dunn, J. Young *Children's Close Relationships: Beyond Attachment.* Newbury Park, CA: Sage Publications, 1993.

Edwards, C. P. "Thinking About Friendship: Fostering and Extending Young Children's Understanding." In *Connecting: Friendship in the Lives of Young Children and Their Teachers,* edited by D. P. Wolf and B. Neugebauer. Redmond, WA: Exchange Press, 2004.

Edwards, C. P., and P. G. Ramsey. *Promoting Social and Moral Development in Young Children: Creative Approaches for the Classroom.* New York: Teachers College Press, 1986.

Epstein, A. S. *The Intentional Teacher: Choosing the Best Strategies for Young Children's Learning.* Washington, DC: National Association for the Education of Young Children, 2007.

———. *Me, You, Us: Social–Emotional Learning in Preschool.* Ypsilanti, MI: HighScope Press, 2009.

Fabes, R. A., and N. Eisenberg. "Young Children's Coping with Interpersonal Anger." *Child Development* 63, no. 1 (1992): 116–28.

Farrant, K., and E. Reese. "Maternal Style and Children's Participation in Reminiscing: Stepping Stones in Children's Autobiographical Memory Development." *Journal of Cognition and Development* 1, no. 2 (2000): 193–225.

Fivush, R. "Owning Experience: Developing Subjective Perspective in Autobiographical Narratives." In *The Self in Time,* edited by C. Moore and K. Lemmon. Mahwah, NJ: Erlbaum, 2001.

Friedman, W. J. "Children's Knowledge of the Future Distances of Daily Activities and Annual Events." *Journal of Cognition and Development* 3, no. 3 (2002): 333–56.

———. "Children's Time Memory: The Development of a Differentiated Past." *Cognitive Development* 7, no. 2 (1992): 171–87.

———. "The Development of Children's Knowledge of the Times of Future Events." *Child Development* 71, no. 4 (2000): 913–32.

———. "The Development of Children's Memory for the Time of Past Events." *Child Development* 62, no. 1 (1991): 139–55.

———. "The Development of a Differentiated Sense of the Past and the Future." In *Advances in Child Development and Behavior*, vol. 31, edited by R. V. Kail. San Diego, CA: Academic (Elsevier), 2003.

———. "The Development of Temporal Metamemory." *Child Development* 78 (2007): 1472–91.

———. "Developmental and Cognitive Perspectives on Humans' Sense of the Times of Past and Future Events." *Learning and Motivation* 36, no. 2 (2005): 145–58.

Friedman, W. J., A. G. Gardner, and N. R. E. Zubin. "Children's Comparisons of the Recency of Two Events from the Past Year." *Child Development* 66, no. 4 (1995): 970–83.

Friedman, W. J., and S. Kemp. "The Effects of Elapsed Time and Retrieval on Young Children's Judgments of the Temporal Distances of Past Events." *Cognitive Development* 13, no. 3 (1998): 335–67.

Galinsky, E. *Mind in the Making: The Seven Essential Life Skills Every Child Needs.* New York: HarperStudio, 2010.

Gauvain, M. "Bringing Culture Into Relief: Cultural Contributions to the Development of Children's Planning Skills." In *Advances in Child Development and Behavior*, vol. 32, edited by R. V. Kail. Amsterdam: Elsevier, 2004.

Hartup, W. W. "The Company They Keep: Friendships and Their Developmental Significance." *Child Development* 67, no. 1 (1996): 1–13.

Hirschfeld, L. A. "Children's Developing Conceptions of Race." In *Handbook of Race, Racism, and the Developing Child*, edited by S. M. Quintana and C. McKown. Hoboken, NJ: Wiley, 2008.

———. *Race in the Making: Cognition, Culture, and the Child's Construction of Human Kinds.* Cambridge, MA: MIT Press, 1996.

Hohmann, M., and D. P. Weikart. *Educating Young Children.* 2nd ed. Ypsilanti, MI: HighScope Press, 2002.

Hopkins, S., ed. *Hearing Everyone's Voice: Educating Young Children for Peace and Democratic Community.* Redmond, WA: Child Care Information Exchange, 1999.

Howes, C. "Peer Interaction of Young Children." *Monographs of the Society for Research in Child Development* 53, no. 1, serial no. 217 (1988): 1–92.

Howes, C., and S. Spieker. "Attachment Relationships in the Context of Multiple Caregivers." In *Handbook of Attachment: Theory, Research, and Clinical Applications*, 2nd ed., edited by J. Cassidy and P. R. Shaver. New York: Guilford Press, 2008.

Hudson, J. A. "The Development of Future Time Concepts Through Mother–Child Conversation." *Merrill-Palmer Quarterly* 52, no. 1 (2006): 70–95.

———. "Do You Know What We're Going to Do This Summer? Mothers' Talk to Preschool Children About Future Events." *Journal of Cognition and Development* 3, no. 1 (2002): 49–71.

———. "The Emergence of Autobiographic Memory in Mother–Child Conversation." In *Knowing and Remembering in Young Children*, edited by R. Fivush and J. A. Hudson. New York: Cambridge University Press, 1990.

Hudson, J. A., L. R. Shapiro, and B. B. Sosa. "Planning in the Real World: Preschool Children's Scripts and Plans for Familiar Events." *Child Development* 66 (1995): 984–98.

Kahn, P., and S. Kellert, eds. *Children and Nature: Psychological, Sociocultural, and Evolutionary Investigations.* Cambridge, MA: MIT Press, 2002.

Katz, L. G., and D. E. McClellan. *Fostering Children's Social Competence: The Teacher's Role.* Washington, DC: National Association for the Education of Young Children, 1997.

Katz, P. A. "Racists or Tolerant Multiculturalists? How Do They Begin?" *American Psychologist* 58, no. 11 (2003): 807–909.

Kochanska, G., and R. A. Thompson. "The Emergence and Development of Conscience in Toddlerhood and Early Childhood." In *Parenting and Children's Internalization of Values*, edited by J. Grusec and L. Kuczynski. New York: Wiley, 1997.

Levstik, L. S., and K. C. Barton. "They Still Use Some of Their Past': Historical Salience in Elementary Children's Chronological Thinking." *Journal of Curriculum Studies* 28 (1996): 531–76.

Liben, L. S. "Education for Spatial Thinking." In *Handbook of Child Psychology: Child Psychology in Practice*, vol. 4, 6th ed. Series edited by W. Damon and R. M. Lerner. Volume edited by K. A. Renninger and I. E. Sigel. New York: Wiley, 2006.

———. "Spatial Development in Childhood: Where Are We Now?" In *Blackwell Handbook of Childhood Cognitive Development*, edited by U. Goswami. Oxford, UK: Blackwell Publishers, 2002.

Luov, R. *Last Child in the Woods: Saving Our Children from Nature-Deficit Disorder.* Chapel Hill, NC: Algonquin Books, 2005.

Mindes, G. "Social Studies in Today's Early Childhood Curricula." *Beyond the Journal: Young Children on the Web* 60, no. 5 (2005): 12–18.

———. *Teaching Young Children Social Studies.* Lanham, MD: Rowland and Littlefield Education, 2006.

Musser, L. M., and K. E. Diamond. "The Children's Attitudes Toward the Environment Scale for Preschool Children." *Journal of Environmental Education* 30, no. 2 (1999): 23–30.

National Research Council. *Learning to Think Spatially: GIS as a Support System in the K–12 Curriculum.* Washington, DC: National Academies Press, 2006.

———. *Report of the Committee on Early Childhood Pedagogy.* Eager to Learn: Educating Our Preschoolers. Edited by B. T. Bowman, M. S. Donovan, and M. S. Burns. Washington, DC: National Academies Press, 2001.

National Research Council and Institute of Medicine, Committee on Integrating the Science of Early Childhood Development. *From Neurons to Neighborhoods: The Science of Early Childhood Development.* Edited by J. P. Shonkoff and D. A. Phillips. Washington, DC: National Academies Press, 2000.

Nelson, K., and R. Fivush. "The Emergence of Autobiographical Memory: A Social–Cultural Developmental Theory." *Psychological Review* 111, no. 2 (2004): 486–511.

Newcombe, N., and J. Huttenlocher. *Making Space.* Cambridge, MA: MIT Press, 2000.

Parker, J. G., and J. M. Gottman. "Social and Emotional Development in a Relational Context: Friendship Interaction from Early Childhood to Adolescence." In *Peer Relations in Child Development*, edited by T. J. Berndt and G. W. Ladd. New York: Wiley, 1989.

Quintana, S. M. "Children's Developmental Understanding of Ethnicity and Race." *Applied and Preventive Psychology* 7, no. 1 (1988): 27–45.

———. "Racial and Ethnic Identity: Developmental Perspectives and Research." *Journal of Counseling Psychology* 54, no. 3 (2007): 259–70.

———. "Racial Perspective Taking Ability: Developmental, Theoretical, and Empirical Trends." In *Handbook of Race, Racism, and the Developing Child*, edited by S. M. Quintana and C. McKown. New York: Wiley, 2008.

Reese, E. "Social Factors in the Development of Autobiographical Memory: The State of the Art." *Social Development* 11, no. 1 (2002): 124–42.

Rubin, K. H., W. M. Bukowski, and J. G. Parker. "Peer Interactions, Relationships, and Groups." In *Handbook of Child Psychology: Social, Emotional, and Personality Development*, vol. 3, 6th ed., edited by W. Damon and R. M. Lerner. Volume edited by N. Eisenberg. New York: Wiley, 2006.

Rubin, K. H., and others. "Peer Relationships in Childhood." In *Developmental Science: An Advanced Textbook*, 5th ed., edited by M. H. Bornstein and M. E. Lamb. Mahwah, NJ: Erlbaum, 2005.

Schug, M. C. "Children's Understanding of Economics." *The Elementary School Journal* 87, no. 5 (1987): 506–18.

Schug, M. C., and J. C. Birkey. "The Development of Children's Economic Reasoning." *Theory and Research in Social Education* 13, no. 1 (1985): 31–42.

Seefeldt, C., and A. Galper. *Active Experiences for Active Children: Social Studies.* 2nd ed. Columbus, OH: Pearson, 2006.

Seefeldt, C., and others. *Social Studies for the Preschool/Primary Child.* 8th ed. Boston: Merrill, 2010.

Siegler, R. S., and D. R. Thompson. "'Hey, Would You Like a Nice Cold Cup of Lemonade On This Hot Day?': Children's Understanding of Economic Causation." *Developmental Psychology* 34, no. 1 (1998): 146–60.

Smetana, J. G. "Preschool Children's Conceptions of Moral and Social Rules." *Child Development* 52, no. 4 (1981): 1333–36.

———. "Preschool Children's Conceptions of Transgressions: The Effects of Varying Moral and Conventional Domain-Related Attributes." *Developmental Psychology* 21, no. 1 (1985): 18–29.

Thompson, D. R., and R. S. Siegler. "Buy Low, Sell High: The Development of an Informal Theory of Economics." *Child Development* 71, no. 3 (2000): 660–77.

Thompson, J. E., and K. K. Twibell. "Teaching Hearts and Minds in Early Childhood Classrooms: Curriculum for Social and Emotional Development." In *Handbook of Child Development and Early Education: Research to Practice,* edited by O. A. Barbarin and B. H. Wasik. New York: Guilford Press, 2009.

Thompson, R. A. "The Development of the Person: Social Understanding, Relationships, Self, Conscience." In *Handbook of Child Psychology: Social, Emotional, and Personality Development,* vol. 3, 6th ed., edited by W. Damon and R. M. Lerner. Volume edited by N. Eisenberg. New York: Wiley, 2006.

———. "Empathy and Its Origins in Early Development." In *Intersubjective Communication and Emotion in Early Ontogeny: A Source Book,* edited by S. Braten. New York: Cambridge University Press, 1998.

———. "The Roots of School Readiness in Social and Emotional Development." *The Kauffman Early Education Exchange* 1 (2002): 8–29.

Thompson, R. A., and M. Goodman. "Development of Self, Relationships, and Socioemotional Competence: Foundations for Early School Success." In *Handbook of Child Development and Early Education: Research to Practice,* edited by O. A. Barbarin and B. H. Wasik. New York: Guilford Press, 2009.

Thompson, R. A., R. Goodvin, and S. Meyer. "Social Development: Psychological Understanding, Self-Understanding, and Relationships." In *Handbook of Preschool Mental Health: Development, Disorders, and Treatment,* edited by J. Luby. New York: Guilford Press, 2006.

Thompson, R. A., and K. Lagatutta. "Feeling and Understanding: Early Emotional Development." In *The Blackwell Handbook of Early Childhood Development,* edited by K. McCartney and D. Phillips. Oxford, UK: Blackwell Publishers, 2006.

Thompson, R. A., S. Meyer, and M. McGinley. "Understanding Values in Relationship: The Development of Conscience." In *Handbook of Moral Development,* edited by M. Killen and J. Smetana. Mahwah, NJ: Erlbaum, 2006.

Thompson, R. A., and H. A. Raikes. "The Social and Emotional Foundations of School Readiness." In *Social and Emotional Health in Early Childhood: Building Bridges Between Services and Systems,* edited by D. F. Perry, R. F. Kaufmann, and J. Knitzer. Baltimore, MD: Paul H. Brookes Publishing Co., 2007.

Thompson, R. A., and J. E. Thompson. "Early Childhood Education for Children with Disabilities." *The Special EDge* 23 (2010): 1–6.

CHAPTER 3
Science

Children have a sense of wonder and natural curiosity about objects and events in their environment. Just like scientists, they seek information and actively explore and investigate the world around them, try things out to see what happens, and confirm or adjust their expectations. Children's exploration with water, sand, blocks, and other objects and materials in the preschool environment provide them with opportunities to discover the physical characteristics of objects, to explore concepts such as balance, forces, motion, and ways that solid objects are different from liquids. Observing and investigating plants and animals, both indoors and outdoors, allows children to discover what different living things look like, how they behave, what their habitats and needs are, and how they grow and change over time. Thinking about experiences of night and day, rain, wind, and other changes in weather and the environment raises interesting questions about the nature of earth phenomena, and provides children with opportunities to discover characteristics of the natural world.

Science is a natural and developmentally appropriate focus for young children. Educators and researchers recognize the importance of young children's science experiences and the need to establish educational programs that support science, technology, engineering, and mathematics **(STEM)** in the early years. Preschool science is about active learning, not memorizing scientific facts or watching the teacher perform science demonstrations. The purpose of preschool science is to nurture children's habits of inquiry, critical thinking, creativity, and innovative problem solving, and to foster open mindedness, and the motivation to learn. Preschool science guides children's natural curiosity into opportunities to observe, explore, and inquire about basic phenomena and materials in their world. From infancy, children gain knowledge and develop concepts about living things and physical objects. Preschool science provides children with focused experiences that allow them to learn ways to explore and extend their knowledge. Children begin to adopt scientific ideas and to acquire the basic skills and language of **scientific inquiry** (ways to explore and develop knowledge and understanding of scientific ideas). Making **observations,** posing questions, planning investigations, using tools to gather information, making predictions, recording information, and communicating findings and explanations all combine in an evolving process of developing science understanding and creating a disposition to choose to learn science in the future.

Science can be conducted in any preschool setting. All preschools, regardless of the level of resources and access to nature, can use their existing resources to create a program with meaningful science learning experiences. Pushing cars down an incline, building with blocks, manipulating tubes at the water table, or mixing clay with water are everyday play activities that engage children in experimenting with objects and materials. Collecting leaves, searching for insects in the yard, sorting and classifying fruits and vegetables, and sprouting seeds in pots engage children with living things. Experiences of child-initiated play are important as they provide children with opportunities to construct understandings and integrate knowledge. With teachers' intentional planning, guidance, and support, children's play and interactions with objects can become rich experiences of scientific inquiry and facilitate children's knowledge and understanding of objects and events in the world.

Preschool teachers play a pivotal role in expanding children's understanding of science concepts and developing children's attitudes, skills, and the language of scientific inquiry. The teachers can focus children's attention on particular science concepts, those that are developmentally appropriate, interesting, and engaging for both children and teachers. They can create engaging inquiry experiences, encouraging close observations of objects and events. Teachers help children formulate questions, make predictions, and experiment with objects and materials to test children's predictions. Teachers guide children to reason and

think more deeply about the phenomena they observe, to notice patterns and draw connections. They teach children how to document their observations and ideas and share them with others. For example, planting and sprouting seeds can become a rich process in which children predict what plants will look like as they grow; engage in detailed observations of plants over time; track, measure, and record their plant's growth through drawings, words, and photos; and participate in group discussions, sharing their observations and thoughts. These kinds of experiences deepen children's understanding of how plants change and what they need to grow and develop. Children may draw the connection to their own growth and the growth of other animals and begin to develop a broader understanding of living things. Such experiences of scientific inquiry not only support children's development of scientific knowledge, but provide a natural vehicle for developing children's social skills, and their develop-

ment in mathematics, language, literacy, and other domains.

Preschool teachers do not need to have extensive knowledge about science in order to be able to teach it well, but they should be willing to research and gain general knowledge of the concepts and principles they explore with children. The kind and amount of information or knowledge they need to know is readily available through basic research. Acquiring some background knowledge about the topic helps teachers in planning inquiry experiences and challenging and supporting children through their explorations. Teachers do not need to have answers to all the questions children will raise. Rather than providing children with answers, teachers can use children's questions as a springboard for further investigations. They may say, "I don't know. Let's find out together." It is essential that teachers become "scientists" together with children, model a questioning mind for children and think out loud, expressing interest and enthusiasm. Teachers' thoughtful guidance and support through inquiry experiences builds a foundation for children's understanding of basic science concepts, fosters a positive approach to learning, and develops learning skills and attitudes necessary for later success in science and in other subjects.

Guiding Principles

The following principles guide teachers in establishing a preschool science program that fosters children's curiosity and develops their skills and habits to explore and learn about their world. These principles are consistent with a constructivist approach to learning, where children actively construct knowl-edge through physical and mental interactions with objects and people in their environment. The principles are drawn from current research-based models and approaches to early childhood science[5] and are consistent with the National Association for the Education of Young Children (NAEYC) guidelines on developmentally appropriate practice.[6]

▶ **The preschool environment supports children's curiosity and encourages inquiry and experimentation.**
Teachers can create an environment that sparks children's curiosity and supports children's natural inclination to engage in scientific inquiry. The physical environment provides children access to a wide variety of objects and materials to explore and investigate and tools to support their investigations. The social environment fosters attributes important for learning such as curiosity, open-mindedness, critical reflection, respect for evidence, independence of thought, perseverance, and cooperation. In a preschool environment with a culture of inquiry, the teacher:

- acts as a researcher, joining children in exploring their world;

- asks **open-ended questions** to encourage children to think and talk;

- introduces children to new vocabulary, including scientific terms such as *observe, explore, predict,* and *measure;*

- demonstrates appropriate use of scientific tools;

- invites children to reason and draw conclusions;

- encourages children to share their observations and communicate their thoughts;

- models respect for nature.

▶ **Content of inquiry is developmentally appropriate and builds on children's prior experiences.**

Young children have rich knowledge of the natural and physical world.[7] Some areas of knowledge appear early and provide robust foundations for science learning. Preschool science supports children in developing competencies they are ready to acquire. The preschool learning foundations in science present skills and concepts that are developmentally appropriate for preschool children. Children's intuitive understandings of scientific concepts vary based on their cultural beliefs, language, and the daily experiences in which they are immersed. These differing backgrounds that children bring with them as they enter preschool serve as the foundation on which they build new knowledge and understanding. It is critical for teachers to take into account children's existing knowledge and beliefs and build on this base when introducing new concepts.

▶ **Scientific inquiry experiences are interesting and engaging for children and teachers.**

The most engaging science activities are drawn from the world around the child, are relevant and connected to children's daily experiences, and

reflect children's questions and interests. The teacher's own level of enthusiasm, engagement, and interest in the topic of study is of equal importance. If the teacher is interested in the content of study, she or he is more likely to be engaged and motivated to participate with children as a researcher, and to generate ideas and activities. Moreover, the teacher enthusiasm will transfer to the children. The adult's excitement will help develop and maintain children's curiosity, joy of discovery, and positive attitudes about learning.

▶ **Children explore scientific concepts directly through active, hands-on, minds-on playful experiences.**

The preschool environment provides children with numerous opportunities to explore objects and phenomena drawn directly from their world, using all of their senses. Multiple hands-on activities with concrete objects benefit all children, including children who are English learners and many children with special needs for whom learning through authentic experiences with concrete objects is very important. Magical science such as the combination of materials to produce an exciting reaction (e.g., an exploding "volcano") compels attention, but it does not help children to understand the connection between the adult actions and the resulting reactions They do not learn how variations in actions can produce different responses. While children interact with materials, teachers can encourage them to engage in simple experiments. Children can learn to observe carefully, to put forward their ideas and thoughts, to ask questions, and to make and test predictions. Such hands-on, minds-on activities reinforce children's natural interests and curiosity while strengthening their reasoning skills.

▶ **Children explore scientific concepts in depth through multiple, related learning experiences over time.**
In order for children to build a deeper understanding of a concept, they need to have many opportunities to work with a concept and to explore it from different perspectives over an extended period of time.[9] A range of conceptually related experiences that continues for weeks, or even months, allows children a deep exploration of the scientific concept, and results in learning that is more effective, powerful, and long-lasting.

▶ **Children construct knowledge through social interactions with peers and adults.**
Interactions with peers and adults facilitate children's construction of scientific knowledge while developing children's social, language, and communication skills. Children and adults co-construct knowledge as they explore and investigate together. Through a collaborative inquiry process, children and teachers seek to make meaning of the situation they explore. At the same time, adults ask questions to challenge and expand children's thinking and guide and scaffold them through the learning process. When children interact with peers and adults, they learn to work cooperatively, take turns, share, listen to others' ideas, respect different views, think flexibly, sometimes hold to their own ideas, and assist each other when needed.

▶ **Children use language and other forms of communication to express their thoughts, describe observations, and document their work.**
Communication is an integral component of children's learning and formation of scientific concepts. Children use language when describing their

observations, reflecting on their work through collaborative discussions and sharing their ideas and thoughts with others. They also learn to use the vocabulary associated with science and gradually begin to use terms such as *predict, observe, measure,* or *experiment.* Children can communicate in their home language, sign language, or English. Children also use different forms of communication to record and document information, including drawing, gesturing, dictations of words or sentences, signing, and symbol boards. The use of language enriches children's scientific experiences and facilitates their understanding of scientific concepts.

▶ **Teachers support children who are English learners in understanding and communicating scientific knowledge and skills.**
Scientific experiences provide natural opportunities to expose children to new

words in English and in their home language and to use these words in a meaningful context. During initial stages, children who are English learners may not yet have the vocabulary to describe their observations and express their thoughts in English. Teachers can encourage children to express themselves, whether in English or in their home language. Teachers may need to scaffold communication with children in focused small-group interactions, by using gestures and visual cues, to describe, clarify, or demonstrate by acting out the meaning of a word or phrase presented in English, and to expand and extend the child's language. Children who are English learners benefit from using the home language in learning of concepts in English and from having a strong family–school partnership.[10] Adult family members and older siblings can be a resource for teachers for science vocabulary words in children's home languages. For more information about strategies to support children who are English learners, see the *California Preschool Curriculum Framework, Volume 1*, chapter 5, "English-Language Development."

▶ **Science is embedded in children's daily activities and play and provides a natural vehicle for integrating mathematics, literacy, and other content areas.**

Science can be integrated throughout the day and included in a wide range of activities throughout the preschool environment. Rather than isolating science to one particular time slot, or one particular area of the learning environment, the teacher can encourage children to pursue science ideas while playing with blocks, at the water table, or in the sandbox. The nature of science explorations facilitates curricular integration and provides meaningful situations in which to develop math, literacy, writing, art, and social skills.

▶ **Individual differences are recognized, and all children are included and supported.**

Children are different from one another and enter preschool with various levels of social, linguistic, motor, and cognitive abilities as well as sensory preferences. Yet, they all share a natural curiosity and desire to explore their environment and make sense of their world. Science is for all children regardless of their age, sex, cultural or ethnic background, ability, aspirations, or interest.[11] The amount and kind of support children need varies from child to child and may include physical, linguistic, cognitive, and/or social support. As stated in the NAEYC guidelines on developmentally appropriate practice, "Teachers should incorporate a wide variety of experiences, materials and equipment, and teaching strategies in constructing a curriculum to accommodate a broad range of children's individual differences, prior experiences, maturation rates, style of learning, needs and interests."[12] If children are receiving special education services, teachers can ask for ideas from families and specialists in order to adapt activities as needed. Talk with family members about the interests, abilities, and preferred style of interaction of those children with special needs. Make adaptations to materials and activities to increase successful participation of all children.

▶ **The preschool environment, home, and community are connected through science.**

Children's learning is enhanced when parents and family members are involved in children's learning and share with them the excitement and joy of discovery. The science domain, in particular, bridges across different cultures and languages. The life cycle of a butterfly or the properties of objects and materials can be described in different languages, but are the same in all cultures. Parents and family members can support children's learning of science and enhance their knowledge base in the home language. They can use everyday situations to extend and enrich children's knowledge and understanding of scientific concepts and take an active role in children's science experiences at home and in the preschool environment. By partnering with families, teachers can also learn about children's interests, cultural beliefs, and home experiences related to science. In addition to families, numerous community resources can be tapped to enrich science activities. Local facilities and businesses can host field trips, and professionals (e.g., veterinarians, engineers, nurses, scientists) can make presentations that provide valuable information to children and teachers alike.

Environments and Materials

The Physical Environment

The indoor and outdoor environments provide the context for children's physical and social explorations and construction of scientific concepts. The following section includes strategies for helping teachers set up a physical environment that is rich, stimulating, and conducive to children's construction of knowledge.

▶ **Be thoughtful about what objects and materials to include in the environment.**
The selection of objects and materials that stimulate children's interest and provide the means for scientific investigation is vital. Children need meaningful hands-on explorations of objects and materials to learn about concepts of science in an authentic way. It is important to consider all children, including those with special needs, when designing the environment. Accessibility of a wide variety of objects and materials, particularly those that focus children's attention on important aspects of the scientific phenomena they are studying, acknowledges individual differences and permits individual choice approach. The appendix at the end of this chapter provides examples of suggested materials that support learning in the physical, life, and earth sciences.

▶ **Provide a variety of natural materials to observe and investigate.**
As part of children's playful explorations, they discover the properties and characteristics of natural objects and how they change under different conditions. Water, sand, and clay are natural materials that are traditionally found in early childhood settings and invite scientific investigation. Twigs, leaves, bark, seeds, pinecones, crystals, shells, pebbles, and different kinds of rocks come in a variety of colors, shapes, sizes, textures, and patterns and are fascinating and intriguing for children. They encourage sensory exploration and close observation. They provide opportunities to label, sort, classify, order, compare, and contrast. For additional suggestions of natural materials, see the appendix at the end of this chapter.

► **Include objects and materials that allow for creativity and open-ended investigation.**

Open-ended materials are materials that can be used in multiple ways and therefore allow for creativity and investigation and problem-solving. These are different from objects that were designed with a particular use and only one way of operation. For example, in a prefabricated marble run, all children need to do is drop the marble in and watch it roll. This is very different from a roadway for marbles created by children using blocks and different kinds of gutter materials.[13] Open-ended materials, such as blocks, boxes, cardboard, foam, and other construction materials, can be used in different ways for different projects, encouraging experimentation. A variety of **reclaimed materials** will spark children's curiosity, enhance children's playful explorations, and models for children ways to reuse and recycle materials.[14] For additional suggestions of open-ended materials, see the appendix at the end of this chapter.

► **Include living things in the preschool environment.**

Experiences with plants and animals, including human beings, expand children's ideas about the appearance, behavior, and habitats of living things. Taking care of pets and plants, observing them grow and change, helps children become more aware of the basic needs and life cycles of living things. They learn that living things need to be treated with care and respect to keep them healthy and safe. Plants in the preschool environment can range from experimenting with seedlings in small cups or pots, to a terrarium, an open container with soil, a collection of plants in the room, or large outdoor

pots and gardens. The preschool environment may also include pets such as birds, guinea pigs, fish, or hamsters, providing opportunities to observe changes in animals as they grow. Caring for caterpillars or tadpoles allows children to learn about transformations related to the **life cycle**. Before deciding which pets or plants to include in the room, it is important for the teacher to be knowledgeable of the plant or animal's requirements, local program policies regarding pets, and toxicity of plants. It is also important to find out whether any of the children or staff members are allergic to either the plants or the animals, and about children's fear of certain animals.

► **Include scientific tools for observation, measurement, and documentation.**

Magnifiers, hand lenses, measuring cups, and a balance scale are some

of the scientific tools that help in the observation and measurement of objects. Magnifiers (such as handheld lenses and microscopes) help children observe details in living things or other objects (e.g., feathers, insect eggs, salt crystals, water droplets). Tools, such as a balance scale, rulers, measuring tape, measuring cups and spoons, and a thermometer, introduce children to ways in which attributes such as weight, length, volume, and temperature can be measured. Children also need tools such as clipboards, paper, journals, pencils, markers, and cameras for recording data and for documenting their work. Preschool children are not expected to know how to use these tools on their own. With guidance from teachers, they can become familiar with the tools and learn about the function of different measuring devices. See the *California Preschool Curriculum Framework, Volume 1*, chapter 6, "Mathematics," for more information about opportunities to promote measurement concepts in the environment.

▶ **Make scientific tools available throughout the preschool environment.**
Optimal learning opportunities may be created by making scientific tools available daily and accessible to all children in different interest areas. For example, measurement tools can be part of the playhouse, and clipboards and measurement tapes can be part of the block area. Teachers may choose to have a science table devoted to scientific tools, objects, and materials related to the current focus of study in addition to those placed in other parts of the room. The mere presence of scientific tools does not invite children to use them in a purposeful way. Tools introduced to the children and dem-

onstrated by a teacher, individually or in small groups, are more likely to be used as intended. It is helpful to start with a few tools and add or rotate tools in planned activities as investigations expand.

▶ **Consider adaptations in scientific tools and materials for children with special needs.**
Encourage all children, including those with special needs, to discover properties of objects and materials in new and different ways. Children with visual and/or motor challenges may need assistance from an adult or peer to manipulate objects, or use scientific tools. Simple instructions and rules for safe use; providing pictures of tools and possible uses may facilitate participation by more children. For example, putting a bigger grip on the hand lenses can help children with low muscle tone. Consultation with specialists can be helpful to find or adapt materials that allow for discovery and that can easily and safely be used by children with physical disabilities or other special needs.

▶ **Use technology to support children's scientific experiences.**
Technology is part of a child's world. It can augment and enrich children's

scientific exploration when used appropriately. Computers, particularly those with access to the Internet, provide expanded resources and enable teachers and children to obtain a great amount of information quickly. Teachers may use the Internet to obtain background information on any topic of inquiry and to show photographs or videos on a range of topics. In addition to computers, other technologies such as video and digital cameras and tape recorders can be used to support children's documentation practices. These can be powerful tools in recording observations and tracking changes in objects and materials.

▶ **Present documentation of science-related experiences in the preschool environment.**

When engaged in scientific explorations, children are encouraged to record and document information in drawings, charts, and photos or by constructing three-dimensional models. For example, to record the growth of lima beans, children, with the assistance of the teacher, may create a chart with drawings or photos of the lima beans before and after sprouting and growing. Making children's and teachers' **documentation** visible in the room allows children to revisit an experience, provides a focus of conversation for children and teachers, and makes the process of inquiry visible for children and for families. It also gives a positive message to children about the importance of their investigations and the value the teacher places on their work.

▶ **Include children's books with science-related content.**

Children's books provide powerful ways to extend children's firsthand scientific experiences. Nonfiction,

informational books about things and events in the world, such as insects, animals, seeds, the seasons, fruits and vegetables, or the human body, provide resources for children's investigations through pictures and descriptions, and enrich children's knowledge about their world. Numerous story books, such as *The Tiny Seed* by Eric Carle or *The Happy Day* by Ruth Krauss, have science connections and can be starting points for discussing concepts such as growth or seasonal and weather changes.[15] Teachers can use books to introduce scientific concepts, to encourage the use of scientific language (e.g., "What do you predict will happen next?"), and to develop skills of scientific thinking. Reading for information supports language development and comprehension skills as well as the learning of science. Not all books need to be purchased. Public libraries are a great resource. Teachers can create their own books, often by using documentation of children's work such as drawings, quotes, and photos (see the example on page 167).

▶ **Use the outdoors for natural explorations and investigations.**

The outdoor environment is where children can experience their natural surroundings first hand, and learn about concepts related to living things, physical objects, and earth materials and phenomena (e.g., rain, wind, a rainbow). It provides ideal sites for explorations of natural objects such as insects, plants, rocks, clouds, shadows, water, light, weather, and the motion of objects. Outdoor explorations also connect children with nature and teach them to be respectful of living things and the natural environment. There are endless opportunities for children to experience and do sci-

ence outdoors.[16] They can observe and investigate plants, insects, and other small animals in their natural habitats. These experiences will broaden their understanding of and respect for living things. Access to books enriches children's outdoor explorations and allows them to cross-reference what they observe with information in the book. The outdoor environment can include space and resources for children's large-scale construction projects and exploration of physical science, in which they investigate force, balance, and properties of different materials. Open space to experiment and interact with moving objects such as balls, wheeled items, and slopes is found outdoors. Such outdoor explorations promote collaboration, teamwork, and positive attitudes toward nature.[17]

▶ **Organize the space in ways that promote children's explorations.**
In thinking about the arrangement of the indoor environment, teachers can plan to allow space for long-term investigations and small-group and large-

group explorations and discussions. Several considerations in organizing the indoor physical space can facilitate the smooth flow of playful explorations throughout the environment, as well as promote social interactions among children.[18]

- **Space.** Allow space for observations and for objects, materials, tools, and resources related to science. Some investigations last for extended periods of time and may require storage and display space, and open space set aside to preserve ongoing investigations, whether indoors or outdoors.

- **Flexibility.** The amount of space and kind of setups needed for different activities changes based on the nature of children's investigation. Allow for flexibility in the use of physical space and furniture to accommodate the changing needs of each activity.

- **Accessibility.** In order to promote self-direction and free explorations, tools and materials need to be accessible and consistently available to children. Scientific tools (e.g., magnifiers, tweezers, clipboards), books, and the objects and materials children explore should be placed on low shelving or tables and be accessible to all children.

- **Social interactions.** Social interactions are necessary for conceptual growth and the development of communication skills. The arrangement of the physical space can facilitate children's interactions with each other. For example, the setup of an activity suggests to children whether they should work alone or with other children. Environments that are most successful allow for children's solitary play and individual explorations, as well as for social interactions and collaborative investigations, in small or large groups, minimizing conflict caused by crowding or interfering with the path of travel.

▶ **Always be aware of children's safety.** Safety is an important consideration in indoor and outdoor activity plans and the materials selected for the activity. Some materials or plants, for example, are poisonous and should not be studied with children. Children or staff members may be allergic to certain plants or animals, and some materials may also produce allergic reactions. Ask parents or family members and check children's records for information about any allergies. Talk with children and demonstrate how to practice safety when using tools and manipulating different materials. For instance, safety goggles that fit young children

may be used in activities that have any potential for liquids or solids accidentally getting into the eyes. Good safety practices should also be part of children's outdoor explorations of plants and insects. Make sure the area is free of poisonous plants or undesirable animals. Check your local licensing regulations for any safety-related issues.

The Social Environment: Establish a Culture of Inquiry

While a physical environment with a wide range of objects and materials is necessary for fueling and encouraging children's experimentation, the social environment must support exploration and investigation and encourage children to pursue their own questions and develop their ideas. In a preschool environment with a culture of inquiry, the teacher is a researcher, joins children in exploring the world, and models a questioning mind for children. The teacher observes children closely, fosters children's curiosity and questioning, and asks open-ended questions (i.e., questions that do not have a single right answer or that ask for only a yes or no answer). The teacher engages children in conversations and enhances their enthusiasm and motivation to learn.

VIGNETTE

Ms. Lucinda notices that Yau and Tommy are very excited about the ramp they built in the block area. They put the car at the top of the ramp and watched it go down slowly by itself. They did it over and over. At some point, Tommy raised the board and made the ramp steeper. They put the car at the top and let it go again. Both of them got excited when they noticed that the car was going down faster. "Wow, that was fast," Ms. Lucinda said. "It was faster. I wonder what you did to make the car go down faster." Tommy said, "I was holding up the road. You see, like this." Ms Lucinda asked, "How can you change the ramp so the car goes down fast, even when you are not holding it up?" Yau tried to place more blocks under the higher side of the ramp (making the ramp steeper). Tommy then placed the car at the top and let it go, and they watched the car go fast, "really fast." At circle time, Ms. Lucinda asked Yau and Tommy to share how they learned to make the car go down the ramp faster.

TEACHABLE MOMENT

▶ Observing Yau and Tommy playing in the block area, the teacher notices they have discovered, through play, how to make objects go downhill faster. She intervenes and asks, "I wonder what you did to make the car go down faster." Yau and Tommy were quickly engaged, and Ms. Lucinda observed them solving the problem on their own. She later invites them to share what they discovered with the rest of the group. She also could have taken a photo or suggested to the children that they draw what they had done, or count and record how many blocks they used to make the car go faster. The physical science of movement is exciting for young learners because they can see immediately the cause and effect. They can test and retest their solutions, get results, and draw conclusions.

▶ **Foster children's curiosity and questioning.**
As children interact with objects and observe their environment, they express curiosity and raise different questions: "Do snails have eyes?" "Why doesn't the ball come out?" "Where is the rain coming from?" The teacher welcomes and values children's questioning, rather than provide answers, and encourages them to pursue their ideas and questions. Children who are English learners should be encouraged to ask questions in their home language whenever possible, as these questions are likely to be more complex. Not all children use words to express curiosity. Children may express their questioning and interest nonverbally, through their facial expressions, body language, and behaviors. For example, they may be absorbed in an exploration for a long time, try out different ideas, or repeat the same experience over and over. Teachers can scaffold the child's interest by thinking out loud: "It looks like you enjoy mixing the sand with water. I

wonder what happened to the water, or I wonder what would happen if you put some of the wet sand in the sun."

▶ Guide children in exploring their questions.

The teacher's interest in the children's questions indicates to them that their thoughts are valuable and important. Some of the children's questions can be explored directly with appropriate experiences, additional support, and materials to extend their learning. Other questions can be answered by using resources, such as books, the Web, or an expert.[19] In some cases, teachers may not know the answers to children's questions. They can invite children to explore together: "I don't know. Let's find out together." Teachers often need to do some investigations of their own so they know where to take the children in future investigations. Modeling inquiry practices for children is a powerful way to establish a culture of inquiry in the preschool environment. Teachers' enthusiasm for exploring and investigating is relayed to children in the group.

▶ Be an active observer.

Spending time with children and observing them closely, both inside the room and outside in the yard, is key to supporting children's learning. Observations enable teachers to find out what themes are of interest to the children in the group, what they do with different materials and activities, and what questions they have. Through in-depth observations, teachers enrich their understanding of children's diverse cultural backgrounds and language abilities in a genuine way, and learn to consider multiple perspectives when formulating goals for children.[20] Such information can guide teachers in selecting a focus of inquiry that is relevant and responsive to children's questions, interests, and abilities and build on children's existing knowledge and understanding. Based on this information, teachers can decide what experiences to offer children next, how to deepen their understanding, and how to support the needs of individual children in the group.

▶ Talk with children and engage them in conversations.

While observing and listening to children as they work, teachers ask questions, challenge their thinking, and engage them in conversations about their work: "What can you do to make the bridge higher?" "Why do you think roly polies roll up?" "Tell me about your rock. Where did you find it? Are there more rocks like this around?" Remember to pause and give children enough time to respond. Interactions of this kind guide children's thinking and provide them with opportunities to use language to describe, explain, reflect, and engage in conversations with adults and peers. More specific strategies about how to engage children in conversations about their work are in the Scientific Inquiry strand: Substrand 2.0, Documentation and Communication.

Model the use of scientific vocabulary.

Experiences of scientific inquiry provide the context for introducing children to scientific vocabulary such as *observe, predict, measure,* and *experiment.* With teachers' modeling the use of these words in meaningful contexts, children will begin using relevant scientific terms such as, "I observe . . ." or "My prediction is . . ." across a variety of experiences.[21] The use of scientific terms enriches children's language and facilitates their scientific experiences.

Key Scientific Vocabulary

- Observe, observation
- Predict, prediction
- Test
- Similar, different
- Compare, contrast
- Count
- Measure
- Investigate
- Explore
- Experiment
- Discover
- Record
- Explain
- Hypothesis

Know when to intervene and when to stand back.

While observing children, teachers make a moment-to-moment judgment about when and how to intervene. When children are intensely engaged, as they experiment with objects or try to figure out a solution to a problem, questions from the teacher may distract them. The effective teacher pays attention to what children are doing, intervening only when it is the appropriate time to further stimulate the child, supporting learning without overwhelming children with too many questions.

Provide children with time.

Scientific inquiry requires time. Children need time to explore materials and tools, to learn skills of inquiry, to investigate a concept in depth, to discuss, and to document. The daily schedule should allow for enough time to explore and interact with materials, and for group times to discuss and reflect. Long-term planning should allow for deep and extended explorations of a concept over time. The explorations of big scientific ideas (e.g., change in materials, growth, form and function of tools) will require more than one week and may require several weeks or even months. Children need time to experience and revisit a variety of activities to deepen their understanding of a concept. There may need to be an area set aside to preserve ongoing investigations.

Research Highlight: Children's Misconceptions in Science

Children bring to science many ideas about how things work. These intuitive understandings or naïve theories that children have constructed often conflict with what is known to be scientifically correct. Children hold preconceptions and misconceptions about different topics of science including forces, changes of matter, light, sound, and earth phenomena.[22] For example, children believe that water disappears when it evaporates or that rain occurs when clouds are shaken. It is important to know how these conceptions differ from the scientific explanation and why children construct these ideas. Children's misconceptions are intuitively reasonable, from the child's perspective, and are used by children to explain the "why" behind physical events. Some of children's ideas may be cultural beliefs that have been introduced at home. The teacher's role is to guide children through numerous opportunities to discover and re-create concepts, without overtly correcting their misconceptions.[23] Remember, science is about experimentation, and the goal is to support children's scientific thinking, not to merely provide the correct answer.

Summary of the Science Foundations

Scientific Inquiry

The scientific inquiry foundations focus on the skills and language employed in the process of scientific inquiry. The first substrand, *Observation and Investigation,* focuses on children's ability to observe and investigate objects and events in the environment. Foundations include key scientific processes such as observe and describe, compare and contrast, predict and check, and draw **inferences.** The second substrand under Scientific Inquiry, *Documentation and Communication,* is about processes and skills employed to document and record observations and to communicate ideas and explanations with others.

Physical Sciences

The foundations in physical sciences are about investigating characteristics and **physical properties** of nonliving objects and of solid and liquid materials, and changes in objects and materials. The first substrand focuses on children's ability to explore and describe properties of objects such as size, shape, weight, texture, and flexibility. The second substrand is about changes and transformations in objects and materials and the motion of objects.

Life Sciences

The foundations in **life sciences** are about core concepts related to properties and characteristics of living things and their growth and change over time. The first substrand, *Properties and Characteristics of Living Things,* focuses on children's ability to explore, observe, and study characteristics of animals and plants in their everyday environment, including their physical characteristics, body parts, behaviors, and habitats. The second substrand, *Changes in Living Things,* focuses on changes and growth in living things over time and the basic needs that must be met in order for them to grow and survive.

Earth Sciences

The foundations in earth sciences are about observing and exploring earth materials and phenomena. The first substrand, *Properties and Characteristics of Earth Materials and Objects,* is about actively exploring and investigating earth materials, such as soil, sand, rocks, water, and air. The second substrand, *Changes in the Earth,* is about observing and describing the movement and apparent changes of natural objects in the sky (e.g., sun, moon), changes in the weather, and changes in the environment due to weather and seasonal changes.

Summary of the Strands and Substrands

Scientific Inquiry
1.0 Observation and Investigation
2.0 Documentation and Communication

Physical Sciences
1.0 Properties and Characteristics of Nonliving Objects and Materials

2.0 Changes in Nonliving Objects and Materials

Life Sciences
1.0 Properties and Characteristics of Living Things
2.0 Changes in Living Things

Earth Sciences
1.0 Properties and Characteristics of Earth Materials and Objects
2.0 Changes in the Earth

Scientific Inquiry

Young children's experience of science is an interplay between *content knowledge* (what children learn about) and *inquiry skills* (the skills and processes they apply to explore and develop knowledge and understanding of scientific ideas). Children build knowledge and understanding of concepts through active participation in the process of **scientific inquiry.** Like scientists, children have a natural desire to inquire, but they need guidance in developing the skills of scientific inquiry.

- *Observation and **investigation*** skills involve ways to observe, compare, measure, classify, predict, and to check and investigate objects and events.
- *Documentation and communication* skills are employed to record information and to communicate findings and explanations with others.

Skills of scientific inquiry provide children with the tools for investigating and learning about science topics. Such experiences build habits of questioning, critical thinking, innovative problem solving, communication, collaboration, and decision making.

Scientific inquiry skills are integral to children's ongoing play and explorations and are not taught in isolation. Children develop their abilities to make observations, ask questions, and gather informa-

tion, as part of meaningful exploration and investigation experiences. The following sections provide strategies as to how teachers can establish an environment with a culture of inquiry and facilitate children's use of scientific skills and language through everyday explorations and planned experiences of scientific inquiry.

Basic Inquiry Skills

- Observe and describe
- Use scientific tools
- Measure
- Classify
- Compare and contrast
- Predict and check
- Draw inferences and conclusions
- Record and document
- Communicate

1.0   Observation and Investigation

As children observe and engage with objects, they enjoy trying out things and seeing what happens. Pushing cars, building with blocks, manipulating tubes at the water table, or collecting leaves are all examples of children's investigations of objects and materials. Such experiences provide the context for developing the attitudes, skills, and language of scientific inquiry and allow children to construct understanding and knowledge about objects and events. Teachers can use the experiences to encourage children to observe closely, using their senses and tools, and describe their observations, which helps them in learning about properties and characteristics of objects and materials. Noticing details and recognizing similarities and differences between objects and events underlies children's ability to sort, classify, and compare and contrast, important skills in science and in mathematics. Children can also make predictions about changes in materials and objects based on their intuitive

knowledge or past experience, and then test their predictions through observations or simple experiments. Such experiences also illustrate to children the value of observable evidence. They learn to use evidence to verify their predictions, make inferences, or draw conclusions. The first substrand, *Observation and Investigation*, focuses on scientific skills and language applied in the processes of observing and investigating objects and events in the environment.

Sample Developmental Sequence

Young children actively search for information about objects and events in their environment.
- Infants and toddlers observe, hold, touch and handle objects, and may even examine them with their lips and tongues. They start with brief, simple explorations of objects. They repeat the same experience and then try out different things with an object to see what happens, or how things work. For example, purposely throw a rattle to hear it land or push a ball and watch it roll.
- At the next level, children engage in more sustained and complex manipulations of objects. For example, they build with blocks or other materials not only to knock it down, but also to create something. They demonstrate a broader interest in objects and events in their environment and may ask questions about them.
- As children develop their inquiry skills, they engage in purposeful, detailed observations and simple investigations of an object and event of interest. They can use prior knowledge and experience to make predictions and then test and verify their predictions through observations or simple experiments.

- Children engage in extensive detailed observations, and may use scientific tools such as magnifiers or measurement tools to expand their observations. They recognize similarities and differences between objects and phenomena and engage in comparisons.
- As children get older, they engage in carrying out more complex observations and investigations of objects and events, with the assistance of adults. They may participate in more focused experiments, collect and record data, and analyze evidence.

Promoting the Development of Scientific Inquiry Skills

Observe and Describe

VIGNETTE

In the fall, Ms. Linda brought a big pumpkin to class and placed it on a table. When children came in, they noticed the pumpkin. Alonzo and Lai tried to pick it up and commented, "This pumpkin is heavy." During small-group activity, Ms. Linda invited the children in the group "to observe" the pumpkin, "When we observe it," she explained, "we use our senses to find out about it. We use our eyes to notice carefully what it looks like. We may find out what it smells like and touch it to find out what it feels like. We may even decide to taste it. What do you observe about the pumpkin?" She invited children to examine the pumpkin and make their own observations. Andrea said, "It is big and round." Veronica seemed very interested. She touched the pumpkin but did not share her observations. Slowly, more children became comfortable making observations. Tim said, "It has a stick on it." On a group chart, Ms. Linda recorded each child's name and observation. She touched the pumpkin and said, "It feels bumpy." Kim touched it and said, "I can feel the lines on it." Then Veronica felt comfortable sharing her observation and said, "Hard." Ms. Linda expands Veronica's statement: "Yes, the pumpkin feels hard" and writes it on the chart. After all the children had a chance to share their observations, Ms. Linda said, "Let's see what we observed about the pumpkin," and read their observations to the group. She then invited children to document their observations by drawing a representation of the pumpkin they observed.

TEACHABLE MOMENT

During the fall, children see pumpkins everywhere, but in this type of activity they get to observe a real pumpkin closely. Ms. Linda first introduces the broad meaning of the word "to observe." She encourages the children to observe carefully using their senses and to share their observations with others. She asks questions and models for them how to observe and describe what they see. Modeling is particularly important for children like Veronica who may not be ready to respond to open-ended questions, or who may be developing their English language skills. This type of experience not only introduces children to observation as a science practice, but also provides opportunities for noticing details, building new vocabulary, working as an investigative team, and developing math concepts.

Interactions and Strategies

Facilitate children's observation skills. Observing is the most fundamental scientific skill for obtaining information, constructing meaning, and gaining knowledge about the world. In making observations, children use their senses of sight, smell, sound, touch, and taste to gather information about objects and phenomena in their environment and to notice specific details. Everyday playful explorations and focused investigations provide children with many opportunities to make meaningful observations.

Introduce children to the process of observing. Introduce children to the process of observation by using a simple, familiar object from their daily environment. Encourage them to hold and touch the object. Remind children to use all their senses, instead of "just looking" at the object, and to note specific details.

Introduce the term "observe" to children: "When we observe something, we use our senses to find out about it. We may use our eyes to notice carefully what it looks like. We may use our nose to find out what it smells like, and touch it to find out what it feels like."[24] Teachers may need to spend time talking about the senses and experiment with using each sense.[25] For example, teachers can provide children with experiences where the children can smell something they cannot see or feel, or feel something they can-

not see, or hear something they cannot see or touch. Isolating individual senses will help children understand how they receive and process information from their senses.

Encourage children to describe their observations. Talk with children and ask questions to guide their observations: "What do you notice about this apple?" "What do you observe about your plant?" "How is it different from the last time we observed it?" "What does this rock look like?" "What does it feel like?" "Does it make any sound when you shake it?" Encourage all children to participate at their comfort level and do not correct them or judge them for being right or wrong. Remember, the teacher is encouraging observation, not looking for a right answer. Children who are English learners may be actively engaged by listening to others' observations, but may not yet feel confident or willing to share their observations in English. Invite them to share their observations in their home language whenever possible. When teachers share what they notice, they model for children how to make observations—"This rock is very hard." "It feels bumpy." Children with hearing impairments or motor challenges may communicate with signs, gestures, or devices. Describing observations that depend on use of all senses is a prime opportunity to teach new vocabulary. Invite children to describe the different attributes of objects, including size, shape, color, texture, and other observ-

¿De qué color serán las mariposas?

able properties ("Is it soft or hard?" "Is the rock heavy or light?"). See the *California Preschool Curriculum Framework, Volume 1,* chapter 4, "Language and Literacy," and chapter 5, "English-Language Development," for strategies to support children's vocabulary growth and their ability to use language to communicate their ideas.

Invite children to observe objects and phenomena related to the current focus of inquiry. Observations can focus on living things, nonliving objects and different materials (e.g., insects, plants, body parts, fruits, vegetables, tools, rocks), and different phenomena in the environment ("How does the worm move?" "What happens when they let the ball go?"). Observations are meaningful when built into children's inquiry experiences and allow children to construct knowledge related to their focus of inquiry. For example, while investigating properties of water, children observe drops of water and notice that drops of water are absorbed by fabric. Such observations may suggest related questions and phenomena to be investigated ("Would the drops of water be absorbed by other surfaces? Other materials?").

Invite children to record their observations. Encourage children to draw a representation of their observation and record children's observations by writing down their words ("It is green." "It is smooth." "It is round like a ball." "It is heavy"). This requires them to observe closely and to notice details. Documentation also allows them to track changes over time. For example, when children record the growth of beans, by drawing or taking photos, they can refer to their records and describe changes at different times. The teacher may also write down the comments children make when describing their drawings. These representations may be displayed, made into a book about the investigation, or used in a child's portfolio to document development in drawing and language skills. For more information about strategies to support documentation skills, see the "Record and Document" section, pages 166–167.

Use Scientific Tools

VIGNETTE

While exploring the play yard, children became fascinated with pill bugs (usually called roly polies by children). In the yard, they would look for pill bugs and enjoy watching them curl into balls. One day, Ms. Lopez noticed that a group of children collected pill bugs in a bucket. She invited the children to put the "roly polies" on a tray and observe them closely at the outdoor investigation table. Ms. Lopez said, "Let's use our tools and look really closely at the pill bugs. What do you notice about their body?" Ms. Lopez assisted Jennifer in holding the magnifier above the pill bug: "Wow, it looks so big," Jennifer said. Jose observes the pill bug with a magnifier and gets excited: "I can see its head." Ryan asked, "When is it going to open up again? I want to see how many legs it has."

TEACHABLE MOMENT

▶ The outdoor investigation table includes tools for exploration, such as trays and clear containers, magnifying glasses, rulers, and children's notebooks where they record their observations. Having an outdoor investigation table with tools for observation, measuring, and recording facilitates children's observations and outdoor explorations. The use of magnifiers allows children to observe the pill bugs more closely. Ms. Lopez makes scientific tools available for children so that she can be ready for teachable moments. Over time, children become familiar with the tools on the table and start to use magnifiers and other tools spontaneously and more independently. The observations of pill bugs can be expanded in different ways. Teachers can invite children to record their observations by taking photos or drawing a representation of the pill bugs and dictating to the teacher what they have observed. It can also lead to deeper explorations and discussions about the body structure of pill bugs, how they move, what they like to eat, where they live, how they compare to other animals, and, most interesting for the children in this group, finding out when and why the pill bugs curl up.

Interactions and Strategies

Promote the use of scientific tools to extend children's observations and investigations of objects. Children's investigations of objects and phenomena can be augmented with the use of observation and measurement tools. Magnifiers, such as hand lenses, can help children observe details and objects that are too small to see with only their eyes. The mere presence of scientific tools in the discovery area or throughout the environment does not invite children to use them in a purposeful way. The teacher has an important role in promoting the meaningful use of scientific tools in children's investigations.

Introduce children to scientific tools and their function. Teachers can take time to introduce children to the tools and to demonstrate their functions. Not all tools should be introduced at once. Instead, the teacher should gradually increase the number of tools in the environment. This will increase children's tendency to use tools in the intended way. For example, to introduce magnifiers, the teacher can set up a situation in which children observe an object and need to see details more closely than they can with just their eyes (e.g., in observing ants, seeds, the pattern on a leaf, or grains of sand).

Suggest language to introduce magnifiers to children: "You still need your eyes to see, but the eyes and the magnifiers together allow us to see some things bigger. The magnifiers help us to "observe."[26] As with any new object, children need time to explore, interact, and use it on their own. Teachers can use the opportunity to explain how wearing glasses helps some children to see things more clearly and magnifiers help children to see things enlarged.

Support children in using the tools. After being introduced to tools and experiencing their use with the help of teachers, children may begin to spontaneously pick up the magnifiers or a ruler and ask to use them in context. For example, while observing a worm, the child might say, "I need the magnifying glass to look very close" or "I want to see how big it is." Preschool children are not expected to know how to use a ruler on their own and may need help in holding the magnifier properly. They will need the teacher's

direction and support in using these tools. Children with motor impairments or other disabilities may need more assistance from an adult or peer in using the tools. For example, the teacher may need to hold the hand lenses steady for the children to help them observe closely or offer them the use of a stationary magnifier. As with all materials in the preschool environment, children need to learn to take turns using tools; this is an opportunity to remind children about the concepts of waiting and sharing.

Measure

Young children begin to compare objects by size or weight and use words such as "heavier," "taller," or "longer" to make comparisons. They may compare length by placing objects side by side, and as they get older, they begin to measure length using nonstandard units (e.g., unit blocks, hands). Tools to measure length, weight, or volume extend scientific inves-

tigations by enabling observers to find out how long something is, how much it weighs, and how much space it takes up. **Measurement tools** also allow comparison of one object to another in an accurate way (e.g., "Which is longer?" "Which is heavier?"). Preschool children are not expected to know how to read and use tools on their own; however, with teachers' guidance, they learn that specialized tools are used to measure attributes such as length, height, volume, and weight (see the *California Preschool Curriculum Framework, Volume 1*, chapter 6, "Mathematics," for more information about measurement concepts).

Sort, Classify, and Identify Patterns

VIGNETTE

Following a group discussion about seeds, Mr. Adato set out a tray with a variety of beans of different sizes and colors, including kidney, pinto, and lima beans. He told the children that there were different kinds of beans and mentioned some of their names. The children were engaged in free exploration of the beans. They piled them up and then spread them out on the tray or filled containers of different sizes with beans, and then poured the beans back on the tray. He provided them with small containers on the table and demonstrated, "I am going to put all the white beans here." Children began to sort the beans, mainly by color. He noticed that Lee, a new child to the group, was sorting the white beans by size, and he asked, "I wonder why you put those beans together and those beans together?" Lee pointed to the piles she created and said, "Big here and small here." During group time, Mr. Adato invited children to observe the lima beans and the red kidney beans. He wrote down children's observations and led a discussion about the similarities and differences between the two kinds of beans: "What do you notice about their size and shape?" "What about their color?" "Are all the red ones the same color red?"

PLANNING LEARNING OPPORTUNITIES

▶ Mr. Adato presented children with hands-on experiences exploring beans of different kinds. Learning the names of different beans was less important for him than having children explore a variety of beans, and compare and contrast beans based on different features. He encouraged children to sort beans in different ways and talk about similarities and differences. Lee, a child who is learning English, is engaged in **sorting** the beans and explains her sorting to Mr. Adato. She is empowered when Mr. Adato asks about the way she sorted the beans. This experience encourages children to notice attributes of objects and introduces Lee and other children in the group to new vocabulary in a meaningful context. Following up on the differences and similarities,

Mr. Adato is planning on soaking the beans, then cooking them, and providing more possibilities for comparisons (e.g., comparing the size and texture of raw, soaked, and cooked beans, the tastes of different beans).

Interactions and Strategies

Facilitate children's abilities to sort, classify, and identify patterns. Children's observations and their ability to identify similarities and differences lead naturally to sorting and classifying. Children start putting together objects that belong to the same category, and sorting objects into groups with similar attributes (e.g., "These are big seeds, and these are small ones." "These rocks are smooth, and these are bumpy"). Providing opportunities for children to categorize and **classify** encourages children to focus on physical and other characteristics of objects and provides a foundation for

future understanding of the scientific classification of organisms. Children also start to recognize **patterns** in objects and events, including ones in nature, and are able to predict what comes next based on the repeated pattern (e.g., colors on caterpillars, veins on leaves, rings on the slice of a tree trunk, the pattern of day and night, or everyday routines). Classification and patterning are mathematical skills essential to learning and organizing information about the world. Like other mathematical skills such as counting, estimating, ordering and measuring, they are important in the processes of scientific inquiry. The *California Preschool Curriculum Framework, Volume 1,* chapter 6, "Mathematics," provides strategies to facilitate these mathematical skills.

Compare and Contrast

As children develop skills in observation, they notice discrete elements of objects and naturally begin to identify similarities and differences. The ability to compare builds on the process of observing. In addition to learning about an object by observing its characteristics, children learn more about the object by comparing it with other similar objects. For example, when comparing apples of different colors, children can learn to infer that sometimes color has a relationship to taste. It also introduces children to the concept of variation and diversity. Children can also compare an object to other related objects, or discuss similarities and differences in an object as it goes through changes; for example, different kinds of squash or a caterpillar as it metamorphoses into a butterfly. The ability to compare and contrast is a critical thinking skill and strengthens children's classification skills. It also sets the foundation for children's understanding of experimentation, in which children observe similarities and differences between two objects or events that differ in only one way; for example, observing similarities and differences between two tomato plants growing in similar conditions, except that one plant is in the dark, and another plant is in sunlight.[27]

Interactions and Strategies

Ask questions and model comparative language to introduce the idea of comparing: "How are these alike or similar?" "What is the same about these two things?" "How are these different?" Such open-ended questions may spark a conversation and encourage children to describe similarities and differences. Model comparative language for children who may not be ready to answer open-ended questions: "These apples are different. One is green, and one is red. One is bigger than the other. What else do you notice about these apples?" See the *California Preschool Curriculum Framework, Volume 1*, chapter 4, "Language and Literacy," and chapter 5, "English-Language Development," for strategies to encourage children to use language and engage in conversations.

Invite children to compare and contrast objects and phenomena related to their current focus of inquiry. The skill of comparing and contrasting is a powerful tool for constructing meaning and knowledge about scientific concepts. Comparing and contrasting different kinds of leaves, for example, not only expands children's knowledge of leaves in the environment, but more importantly, introduces children to the concept of *variation* and *diversity*. Similarly, comparing and contrasting an object before and after change due to growth or other transformations (e.g., seeds before and after sprouting, cornstarch before and after being mixed with water; or transformations such as a moth transforming from an egg, to a larva, to a pupa, to a moth) highlights changes in objects, and the concept of cause-and-effect.

Predict and Check

VIGNETTE

Ms. Brown presented children with a big cube of ice. She asked the children to touch or hold it and tell her what they notice about it: "What does it feel like? What does it look like?" Children shared their observations: "It is cold." "It is slippery." "It is very smooth." "It is wet." "It is white." "It is square." Ms. Brown asked the children, "What do you know about ice?" Some children shared their ideas: "We keep it in the freezer." "It's very, very cold." "If you put it in water, it disappears." She invited children to draw their observations of the ice cube in their notebooks. The next day, Ms. Brown told the children that together they are going to explore what will happen to ice when it is left outside of the freezer. She has asked children: "What do you think will happen to this ice cube if we leave it in this bowl? What is your prediction?" "Will it stay the same?" "What will be different?" Children made predictions, and she wrote them on a chart (e.g., "It will not be so cold anymore." "It will turn into water"), "After lunch, we'll check our ice cube and find out what happened."

PLANNING LEARNING OPPORTUNITIES

▶ Ms. Brown presented opportunities to explore properties and characteristics of water, including changes in water due to changes in temperature such as freezing and melting. In this particular example, she guides children, through a series of scientific practices in exploring the phenomenon of melting. The children observe the ice and record their observations ("What does it feel like?" "What do you know about ice?"). Next, they predict changes to the ice. Ms. Brown asks questions to elicit predictions and records their predictions. Finally, they observe the ice at a later time to check their predictions. This experience can be expanded into more investigations of melting; for example, by varying the size of the ice cube or the location of the bowl (indoors or outdoors). Children may also investigate how water can turn back into ice.

Interactions and Strategies

Encourage children to make predictions. While observations involve using the senses to gain information about objects and phenomena, **predictions** are about making a reasonable guess or estimation of what is going to happen, on the basis of previous evidence and preexisting knowledge. For example, children can predict whether an object will sink or float in water, where a car will stop after rolling down a ramp, or what is going to happen after planting sunflower seeds. They may not be accurate, but they can make a reasonable guess based on previous experiences and knowledge of objects. The more experiences children have with phenomena or objects, the more likely they are to make reasonable predictions. Children who are English learners may not feel confident or willing to share their predictions in English. Therefore encourage children to make predictions in their home language, whenever possible, and repeat prediction prompts in English and in the child's home language, if possible, to help create the bridge between home and school language. Even though the words **prediction** and **hypothesis** are often used interchangeably in everyday usage, a prediction is not the same as a hypothesis. Unlike a prediction, which is a guess about what is going to happen, a hypothesis is a proposed explanation of observable phenomena that is either confirmed or disproved by an experiment. Teachers may choose to introduce the word *hypothesis* to children, when asking for children's explanations of what they think happened, but use the term *predict* when asking them to make a guess.

Introduce children to the idea of predicting. Children need to be introduced to the process of making a prediction. Gelman and others used the following reasoning with children: "Prediction is kind of like a guess: When we predict, we do not know the answer or what is definitely going to happen, but we usually have some information that helps to make a prediction, to make a guess."[28]

Encourage children to first *predict* and then *check*. When children first predict and then check their predictions with actions, they learn to compare what actually happens with what they thought would happen rather than merely accepting facts without thinking about them ("So your prediction was that if we added a block, the car would go farther. Now let's release the car down the ramp and check how far it went." "You predicted that the water would overflow if you dropped the block into the bucket. What happened when you dropped the block in the water?").[29] By testing and verifying their predictions, children gain new information that informs their future predictions.

Elicit children's predictions by asking questions. Teachers can ask children questions to encourage them to make predictions: "What do you think will happen if we mix the water with flour? What is your prediction?" "Will the flour still look the same?" "What would it feel like?" Some children may not have any prior experience on which to base predictions and thus be hesitant to guess or feel uncomfortable expressing predictions in a large group. Those children may benefit from a one-on-one interaction with the teacher focusing on examples of predicting or guessing. With more experiences of predicting and checking, children feel more comfortable with the process and may spontaneously suggest ways to test their predictions.

Remind children that predictions do not have to be right. In investiga-

tions with a group of children, some children's predictions might be correct and some might not be. Predictions are not always correct. Incorrect predictions should be responded to in a matter-of-fact way ("Oh, that did not turn out like we thought it would. Instead of the car going farther, it fell off the ramp. I wonder why?" "The water did not overflow, but do you notice that something did happen? I wonder why it didn't overflow and how could we make it overflow?"). Some discrepancies between what children have predicted and what actually happens may lead to further inquiry, and this is the beauty and fun of science. Children need to be encouraged to make a prediction and not be afraid of being wrong. Communicate to children that predictions are like estimations and do not have to be right. Over time, with more data or information, children's predictions may change and become more accurate. Remember, the goal is to support children's scientific thinking. They will come up with predictions, hypotheses, and ideas that teachers know are incorrect. It is more important to support their critical thinking skills than to merely provide them with the correct answer.

Record children's predictions. Documentation facilitates the comparison of what they predicted with what actually happened. Writing down children's predictions conveys to children that their predictions are valuable and that documentation is integral to the process of scientific inquiry. A small-group activity, in which each child expresses her prediction and the teacher records it on a chart, illustrates for children that not all predictions are the same, and each child can have her own prediction.

Draw Inferences and Conclusions

Interactions and Strategies

Facilitate children's ability to make inferences and draw conclusions. Predicting and inferring are processes of reasoning that rely on observable information. When predicting, children guess what will happen next and then check their prediction. When inferring and drawing conclusions, children observe what happened and make an assumption about the cause. Their assumption is based on previous experience, even though they cannot observe the cause directly. For example, noticing that the grass is wet, a child may infer that there was rain before he went outside. Children constantly try to make meaning of their observations. From a very young age, they use observations to make inferences. For example, a child notices that the plant is wilting and infers that it needs water. The teacher can help children draw connections to previous experiences: "Remember the time we forgot to water the plants over vacation?" or "I remember the last time we went outside and the grass was wet."

Use everyday observations to model inferring. Everyday interactions and observations provide many opportunities for making inferences. For example, the sky turns dark, and the teacher says, "It looks like it is going to rain soon." During mealtime, the teacher can lead the children to make a similar inference; for example, drawing the children's attention to the steam rising from the soup, asking what they notice and what it might mean, leading them to infer that the steam they see indicates the soup is hot.

Encourage children to explain the reasoning behind their inferences. When children make inferences and draw conclusions, encourage them to explain their reasoning: "What makes you think the plant needs some water?" "What tells us that it is probably cold outside?"

2.0 Documentation and Communication

Integral to children's processes of scientific inquiry is their **communication** about what they are doing and thinking. As illustrated by the vignettes in the previous section, experiences of observations and investigations provide children with many opportunities to use language (verbal, sign language, or other forms of communication) to describe, explain, and reflect on their work. They describe their observations using their own words (signs or symbols), explain the reasoning for their sorting and classifications, discuss similarities and differences, make predictions, and describe and record findings. Children also communicate and reflect on their experiences through the documentation of their work. They may use drawings, words, photos, charts, and other forms of communication to **record** and document information. Such experiences build children's language and communication skills. Through conversations with adults and peers, children expand their vocabulary, and learn to share their thoughts and become aware of the ideas of other children. Sharing and reflecting on their experiences also help children think more deeply about their work and facilitate their understanding of science knowledge.

Sample Developmental Sequence

- At a very young age, children may communicate their observations about characteristics of objects or events nonverbally, using a variety of gestures, or with short phrases of one or two words (e.g., "big ball").
- At the next level, they communicate observations of objects or events, using simple phrases to describe and compare physical characteristics.
- As children develop their inquiry skills, they begin to create representations of their observations and to record information in a variety of forms, including drawings, words, photos, and models.
- Over time, preschool children record and document their observations in greater detail and engage in conversations related to scientific inquiry. They share observations, make predictions, and discuss similarities and differences between objects and events.
- Children use more complex forms to collect and record information, including tallying, charts, and simple graphs. They also engage in deeper discussions in which they communicate their thoughts and share findings and explanations.

Record and Document

VIGNETTE

The children in Ms. Moreno's group are taking turns bringing home the picture book they created as a group. Today, it is Emilia's turn to take home this book. This picture book was created to document the growth of their plant. Emilia points to the photos in the book (taken by Ms. Moreno to document the process) and to children's drawings. She tells the story out loud to her grandmother, who is picking her up, "First we had to buy seeds (points to a photo of the seeds packet on the first page), then we put the soil, and then we put the seeds inside the dirt . . ." Emilia continues with more details while looking at the pictures in the book: how they put the pot in the sun, watered the plant, and measured its growth. "Here it was one inch, and here it was bigger, and here it was very tall, and it has many leaves." At home, Emilia will share it with her family, and together they will retell the story in her home language.

TEACHABLE MOMENT

▶ A book with photos and children's drawings made by the group makes the process of growth visible. It allows children to revisit the experience and to notice changes in the plant over time. Creating a class book not only facilitates science learning, but it also becomes a focus of discussion and storytelling and supports the development of language and literacy (e.g., developing age-appropriate vocabulary such as seed, soil, plant, and the ability to retell a story, including key details in the text). It is also useful for children new to the program and for children who are English learners as they revisit an experience, recall the terms used, and express their memories in either or both their home language and English.[30] Sending the book home engages families and supports children's learning.

Interactions and Strategies

Encourage children to record observations and document investigations and findings. Recording and documenting facilitates children's understanding about what they investigate and provides a tool for communication. The entries children make in their journals are conceptual representations that are important for the child's understanding of scientific concepts and concepts of print. In recording and transcribing the child's own words, teachers validate the child's ideas while showing the importance of writing. It develops children's understanding of symbolic representations, as they begin to use drawings and print to record information.

Introduce children to the idea of recording. Children need to be introduced to the process of recording and documenting. Gelman and others used

the following reasoning with children, "Like scientists, we record things to keep track of our observations and ideas. We can look at them later to remind us of the things we observed and the ideas we had."[31]

Promote the use of different forms to record and document information. Children may create a representation by drawing a picture, making a three-dimensional model, or taking a photo. They may have a specific science notebook or journal, which they use on a regular basis, to record their observations with drawings and verbal or sign language dictations. They may also participate in recording information on a group chart or by keeping data logs; for example, tracking the height of their plant or the temperature outside at different times of the day. Different forms of documentation provide children with multiple ways to process information and express their ideas, using verbal and nonverbal means of communication.

Consider adaptations for children with special needs. Children with speech or language delays also benefit from expressing themselves using nonverbal means of communication. Children with motor delays or other disabilities may appreciate dictating their drawing ideas or "directing" the teacher to photograph something for their journal. A child who is not physically able to draw can benefit from holding the object on her wheelchair tray while the other children draw or take photographs from various angles for her to use as her observation record.

Encourage children to describe their representations while you write their words. Creating a representation of an object or event is a skill that develops over time. Sensitive adult guidance and encouragement are often necessary to

promote and extend children's recording (e.g., "Let's look at it again. How many branches are coming out of the stem?"). Remember, it is the process that is important, not the final product.[32] Children's descriptions of their drawings, models, or photos will reveal their conception and understanding of the object or event they recorded, regardless of whether their representation is accurate. Refrain from making judgments about children's representations; instead, ask them to describe what they have drawn. For example, the teacher said to the child, "Tell me about your drawing (or model or photo)," and the child explained, "This is the snail, and this is the leaf, and this line is how the snail got from here all the way to the leaf." The teacher can record in writing children's explanation of their drawing and display drawings on the wall, so that children (and families) can view all the different representations of the same object (e.g., a pumpkin). See the *California Preschool Curriculum Framework, Volume 1*, chapter 4, "Language and Literacy" (Concepts about Print) for strategies to incorporate print and use print as a tool to record information.

Encourage different means of communication. Children may use many means of communication to describe their observations and thoughts, including home language, sign language, and communication devices. Children who are English learners may be at a stage in which they are still developing their confidence and ability to express themselves in English. They may benefit from recording their ideas nonverbally and then describing them in the home language to teachers who share the child's home language, and describing them in English when possible. Having an adult encourage, prompt, and scaffold the use of expressive language in English and in the child's home language whenever possible, would support the child's overall development of scientific knowledge and language skills.

Invite children to record collaboratively, using charts, graphs, or models. Some forms of documentation, such as journal entries and drawings, are more appropriate for individual work, while others can become a group collaboration of data collection and recording activity, guided by the teacher. For example, children recorded on a chart their prediction of lemons having seeds inside, by writing down their name (or other symbol), either under the "Seeds" column or the "No seeds" column. During group time, the teacher invited the children to count the number of names under each column, and together they created a bar graph that represented how many children think lemons have seeds inside and how many children think lemons do not have seeds. In the next small-group activity, children investigated what is inside a lemon and compared what they found with the predictions the group had made.

Communicate

VIGNETTE

Maya fills up a cup with water and pours the water into the opening of a long, clear tube, watching the water going down the tube and coming out at the other end. She repeats it over and over. Seth is holding his hands at the other end of the tube, touching the water that is coming out. Then, Seth puts a bucket right underneath the bottom of the tube.

Maya and Seth pour water into the funnel and watch the water flowing down the clear tube and filling up the bucket. "More, more water!" He tells Maya. "Let's fill it all the way up to here." He points to the top of the bucket. "Ms. Ruben, look! We are filling the bucket with the tube."

Ms. Ruben says, "Tell me how you do it." Maya explains, "We put water in this hole, and then the water goes in here and down to the bucket." Ms. Ruben says, "You used the tube with a funnel to make the water fill up the bucket. What an interesting way to make the water flow down. I wonder what would happen if the tube is held this way (she holds it horizontally)? (Pause) What do you predict? What do you think the water will do?"

TEACHABLE MOMENT

▶ Ms. Ruben observes the children as they play and explore with water and materials at the water table. She waits for the right moment to intervene and is invited over by the children. She asks questions to engage children in talking and reflecting on their experience of making the water flow down the tube. She asks questions to encourage them to describe and explain what they were doing and to predict what might happen if the position of the tube is changed. She wants the children to think about how water moves and what they can do to affect its movement. The teacher also plans ahead for the next time the children will be at the water table. She will add tubes of different sizes and diameters and different size buckets to facilitate children's work and provide them with more opportunities to discover how water moves.

Interactions and Strategies

Ask open-ended questions. One effective way to encourage children to think and talk about their ideas is to present them with open-ended questions. Unlike questions with yes or no answers (e.g., "Is it black?") or questions with one defined answer (e.g., "What color is it?"), open-ended questions have a multitude of answers (e.g. "What will happen if . . ." "How did that happen?" "What kinds of things do you think look like that?"). The goal is to challenge children's thinking and encourage children to put forward their ideas and thoughts, not necessarily give the answer the teacher is looking for. Questioning also supports language acquisition by embedding new words into open-ended questions. Children who may not be ready to respond or whose English is limited would benefit from teachers' modeling of possible responses and the teacher's expansion of children's initial observations.

- **Questions to encourage children to share their observations:** *"What did you notice* when you observed the snail?" *"What happened* to the ice cube when we left it outside?"

- **Questions to facilitate children's problem-solving and investigations:** *"What do you think we could do* to make the ball roll down in this direction?" *"Can you think of another way* to make the clay softer?" *"How could we find out* what worms like to eat?

- **Questions to elicit children's predictions and explanations:** "*Why do you think* this plant grew and this one did not?" "*Why do you think* the pill bug turned its body into a ball shape?" "*What do you think* would happen if you mix salt with water?"

Engage children in collaborative discussions. A powerful way to encourage children to discuss their ideas, share their experiences, and listen to others' perspectives is through small- and large-group discussions. While children interact with adults and peers, they learn to express their ideas and thoughts in a way that others can understand them. They learn to take turns and understand that other children in the group may have a different idea from theirs. Teachers support children's understanding of concepts through effective adult–child interactions and scaffolding. They may ask children to describe their observations, make predictions, and challenge them to give reasons and explanations for their ideas: "Leah, what did you do to make your tower stable?" "Kim, how did you get the water to flow through the tube?" "Which ball do you think will roll farthest when we let go of it at the top of the slide?" Discussions are richer when children refer to concrete examples, including children's representations, documentation, and the actual objects and materials they discuss while sharing their experiences.

Bringing It All Together

Ms. Linda had noticed how engaged children were in observing the pumpkin in the room and looked for ways to extend their explorations. She remembered that whenever she gave her children opportunities to compare objects, the children learned more about each of them. She brought in several more pumpkins and other squashes in various sizes, shapes, colors, and texture (e.g., acorn squash, butternut squash, gold nugget, sweet dumpling, zucchini, and yellow squash). During group time, she showed them the variety of squashes and pumpkins, including the pumpkin already in the room, and asked them questions to engage their interest. She wanted to draw the children's attention to the characteristics of the different squashes: "Look at all of these squashes. What do you notice about them? What colors do you see? How are they alike? How are they different?"

These types of questions generated a rich discussion of comparing and contrasting. Children shared their observations: "These are really big, and this one looks like a baby pumpkin." "This one is long, and this one is more like a pumpkin." "The pumpkins are orange and big, but these (pointing to other squashes) are orange and green and yellow." Ms. Linda sometimes rephrased their observations: "So you observed that all the pumpkins are orange, but the other squashes have many different colors." Or, "So you noticed that some are big and some are small." She told the children that the squashes would be available for more observations and explorations during their choice time.

Ms. Linda observed the children exploring the squashes and posed questions or made comments along the way: "So here you put all the orange squashes, and here you put all the green ones. What other ways can we sort the squashes?" The children who placed all the orange squashes together started to order them by size. They explained, "This pumpkin is the biggest, this one is medium, and this one is the baby." They were also excited to find out which of the two larger pumpkins was bigger or heavier. For example, Ms. Linda helped them check how many hands it took to go around each pumpkin. She also showed them how they can measure the circumference of both pumpkins, using a measuring tape, to find out which one is larger.

On a different day, Ms. Linda invited them to predict the inside of a pumpkin. Children came up with different predictions; for example, "seeds," "orange stuff," "juice." Ms. Linda recorded their predictions and asked, "How do you think we can find out?" One of the children said, "Let's cut it and see what's inside." Children observed the inside of a pumpkin. For some of the children who are sensitive to textures, Linda provided gloves and sticks to explore the inside of the pumpkin. They were mostly fascinated with the great number of seeds inside, "Wow! So many seeds." Ms. Linda asked, "How many seeds do you estimate it has inside? What is your estimate? How many do you guess?" Children came up with a wide range, from twenty to one million. Ms. Linda told them that the seeds would be available for their explorations. "You may try to count the seeds to find out how many seeds are inside the pumpkin." "The children recorded their observations of the inside of the pumpkins through drawings and dictations. During group time, Ms. Linda pointed to one of the other squashes *around the room and asked, "I wonder what we will find inside this squash if we cut it open? What do you predict?" One of the children said, "We are going to find many seeds." Ms. Linda asked, "Why do you think so?" and the child replied, "Because it looks like a small pumpkin, so maybe it is also has the same inside." Ms. Linda told the group, "During choice time, we are going to explore what is inside some of our squashes.*

The teacher provided children with multiple experiences over several days of observing and investigating characteristics of squashes. Children had opportunities to explore the outside and inside of squashes while developing their inquiry skills of observing closely, describing, predicting and checking, recording, and discussing their observations. Exploring squashes also provided the context for building children's language skills and expanding their vocabulary as they describe, compare, and predict the different attributes of squashes (e.g., words to describe color, size, or texture). Furthermore, it also involved the application of different mathematical skills, including sorting, ordering, measuring, estimating, and counting. By providing children with squashes in different colors, sizes, and shapes, the teacher introduced children to the concept of variation and diversity in living things. The zucchini, for example, looks very different from the pumpkin, yet both are called "squash." This activity provides an opportunity to challenge children's thinking about ways that things are the same and ways that they are different. Sorting squashes into groups based on similarities and differences provides a foundation for future understanding of scientific classification.

Engaging Families

✔ Science is a bridge across different cultures and languages. The content of science is the same in any language or culture. Parents and families may differ in their cultural perspectives related to concepts of science, but they all share a fundamental knowledge about living and nonliving things (e.g., that living things need food) and natural phenomena (e.g., weather). Families can support children's learning of science, using their home language, and be partners in the education of their children. Use science learning as an opportunity to involve families by inviting them to the program and by sending home suggestions for activities that they can do with their children. For example, by sending home a picture-only book about children's current focus of study (e.g., on the growth of seeds into flowers, farm animals, or rolling objects), family members and children can add words to describe the pictures, and children who are English learners can make it a dual-language book, describing pictures in the home language and in English. With such experiences, children's concept development and language abilities flourish and thrive.

✔ Communicate to families their important role in supporting children's curiosity and the development of scientific knowledge. Children have opportunities to engage with science all around them through the course of their daily lives. They develop intuitive ideas about the world through informal interactions with family members, through cultural practices, daily activities, books, and media sources. Help families understand the importance of nurturing children's expressions of curiosity. It could be as simple as being patient and slowing down when a child stops to pick up an object that looks interesting or when she asks questions about objects and events in the environment.

✔ Share with family members your approach to science and how you support children's development of inquiry skills. Inform family members and other caregivers about children's current focus of inquiry and the skills children will develop while engaged in processes of inquiry. Share with families the question the children are working on; explain your objectives and why they are important. There

are different ways to connect and communicate with families, including bulletin board postings, newsletters, sending home interactive materials and pictures of what the children are working on, and family night events. Communicating the objectives of children's current focus of explorations is vital to engaging parents and family members as partners in supporting children's development of scientific skills and knowledge.

✔ Learn about cultural beliefs and practices. Invite family members to come and talk with the teacher and children about their beliefs and connections to nature. Cultural differences reflect differences in people's basic orientation for relating to nature.[37] Native Americans, for example, have a spiritual connection with nature that goes beyond science and a tradition that honors humans living in harmony with nature rather than being in control of it. Cultural beliefs are transmitted to children by adults through practices and in their comments regarding nature. Such beliefs shape children's perception of the natural world.[38] There are also cul-

Research Highlight: Family Activities Benefit Children

There is a growing recognition that out-of-school activities, including family social activities, dinner table conversations, access to books, and visits to nearby parks, museums, zoos, or libraries have a cumulative effect on children's science learning.[33] Studies of dinner table conversations, visits to the zoo, and other everyday activities have uncovered rich conversations on a variety of scientific topics.[34] Families of all backgrounds engage with children in everyday conversations about a range of topics related to science. Through these kinds of interactions, children engage in questioning, explaining, and making predictions.[35] Evidence indicates that parents' involvement and their explanations to children during a museum visit or while watching TV (e.g., an educational children's program) enhance children's learning experience and make it more beneficial and productive for children.[36]

tural differences in child-rearing practices.[39] In some cultures, children are
encouraged to question and speak up,
while in other cultures they tend to
be silent observers and are expected
to listen rather than question. Know
the families in the program and
respect cultural differences, such as
their connection to nature and the
way children display questioning and
exploring behaviors. This knowledge
will help engage families appropriately
and respectfully.

Questions for Reflection

1. What could you add to your program's physical environment to enhance and facilitate children's experiences of scientific inquiry?

2. How would you incorporate practices of scientific inquiry (e.g., observing, predicting, comparing, and measuring) to engage children in learning about topics typically in your curriculum (e.g., autumn, fruits and vegetables, rocks)?

3. How would you facilitate children's thinking skills through everyday observations and interactions?

4. What are different ways you can encourage collaboration among children to facilitate scientific investigations?

5. What sorts of strategies can you use when engaging in scientific explorations to develop children's language and communication skills?

6. What is a current topic of interest of your group? How can you help them explore it directly through hands-on observations and investigations? What questions would you like them to think about?

Physical Sciences

Young children's inquiry in physical science involves the active exploration of nonliving objects and materials and of physical events in their everyday environment. When children build with blocks; play with different balls; push or slide objects of different kinds; play with water, sand, clay, and other objects in the preschool environment; they explore materials in different ways and begin to form ideas about the physical properties. They manipulate objects, act on them, and observe what happens. They may try a certain strategy over and over to see if the same result happens again. Through such exploratory interactions with objects and solid and nonsolid materials, children can learn about cause-and-effect relationships, the physical properties of objects and materials (e.g., size, shape, rigidity, texture), and about changes and transformations of objects and materials. For example, when building with various kinds of blocks, children may learn about the size and shape of the blocks and about the characteristics of the materials used to make the blocks (e.g., wood, foam, plastic). They may discover that the big cardboard blocks should be used at the bottom of a tower and the small unit blocks on top in order to create a strong and stable tower. When playing at the water table, they experience how water flows down and takes the shape of the container.

With teachers' guidance, children's everyday play can become rich, hands-on inquiry experiences of the key concepts in physical sciences. Teachers can provide children with materials to broaden their investigation. They encourage children to try out their ideas, even if the teacher knows the child's strategy will not create the desired result. Teachers challenge children's thinking by asking questions that focus attention on key science concepts being investigated: "What can you do to make the bridge higher?" "How can we make mud?" "Why did the ball roll down in this direction?" Interactions of this kind provide children with opportunities to extend their experimentations with objects, to notice patterns of cause-and-effect, to reason and think more deeply about the phenomena they observe, and to use language to describe, explain, and reflect on their work.

Key Concepts in Physical Sciences

In exploring objects and materials, children develop understanding of key concepts about the physical world.

- They learn about the size, shape, weight, texture and other properties of objects and materials.
- They learn about the form and function of objects and that the form of an object supports its function.
- They continue to learn about cause and effect—that certain actions lead to certain reactions.
- They learn about changes in objects and materials. For instance, how mixing, heating, or cutting will produce changes in materials and that some changes are reversible and some are irreversible.
- They begin to understand that objects not in motion are in a state of balance.
- They learn more about force and motion (inanimate objects are set in motion; pushing and pulling put objects in motion; objects can move in different ways).

The following section provides practical strategies to engage children in rich, playful explorations of the physical world.

1.0 Properties and Characteristics of Nonliving Objects and Materials

Children's natural interest to examine objects and act on them leads them to discover with their senses the physical properties of objects such as size, shape, weight, texture, sound, flexibility, and rigidity. The teacher has a significant role in providing children with opportunities to notice and explore the inherent properties of solid materials they encounter daily such as wood, metal, rubber, foam, or clay, water, and other liquids. Teachers encourage children to observe objects closely, and in some cases, to use simple observation and measurement tools such as magnifiers and measuring devices to extend their observations of objects and materials. The teacher invites children to sort, classify, and reflect on the similarities and differences of objects and materials; to describe the characteristics of objects and materials in greater detail; and to think about their function.

The preschool foundations in science separate aspects related to properties and characteristics of objects and materials (Substrand 1.0) from aspects related to changes in objects and materials (Substrand 2.0). But in reality these aspects of physical sciences are interrelated. While acting on objects and experimenting with different materials, children notice changes in the shape, size, form, or substance. Physical properties of objects and materials have a direct effect on how objects move, what they sound like when tapped, and how materials change and behave when squished, wet, heated, or mixed together. Children learn about the physical properties of objects and materials while manipulating objects and investigating how they move and change. The following strategies, as well as the ones in the next section (Substrand 2.0, Changes in Nonliving Objects and Materials), will broaden and deepen children's awareness and understanding of properties and characteristics of objects and materials.

VIGNETTE

Jin is busy building in the block area. He places two flat rectangle blocks one on top of the other. On the top block, he puts two cylinders and spreads them apart. He then looks for another rectangle block. He notices that the rectangle block he picked is not big enough to cover both cylinders. Instead, he grabs a bigger, flat rectangle block and places it gently on top of the two cylinders, trying to balance the structure, moving the rectangle block more to the right. Then, on top of it, he stacks smaller rectangle blocks vertically, one on top of the other, until the structure begins to lose balance. He takes away the last rectangle block that he added on top and tries to balance it again. He gently adds to the top small foam blocks, one on top of the other, and a small triangle block at the very top. As he sits back and

observes his tower, the teacher tells him, "Jin, you built a really tall building. Tell me about your building. How did you build it? What kind of blocks did you use?" Jin points to the rectangle blocks, saying the shape name in English. The teacher expands Jin's description of the different parts of the tower, "Yes, you chose rectangles made of wood and rectangles made of foam." Then she adds, "I also noticed that you were trying to make it strong. You put heavy, wood blocks at the bottom and the small foam blocks at the top." She points to a large foam block on the floor and asks, "What do you think would happen if we put this block at the bottom?"

TEACHABLE MOMENT

▶ The teacher is observing Jin's actions very closely, and acknowledges his play with a smile, but does not interfere while he is engaged in building the tower. She notices that he is trying to choose blocks that are likely to balance and is keeping the tower from falling down. Jin demonstrates an understanding of balance and stability and of characteristics of different materials.[40] When it is clear that Jin is done building the tower, she invites him to share and reflect on his experience by asking guiding questions. Jin is learning English. He does not yet have the confidence to talk in a big group, and his vocabulary is very limited. This type of one-on-one interaction with the teacher provides him with an opportunity to express himself, and to build his vocabulary, particularly words to describe shapes, different materials, and the position of objects (e.g., bottom, top, above, below). It also sends the message that the teacher values and is interested in what he is doing. Taking the time for one-on-one interactions is also helpful for children who may not communicate easily in the group because of temperament differences, use of sign language, cognitive delays, and the like.

Interactions and Strategies

The following interactions and strategies promote children's understanding of the properties and characteristics of nonliving objects and materials.

Provide children with opportunities to explore a variety of objects and materials in the daily environment. Children learn about the properties and characteristics of objects through direct hands-on manipulation of real things. They need lots of experiences with a variety of objects made of different materials and with different **substances** and liquids. Children with physical disabilities may need special accommodations to manipulate or experience materials. Guidance for adaptations can come from the family members or specialist working with the child. Children can explore the properties and characteristics of a variety of materials in different areas of the preschool environment. A collection of fabrics and household objects made of different materials (e.g., wood, metal, plastic) in the dramatic play area and different kinds of papers (e.g., construction, tissue, wax paper) in the art area enrich children's experiences. During lunchtime or a cooking activity, young children can be encouraged to describe how various liquids such as water, milk, juice, or oil and various kinds of food differ in taste, smell, texture, and so on. By having wood, plastic, cardboard, foam, and plastic blocks at the block corner, children experience similarities and differences in how materials behave, and how the material affects the strength and stability of their constructions. Similarly, by playing with a variety of balls (e.g., tennis, soccer, rubber), children experience how some balls bounce higher or go farther, and with teacher's guidance, they

may begin to make predictions and draw conclusions related to the properties of the balls.[41]

In some cases, the teacher needs to add certain tools and materials to facilitate children's explorations of certain materials. For example, to help children explore how water flows, the teacher may need to be sure the water table has containers, tubes, basters, funnels, and droppers. Similarly, to investigate the properties of sand, children will need containers of different sizes, funnels, plastic bottles, magnifiers, and access to water. Initial demonstration or suggestion of possible uses of materials is helpful to foster exploration, particularly for some children with special needs. The teacher may call attention to the new materials by noting, for example, "Today we added funnels to the water table. How might we use funnels when we explore how water moves?"

Prepare yourself and be purposeful about the scientific concepts children will investigate while engaged with objects and materials. Ask yourself, "What scientific concept(s) will children explore while engaged in this activity or project?" Have a clear set of goals for children's exploration projects (see page 177 for key concepts in physical sciences).

When teachers have a basic understanding of the scientific phenomena embedded in children's activities, they are more likely to be thoughtful and selective about the materials they provide children and to guide children toward exploring and thinking about concepts of physical science. To have clear goals for children's scientific explorations, the teacher needs to prepare herself and acquire background knowledge about the topic. For example, in preparation for a project that involves explorations of different materials, teachers may need to read and think about the different materials in the children's environment (e.g., wood, metal, plastic, water, juice, paper, glass, fabrics) and how they react in different ways. The teacher may want to gain basic knowledge about the three different forms that materials can take (solids, liquids, and gases), and about how materials change. Some changes in materials such as freezing and melting of water, are reversible (physical changes), and others are irreversible, as in cooking (chemical change). The teacher does not need to become an expert on these topics and should not introduce theoretical information to young children, but rather have a basic understanding of the scientific phenomena children investigate in order to support and challenge children through their explorations. Please refer to the "Teacher Resources" section for more informational sources.

Engage children in projects that allow them to explore, experiment, and invent with objects and materials for an extended period of time. Children need extended opportunities to explore and investigate concepts of physical science. They need time to experience and revisit a variety of activities with the materials to deepen their understanding of a concept. The more experiences children have with the same objects and materials, the more likely they are to become aware and reason about their properties, and be creative in their experimentation with objects. A project exploring water or building structures can last for weeks and even months.[42] Long-term projects allow children a deep exploration of the phenomena they investigate and result in effective and powerful learning. This may necessitate designating some space to store projects between explorations.

Experiment with materials and objects before offering them to children. It is important that the teachers themselves experiment with the materials and objects children will investigate prior to offering them to children. By experimenting with objects directly, teachers can learn first-hand about the characteristics and how the objects behave. For example, prior to introducing children to a variety of materials to explore sound, teachers need to experiment with actions and materials to produce different sounds and engage in some of the science experiences and concepts children are likely to encounter in their explorations. Similarly, before teachers introduce children to a variety of building materials and tools, they need to work with the tools and learn about the form and function of each tool. It will prepare teachers in guiding children's investigations and will help them anticipate children's questions, challenges, and interesting ideas for investigation.[43] Beyond this, teachers themselves can experience the pleasure of working with materials and experimenting. Through this preparation, the teacher can also be more aware of any safety issues, particularly if there are children with special needs who may use materials in different ways (e.g., may still explore objects with their mouths).

Invite children to observe and describe the characteristics and physical properties of the objects and materials they investigate. Objects may be hard, soft, rough, smooth, heavy, light, springy, firm, shiny, dull, and so on. Create opportunities for children to observe, describe, and document their observations of objects. Encourage them to touch or hold the object, when possible, and to note specific details about the inside and outside of the object. Children may use tools such as a magnifier, a ruler, or a scale to observe and study it more closely. Talk with children and ask questions to guide their observations: "What do you notice about this maraca?" "What does it sound like when you shake it?" "What does this wagon look like?" "How is it different?" "What does this blanket feel like?" For more information about strategies to support observation skills, see the Scientific Inquiry strand, pages 156–157.

VIGNETTE

It is Emma's turn today to bring an object from home, hidden in a brown bag, and share three clues about it during group time. The rest of the children try to identify what is inside the bag without looking inside. Emma shares with the group: "It is red, it is rectangle, and has holes on one side." The children make guesses: "Is it a piece from a game? "Is it a car?" "Is it a box?" Emma shook her head "no." The teacher makes a suggestion: "Let's ask Emma some questions about her object. Emma, can you please feel the object with your hand and tell us whether it is hard or soft?" Emma touches the bag and answers, "It is hard." Jamie asks "Is it heavy?" and Emma says, "No, it is not heavy." Jamie asks if he can hold the bag and Emma lets him hold it and feel its weight. Julia asks, "Is it something you can eat?" Emma says, "You cannot eat it. You can only play it with your mouth, and it makes music." The teacher clarifies, "So it is a musical instrument?" Emma says, "Yes." Ron asks, "Is it a flute? Emma says, "No." The teacher asks the children, "What other instruments do we play with our mouth?" Then she asks Emma, "Can you turn around and play it with your mouth? We'll listen to the sounds it makes and try to guess what instrument it is."

TEACHABLE MOMENT

▶ This routine activity encourages children to notice specific characteristics and properties of objects and use words to describe them. Because the teacher has given families some guidance in helping their children choose the hidden object and develop good clues, Emma not only brought an appropriate kind of object but also provided useful clues. The teacher facilitated the conversation, helping children to ask questions about characteristics of the objects (e.g., "Is it hard, heavy, or edible?"). This type of activity not only encourages children to think about the characteristics of objects and materials, but also provides a natural opportunity to expand

---

children's vocabulary and develop their communication skills. See the *California Preschool Curriculum Framework, Volume 1*, chapter 4, "Language and Literacy," and chapter 5, "English-Language Development" for strategies to support children's vocabulary growth and their ability to use language to communicate their ideas.

Interactions and Strategies

Plan opportunities for children to sort and classify objects and materials and reflect on similarities and differences. Classification of objects into groups requires children to pay close attention to properties of objects and to identify similarities and differences among objects and materials. Children may classify objects and materials with similar physical properties, such as the properties they can see, feel, or hear. For example, explore different materials such as feathers, wood chips, rocks, foam pieces, and sort them by different criteria ("Which materials are rigid and which are soft?"). Children can also classify or categorize objects that belong together because they have a similar function (e.g., kitchen tools, types of clocks). They may observe objects that belong to the same category (e.g., bicycle, car, motorcycle, wagon), and discuss in what ways they are similar or different: "What is similar about these objects?" "What is different?" "What materials are they made of?" Classification of common objects and reflection on their similarities and differences increase children's understanding of the characteristics of objects and provide a foundation for more abstract ideas of physics.

VIGNETTE

Ms. Yen introduced children to a variety of solid materials, including feathers, wood chips, pennies, foam pieces, marbles, and eggshells. After the materials were introduced, she left them for children's free exploration in the discovery center. The center also included tools such as magnifiers, trays, cups, and a balance scale to expand their observations of the materials, and the children were familiar with how to use them. Children enjoyed exploring these materials, especially finding out how they are similar or different from each other. One question they investigated was, "Which materials are rigid and which are soft?" Children tried pressing, poking, twisting, tearing, and breaking the different materials and shared their conclusions with their classmates as they worked: "The pennies are hard." "The feathers are very soft. You can bend them, and they do not break." "The eggshell breaks when you press on it, and these (points to foam pieces) are soft, and you can break them like this (the child demonstrates how they break easily)." "The wood chips are very hard, too." With the teacher's assistance, some children recorded their findings on the chart, by gluing a sample of each material under "Rigid" or "Soft."

To broaden children's experiences with materials, Ms. Yen decided to invite children to explore various materials that are different in texture, weight, rigidity, color, and shape. Exploring how various materials are similar or different in properties (e.g., rigidity) is an interesting and engaging experience for children. They learn about properties of materials through a process of active inquiry. The teacher encouraged children to observe objects closely, identify similarities and differences among materials, sort and classify, make predictions, check evidence, and record their findings.

Provide children with opportunities to build and experiment with simple machines. *Simple machines* refer to six mechanical devices that make it easier to move or lift something: levers, a wheel on an axle, a pulley, an inclined plane, a wedge, and a screw. Simple machines are the elementary building blocks of many complicated machines that are used daily. For example, a wheel on axle is used in cars, bicycles, ferry wheels, door knobs, clocks, steering wheels, even in a toilet paper holder. Encourage children to find examples of wheels on axles and other simple machines in the preschool and in their home environment.

Children can build their own simple machines using blocks and other materials. For example, they can build an inclined plane (a ramp) with a board or a long block and use it to run cars or other rolling objects down the ramp. Teachers can also help children set up a lever in the block area. Children may experiment with lifting loads of different weights, such as a pillow, a book, or a block. Children will discover when more effort is needed to push down the opposite side of the lever to lift the load. Experiences of building and experimenting with inclined

planes, levers, or wheeled objects provide children with concrete experiences of the principles related to forces and the motion of objects.

Provide children with opportunities to investigate the form and function of different tools and machines. Children encounter different tools in their daily environment. Garden tools, kitchen tools or building tools differ in shape, size,

the materials they are made of, and the function they serve. Encourage children to observe tools and machines closely; describe what they look like, inside and outside; and the function of specific parts (e.g., "This one is sharp because it was designed for cutting." "This was created with wheels so that we can move it easily from one place to another"). Talk with children about the physical characteristics of different tools, what they are used for, and what materials they are made of.

This discussion may lead to an investigation about whether different tools could still serve the same function if made of different materials. Children should have opportunities to operate and use tools and machines. They will learn best about their function through use and operation, whenever possible. Children with motor impairments, visual impairments, or other disabilities may need assistance from adults or peers while operating tools.

Research Highlight: Understanding Cause-and-Effect

Understanding cause-and-effect relationships is fundamental to children's understanding of the world. Based on their understanding of cause-and-effect, children are able to make appropriate predictions, provide causal explanations, and draw inferences. Evidence suggests that three- to five-year old children can think about cause-and-effect in a wide range of contexts, including how physical objects cause movement,[44] the causes of growth,[45] and how emotions, desires, and beliefs cause human actions.[46] By the age of four, children demonstrate knowledge about the causal relationships between object properties and object motion.[47] They assume that a physical event has a cause and search for it. They believe that causes must precede effects and can reason about the kind of mechanism that can or cannot produce certain effects.[48]

Young children are sensitive to evidence of cause-and-effect relationships in the course of free play. When playing with a toy, they figure out which parts activate the toy, for example, make the toy light up and play music, based on patterns of evidence.[49] When evidence is not consistent (e.g., a lever that sometimes does and sometimes does not cause an effect), young children are motivated to continue exploring the toy, preferring to play with it over other novel toys, until they figure out how the toy works.[50]

2.0 Changes in Nonliving Objects and Materials

Changes in Objects and Materials

While interacting with objects and materials—building, cutting, combining, squishing, or mixing—young children make them change. Some changes involve the rearrangement of existing parts and structures to produce a new structure, such as in building with blocks, pipe cleaners, or play dough. Other kinds of changes involve combining, mixing and heating materials, creating mixtures or solutions, and may result in changes of the structure of materials in some way. Young children can reason about changes and transformations of objects and materials. From a very young age, most children understand the cause-and-effect relationship in everyday physics, and that certain actions produce certain outcomes. They also have an intuitive understanding about some properties of materials. Through various exploratory interactions with objects and materials, children experience different kinds of changes. Physical changes in materials, as in creating with play dough, building with blocks, or melting ice, are usually reversible changes (i.e., materials can be transformed back to their original state). In chemical changes, as in cooking, or other activities of mixing and combining different materials, changes are irreversible. Children cannot bring objects or materials back to their original state. As children combine, mix, and attach different objects and materials together, they begin to develop an understanding of how things change and react with one another.

Movement of Objects

Everyday play activities (such as rolling, dropping, or throwing balls; riding tricycles; swinging; pulling a wagon; or pushing cars) are experiences in which children produce movement by their own actions, and increase their understanding of the movement of objects. Through interactions with objects, children learn about cause-and-effect relationships in the movement of objects. They understand that inanimate objects cannot move themselves and need to be moved in order to change their position and location. They experience the force of gravity and notice that some objects move by falling or sliding on an inclined surface. By moving things in different ways, children also discover that the movement of an object depends on various factors such as the force that produced the movement (e.g., through pulling, pushing, throwing, or rolling), the physical properties of the object such as size, mass, shape, the

materials of which the object is made of, and the friction created by the surface on which the object is moving. A stimulating preschool environment provides children with opportunities to experiment with objects and make them move; to describe the direction, speed, and way they move; and to investigate and reason about the different factors that affect the movement of objects.

Inquiry in physical science must involve hands-on direct explorations with objects and materials, whether about changes in objects and materials, or the movement of objects and changes in their position. Kamii and Devries proposed four criteria for good activities: (a) the child must be able to produce the phenomena by his or her action; (b) the child must be able to vary his or her action; (c) the reaction of the object must be observable; (d) the reaction of the object must be immediate.[51] These four criteria were used as guidelines in developing the following strategies to broaden and deepen children's experimentations with objects and materials and their understanding of cause-and-effect.

VIGNETTE

While outdoors, Ms. Rosalinda notices that Darren is rolling the ball down the slide over and over. He is letting go of the ball at the very top of the slide and watching it roll down. Jasmine is sitting on the ground about three feet from the bottom of the slide, facing the slide, and watching the ball roll down. "Roll it all the way to me," she tells Darren. He goes up the slide, and this time, instead of just letting go of the ball, he pushes the ball slightly when rolling it down the slide. They observe the ball rolling down all the way to Jasmine. Jasmine and Darren get really excited, exclaiming "Let's do it again!" Now Jasmine takes the ball up the slide, pushes it down even harder at the top of the slide, and watches it roll down all the way to the tree. "You made the ball roll all the way to here," Ms. Rosalind remarked. "How did you do that?" Jasmine says, "You have to push it hard, and then it goes all the way to here." Ms. Rosalinda brought a small ball and asked, "What do you think will happen if we used this ball instead, and just let go of it at the top of the slide? How far do you think it will go?"

TEACHABLE MOMENT

▶ When children push, roll, kick, throw, and bounce balls, they have opportunities to explore phenomena in physical science. At first, Darren is watching the ball roll down due to the force of gravity, but it stops before it reaches Jasmine. Darren and Jasmine discover that to make the ball roll down farther, they need to push it, to apply force to the ball. Ms. Rosalinda asks them questions to raise their awareness of how they made the ball roll farther. She also encourages them to try using a different type of ball and find out whether they would get the same result. This could evolve into a series of experiences in which children roll balls of different sizes and different materials down the slide. Children who have had experience playing with balls can predict and test which balls roll fast or slow and how far different balls would go. For additional support in extending this activity, see *Ramps & Pathways: A Constructivist Approach to Physics with Young Children* by Rheta DeVries and Christina Sales.

VIGNETTE

During the last cooking activity Ms. Moreno noticed that the children were fascinated when they mixed the flour with water. The children's reactions gave Ms. Moreno an idea for extending the group's explorations with dry materials and engaging them in exploring mixtures. In small-group time, Ms. Moreno introduced the children to different dry materials, such as salt, flour, cornstarch, and sugar, and invited them to explore them. She then suggested that they mix some of these materials with water. The teacher asked the children questions to invite them to make predictions: "What do you think will happen if we add salt to water . . ." As the children watched the salt crystals disappear, they discovered that when salt is mixed with water, it cannot be seen anymore. The teacher immediately asked questions that encouraged the children to check their predictions. Ms. Moreno asked the children, "What happened when you stirred the salt in water?"

Children came up with different answers: "It disappears." "It is inside the water, but you cannot see it anymore." Ms. Moreno invited the children to taste plain water and the water stirred with salt, and tell the difference. When the children communicated that they tasted the salt and that

it was still in the water, the teacher introduced the word dissolve to the children and explained that the salt dissolved in water to make salt water. The children tried out different materials and discovered that some dissolve in water and others, such as flour or sand, do not. The next day, the children tried mixing other materials such as glue, lemonade powder, tea leaves, and play dough to find out what happens to each of these materials when mixed with water.

PLANNING LEARNING OPPORTUNITIES

▶ Cooking activities provide children with opportunities to explore a variety of dry and wet ingredients and to discover how materials change when mixed together. The teacher built on children's last cooking experience and extended their explorations of dry and wet materials. She invited the children to explore how different solid materials react when mixed with water. Ms. Moreno facilitated the children's inquiry process by providing a variety of materials, some that dissolve in water and some that do not, and by encouraging children to predict and check what happens to different materials. She introduced children to new words such as *mixture* and *dissolve* to describe the scientific phenomena they explored. Children can also investigate how different materials (e.g., sponge, cotton balls, paper, wax paper) differ in the capacity to absorb water.

Interactions and Strategies

Avoid presenting children with activities of "magical" science. Often, commercial science activities for young children involve combining materials to produce an unusual, radical reaction that is exciting and fascinating for young children. For example, chemical "snow," combining baking soda and vinegar to create an exploding "volcano," or other chemical reactions involving foam, bubbles, and magical potions. Such "mad science" activities may be fascinating for children, but they do not help children to understand the connection between what they do and the reaction of materials and how different actions can produce different responses. The magical transformation is the whole point of the activity. Furthermore, in activities of "magical" science, children usually are only observers and are not given the opportunity to explore the properties of the materials used or to understand what typically happens when different materials are mixed together.

Select activities or projects in which children can vary their actions on objects and observe the immediate reactions to their actions. Children's ability to observe the effects of their actions on objects is maximized if they are able to manipulate objects directly and produce the reaction by their own actions. They must not be passive and simply observe an adult performing the activity. In order for them to see the connection between their actions and the effect, the reaction must be observable and immediate. A delayed reaction makes it difficult for the child to make a connection between their actions and the reactions of the objects. Furthermore, the activity must provide children with ways that their actions can be varied; for example, when mixing clay with water, adding different amounts of water, and observing the effect on clay. When rolling a ball down a ramp, vary the height of the ramp or the type of ball, and observe how far the ball will go. This kind of variation makes experimentation possible. Otherwise, children reproduce only the same action over and over and cannot explore the effect of their own actions on the outcome.[52] Some children tend to engage in more repetitive actions and will need to be encouraged to explore variations.

Use cooking activities as opportunities to reason about transformations in materials. Cooking activities invite experimentation and provide opportunities to integrate math, science, literacy, and social studies in meaningful ways.[53] Cooking is also an opportunity to explore recipes, ingredients, and utensils used by children's families. Cooking not only increases children's knowledge of food and nutrition, it can also stimulate children's scientific reasoning and illustrate concepts of chemistry and physics. For example, through cooking activities children learn that heat changes things. It makes some things harder (e.g., eggs) and other things softer (e.g., potatoes). They distinguish between dry ingredients and wet ingredients. They also experience what happens when liquid is added to a dry mixture and how materials change when chopped, ground, or blended together. Allow children to try out their ideas and variations in recipes. Children begin to see the relationship

between what they do and the outcome they obtain.

Invite children to set up an experiment and collect and analyze data. Older children in the group can also participate in focused experiments and collect and analyze data. For example, they may investigate the characteristics of the ramps they build and explore how the height of the ramp and its steepness affect how far the ball would roll. They may vary the height of the ramp and measure the distance from the ramp to the point where the ball stopped, using a yardstick or unit blocks, with the assistance of an adult. The teacher can also help children use a chart to record their data and think about the evidence. Collecting data and analyzing evidence help children reach conclusions such as "a really steep ramp matters."[54]

Focus children's attention on the effect of one aspect (variable) at a time. In order to help children reason about the relation between their action and the outcome, teachers may need to help children vary only one aspect (variable), and leave the other constant. For example, while exploring the relationship between the steepness of a ramp and how far the ball would go, children need to vary the height of the ramp, and other variables such as the surface of the ramp or the kind of ball rolling down should not vary. Another example is when children experiment with different materials (e.g., beads, pebbles, sand) to find out which materials inside a maraca make a softer sound and which make a louder sound. The teacher may need to make sure that other variables, such as the external material of the maraca[a] or the amount of beads or pebbles inside, is about the same. This helps children attribute differences in the sounds only to the content of the maraca, and not to other variables.[55]

Lead children to make predictions about what they expect to happen. In physical sciences, children can have many opportunities to try things over and over and see what happens. Because the reactions are immediate and observable, children can first predict what they expect to happen, try out their ideas and immediately return to the evidence and check their prediction; for example, whether an object will sink or float in water, where a car will stop after rolling down a ramp, or what is the result after they mix the lemonade powder with water. Encourage children to make predictions by asking them questions: "What do you think will happen if we mix the flour with water?" "What do you predict will happen to this block when we drop it in the water?" "What will happen if you let the ball drop in this direction?" They may not be accurate, but they can make a reasonable guess based on their previous experiences and knowledge of objects. For more information about strategies to support the skills of predicting and checking, see the Scientific Inquiry strand, pages 163–164.

Ask questions to raise children's awareness of how they produced an effect. Offer opportunities for children to reflect and become conscious about how their actions produced a reaction in an object or material: "How did you make the ball roll down faster?" "Can you do that again?" "What did you do to make your tower stronger?" "How did you get the water in the tube?" "Which ball do you think will slide farthest when we let go of it at the top of the slide?" Encourage children to describe what they have seen and done and to give reasons and explanations for their ideas. Such teacher–

child collaborative discussions encourage children to put their thoughts into words, challenge children's thinking, and facilitate their understanding of scientific phenomena.

As children reflect, describe and explain, they also learn to use a variety of new words. For example, in experimenting with moving objects, children learn to describe their actions (e.g., pulling, pushing, throwing), and the direction, speed, and different ways that things move (e.g., rolling, sliding, flying). This is especially relevant for children who are English learners and get the opportunity to learn a variety of new words in meaningful, authentic learning experiences.

Encourage children to record and document investigations with objects and materials. Children's documentation and representation of their work is part of children's inquiry in physical sciences. Children may draw a representation or make a model of their constructions with objects, such as their tower or ramp built with blocks. They may also draw a representation of what materials look like before and after being mixed or combined together, what they predict would happen, and what actually happened. The teacher may also use a camera or video to capture elements of movement and actions involved in physical science events; for example, how the ball is rolling down a structure, or the different steps involved in preparing play dough. Experiments with objects and materials also provide opportunities to record data on charts and graphs. For example, record on a chart which materials sink in water and which ones float or how far each ball rolled. For more information about strategies to support processes of recording and documenting, see the Scientific Inquiry strand, pages 167–169.

VIGNETTE

The children were playing at the water table and taking turns toss-ing an object into the water, to find out which objects sink and which objects float. Ms. Schultz held a plastic cup, and asked, "What do you predict will happen to this cup when you put it in the water? Will it sink or float?" David said, "It will float like the other cup," refer-ring to the Styrofoam cup they tested earlier. Dana said, "It will sink because it is more hard than the white cup." Gaby said, "Maybe if we put it in like this (facing up), it will not sink." Ms. Schultz asked, "Why do you think so?" Gaby said, "Because the water will not go inside." She put the cup in the water, facing up, and the children observed the cup floating. "You see! It is floating." David said, "Now, let's put it in like this (facing down)." Ms. Shultz said, "That's a great idea. Let's put the cup in the water facing down and see what hap-pens. What is your prediction? Will the cup sink or float?"

The children predicted that the plastic cup will float again. Ms. Shultz asked, "Why do you think it will float?" David answered, "Because it was floating before." She put the cup in the water, facing down, and everyone, including Ms. Schultz, was surprised when they saw the cup sinking in the water. The children were fascinated with what they discovered. They kept putting the cup in the water, one time fac-ing up and one time facing down, watching it turn from a "floater" to a "sinker."

PLANNING LEARNING OPPORTUNITIES

Ms. Schultz decided to use one of the children's favorite activities—playing at the water table—to focus their thinking on sinking and floating of different objects. Preschool children are not ready to understand the concept of density. In fact, they tend to think that heavy objects sink and light objects float. By providing children with a variety of objects (i.e., light and heavy), made of different materials, the teacher can challenge and refine their theories about why some objects sink and why some objects float. In this example, the same object turned from floater to sinker, depending on whether the space within the cup was filled with air or water. Ms. Schultz encouraged children to make predictions, explain their reasoning, test their ideas, and record their results. In fact, together with the children in her group, she discovered a result she did not expect.

Bringing It All Together

Rolling Objects

Nicholas and Andrea demonstrated how the ramp ride they constructed works, "We put the ball all the way up, and now look how it rolls all the way down." They let the ball go down at the very top of their ramp and watched it roll down into one cylinder and straight down into another long open tube until it stopped.

Ms. Rosalinda decided to build on the children's interest in motion of objects and to offer indoor and outdoor opportunities to explore ways to make objects move. She engaged children in thinking about which objects would be good at rolling downhill. She set up a short ramp using a piece of wood and a large wooden block. During large-group time, she presented children with a collection of objects (some that can roll and some that cannot) and asked, "Which objects do you think will be good at rolling downhill?" Ari, for example, predicted that the car and the truck would roll down because they had wheels. Jared predicted that the can and the water bottle would roll too because they are round. More and more children made predictions and shared their explanations, and Ms. Rosalinda wrote them on a chart. The box with the objects was available next to the ramp during free-play time, and children tried rolling different objects down the ramp. Ms. Rosalinda observed them closely while they explored the objects. She would ask, "Why do you think the block is not rolling down the same way as the ball?" or "Why do you think the rock is rolling down in a funny way?" The children put the rolling objects in a box that said "Rollers," and the other objects in a box that said "Not Rollers." Children got excited and tried rolling other objects

in the room, such as an orange, a paintbrush, and a spoon. During group time, Ms. Rosalinda invited children to share their experiences at the ramp. She asked them why they think some objects roll and others do not.

After giving opportunities over several days to explore characteristics of rolling objects, Ms. Rosalinda wanted children to focus on how they can control and change the movement of rolling objects. She provided children with different materials, such as cardboard rolls, cardboard tubes split in half, blocks, boxes, and wood surfaces, and invited children to construct "a long roadway for the ball."

Building on children's interest, the teacher provided them with related experiences to explore and think about the form and function of rolling objects. She intentionally collected rolling and nonrolling objects in advance of the large-group time. She first engaged children in exploring and describing the characteristics of rolling objects. The children observed the objects, made predictions, checked their predictions by rolling the objects down the ramp, and recorded the results in different ways. Children also had an opportunity to reflect and share their discoveries with rolling and nonrolling objects during group time. To facilitate children's ideas about the characteristics of rolling objects, she later invited them to sort and classify rolling objects and to count the number of objects in each category (e.g., round objects, wheeled objects). The teacher next focused children's attention on the movement of objects downhill and the different ways to control the speed and direction of the rolling object. She provided children with different materials and invited them to plan, design, and construct a track for a ball to roll down. This project not only facilitated children's understanding of properties and characteristics of objects, and the physical science of the motion of objects downhill, but also fostered children's math skills, language skills, creativity, and ability to work cooperatively.

Engaging Families

✔ Learn about children's prior experiences, preferences, and particular interests with objects and materials. Some children may have had many opportunities to play and experiment with different materials (e.g., blocks, sand). Other children may come from cultures where they are discouraged from getting dirty or playing with messy materials. Teachers may need to explain to family members the importance of active hands-on explorations of objects and materials in physical sciences. Some children may have specific interests and are intrigued by particular objects or materials such as cars, blocks, water, or sand, while others may avoid interacting with particular objects or materials. Talk with family members to learn about their approach and children's prior experiences and interests. Such information is vital in connecting with families and in supporting children's explorations in physical sciences.

✔ Inform families about children's explorations and experimentations with objects and materials. Share with parents and family members your goals, what children are focusing on, and why it is important. During

family night, for example, the teacher may provide parents and family members with opportunities to engage in physical sciences through hands-on manipulations of objects and materials similar to those of the children's experiences. Sending home children's work or items related to children's experiences of inquiry is a powerful way to connect with families and to encourage family conversations about children's projects in preschool. Once parents and family members are informed and aware of children's science activities in preschool, they can become more involved and supportive. They can refer children to examples in their everyday life that illustrate the phenomena they learned about in the program. They can help children collect objects in the home environment related to children's current focus in preschool (e.g., rolling objects; a musical instrument, or a tool) to share with other children in their group.

✔ Involve family members as volunteers and rich resources in the preschool environment. Family members can also come to the preschool to share their expertise in a particular area of study. They can make presentations to the children, set up exhibits, or engage children in different activities. For example, as part of the children's experience of building structures with different materials, the teacher can invite a family member who is a builder, architect, engineer, or carpenter to come talk with the children. The visiting parent can tell children what they do and share designs, tools, books and stories related to their work. Children benefit from seeing their parents and family members in the preschool setting, and it benefits the teacher, who may not be an expert in all areas.

✔ Provide families with enrichment and follow-up activities they can do with children at home. There are many opportunities to involve children in science inquiries at home, including observations and discussions during daily routines about phenomena related to physical science (e.g., freezing, melting, rolling; operating a machine; cooking), and home-based activities in which children explore different materials. Baking a cake, taking apart an old machine, and discovering what materials the buildings in the community are made of provide opportunities to engage children in physical sciences.[56] Provide families with suggested activities, questions to investigate with their children, and key vocabulary associated with these experiences.

Questions for Reflection

1. How can different interest areas in the preschool environment (e.g., the block area, the water table, the sensory table, and the playground) be used to enhance children's explorations of objects and materials?

2. Think about your physical environment. What would you add or take away to enhance children's explorations of properties and characteristics of particular objects or materials?

3. Think about one of your group's previous projects or activities with objects and materials:
   - What was the purpose? What did you want them to notice and discover while interacting with these materials?
   - How engaged were the children with the activity? What makes you think so?
   - Did the children produce an effect or a change in objects or materials? Was the effect immediately observable? Were children able to vary their actions and observe corresponding reactions?
   - How did you facilitate children's explorations and experimentations with objects?
   - How did you encourage them to reflect, describe, and share their discoveries?
   - What would you do differently if you had an opportunity to do it again?

4. How can you facilitate the development of children's math and language skills while interacting with objects and materials? How can you use these opportunities as a vehicle to support children who are English learners?

5. What adaptations can you make, to materials or interactions with children, to support children with special needs?

Life Sciences

L ife sciences for young children are about nurturing children's curiosity and fascination with the natural world and building their understanding and appreciation of living things. Preschool children have various opportunities to engage with living things in their preschool environment. When playing in the yard, they may come across small animals or bugs or notice changes in the trees. They may help take care of the class pet or plants in the room. They participate in different planned activities related to living things, such as going on a neighborhood walk to collect different leaves, search for bugs or other small animals in the yard, sort and classify fruits and vegetables, explore various seeds, plant bulbs, sprout seeds, or grow a garden. Such experiences in the preschool environment can provide the context for rich experiences of scientific inquiry about properties and characteristics of living things. The goal is to provide children with opportunities to closely observe living things, including human beings, and to encourage them to question, explore and investigate physical characteristics, behaviors, habitats, and needs. Through ongoing opportunities to observe and discuss what they have seen, children develop their ideas about living things, how they are the same, and how they differ from one another. They start to sort and classify and look for patterns. They begin to recognize commonalities such as the physical structure and basic needs of different living things, but also the diversity and variation among different organisms.

The teacher has an important role in guiding children through experiences of exploring and observing animals and plants around them, whether outdoors, as they exist in nature, or indoors in an environment that is as natural as possible. They deepen children's understanding of living things, including features of their own body parts and processes, by encouraging children to observe closely, raise questions, investigate more about a topic, describe and represent their observations, and by creating opportunities for discussion and reflection.[57] At the same time, they model wonder and excitement of the natural world and an attitude of respect for living things and their habitats.

Key Concepts in Life Sciences

In studying animals, plants, and humans, children develop understanding of key concepts related to living things such as:

- All living things have basic needs that must be met for them to grow and survive.

- The body parts of living things are useful for them in meeting their needs.

- The physical characteristics of living things reflect how they move and behave.

- Living things have their habitats in different environments.

- All living things grow over time and go through changes related to the life cycle.

- There is variation and diversity in living things.

1.0 Properties and Characteristics of Living Things

The following section provides practical strategies for engaging children in thinking and exploring important characteristics of living things, including their physical appearance, body structure, behaviors, habitats, and basic needs. For example, explorations of the *physical characteristics* of living things may include observations of their shape, color, body structure, and parts. It can also involve a discussion about what is inside the body of living things and how it is different from the insides of nonliving objects. Teachers may invite children to investigate how different animals move, what they eat, and where they live (i.e., their **habitat**). Observations of various plants indoors and outdoors, including trees, bushes, flowers and seeds, and different organisms of the same species, highlight for children variation and diversity in living things. The following strategies, as well as the ones in the next section (Substrand 2.0, Changes in Living Things), will broaden and deepen children's awareness and understanding of properties and characteristics of living things.

VIGNETTE

While playing outdoors, Gregory pointed up to the oak tree and shouted, "Look, a squirrel up in the tree." Joanna whispered, "Shhh . . . You will scare the squirrel away." They stood there silently, watching the squirrel. Soon more children joined them. Ms. Leon, watched them observing the squirrel and asked, "What do you think the squirrel is doing?" (Pause) "What do you think he is looking for?" She listened carefully to the children's ideas and questions while observing the squirrel: "It is climbing up." "He is looking at us." "I think he is looking for something to eat." Joanna asked Ms. Leon, "Is that where he lives?" Ms. Leon turned the question right back to her and asked, "What do you think?" Ms. Leon expected this question to come up because recently they were talking about the habitats of different animals and commented that some animals live in trees. Later, during group time, Ms. Leon invited children to share with the group their observations of the squirrel. She brought up her question again: "What do you think the squirrel was looking for in the tree?" Some children said that squirrels were looking for food. Ms. Leon asked, "What kind of food do you think squirrels may find in the tree?" Joanna suggested, "Maybe they eat leaves." Miguel said, "Maybe the squirrel was looking for seeds." Ms. Leon answered, "Oh, so you think that squirrels may eat leaves, nuts, and seeds. Let's get our small binoculars and journals and observe the squirrels to find out what squirrels are doing in the tree and what they like to eat."

TEACHABLE MOMENT

▶ The play yard provides an ideal site for explorations of animals and plants in the everyday environment. The children displayed natural wonder and an interest in observing and learning about squirrels, and Ms. Leon supported the children's excitement. She guides the children toward focused observations by asking questions (e.g., "What does it look like?" "What do you think the squirrel is doing?") and getting them to think about how squirrels' habitats (like trees) help them meet their needs. Squirrels live where there is food, and the tree is a source for food (e.g., acorns, other seeds). She invites children to continue to observe the squirrels and find out more about what squirrels eat. Later, she may bring books from the library about squirrels so that the children can find out more about what squirrels like to eat and where their food is located. She may also bring in some examples of what squirrels eat for the children to examine and investigate.

Interactions and Strategies

Focus children's explorations on key concepts of living things. The teacher should be purposeful about the concept(s) children investigate while exploring living things and offer many opportunities to explore a concept from different perspectives over an extended period (see page 197 for key concepts in life sciences). For example, in exploring the physical structure of living things, children can engage in a series of investigations of the physical characteristics and body structure of animals, plants, and humans and think about the functions of different body parts, and how their form helps different living things function and survive. Similarly, in investigating the concept of growth, children may investigate growth in animals, plants, and themselves and begin to recognize common needs of all living things. Through such conceptually related experiences, children will gain a broader and deeper understanding of liv-

ing things. With various kinds of teacher support, they are more likely to draw connections between one activity and another and to search for patterns and relationships as they think about and reflect on their work.

Take children on outdoor explorations of plants and animals. The outdoor environment provides ideal sites for explorations of living things. Teachers can create opportunities for children to engage in outdoor explorations, either in the play yard or other places in the neighborhood, and observe animals and plants in their natural environment. Such experiences build children's connection to nature, increase their awareness of plants and animals in the environment, and broaden their understanding of living things. Chalufour and Worth recommend the following strategies in guiding children's outdoor explorations:

- **Model curiosity and interest in nature.** Children become interested in exploring nature through interactions with adults who model deep curiosity and interest in studying living things. Share your excitement with children, look closely at plants and animals, wonder aloud, and comment on interesting features: "Look at this leaf. What does it look like? What tree do you think it came from?" "I wonder if we can find some bugs under this log." "What do you think we will find under the rock?"

- **Remind children to be respectful of nature.** While teachers model deep curiosity and interest in living things, they should also convey an attitude of respect toward living things and their habitats. Help children understand that they study animals and plants by looking at them carefully and that animals and plants are living things and need to be treated with respect. The more aware children are of the unique needs of plants and animals, the more likely they are to interact with them in ways that keep plants and animals healthy and safe.

- **Engage children in conversations about what they notice and point their attention to important aspects of living things.** Encourage children to talk about what they notice and find: "What did you find in the dirt?" "What does it look like?" "How is it moving?" "Who else found living things under the log?" Use expansive language while communicating with children: "Some of you found leaves in the dirt. Some of you found roots and rocks. Some even found insects." Draw children's attention to key concepts related to living things such as their physical structure, habitats, and the changes in local plants and animals over time (e.g., leaves that change color or fall or the growth of buds, flowers, or fruits).

- **Document children's outdoor explorations.** Encourage children to draw a picture of what they observed to document their explorations. Take photographs or draw sketches of the plants and animals that captured children's interest, and write down children's questions and snippets of conversations or words they use to describe what they observe. During group time, children can share their drawings of a plant or animal they observed outdoors. The teacher can also make children's and teachers' documentation visible in the room, to allow children to revisit an experience, and to use it as a focus of conversation for children.[58]

Provide children with tools for explorations of living things. The study of life sciences has a strong basis in observation. It is about observing and exploring the life of different organisms through direct sensory experiences. It also involves the use of tools such as hand lenses, digging and collecting equipment, and measurement tools, to extend the ability to see details and take exact measurements. Magnifiers, such as hand lenses, can help children observe details in plants or animals that are too small to see without tools. Penlights help children see plants or animals that live under rocks or in other dark places. Small sticks (e.g., tongue depressors), tweezers, containers, and other digging and collecting equipment can be used to safely collect living things. Children also can use a clipboard, paper, pencil, and art materials to record and represent what they discover. Learning how to use tools properly and safely takes time and practice. The teacher should take time to introduce the tools and support children in using them. For more information about strategies to support the use of scientific tools, see the Scientific Inquiry strand, pages 158–160.

Include plants and animals indoors.
Plants and animals in the indoor environment provide opportunities for children to look more closely at characteristics and needs of living things and learn how to treat plants and animals with care and respect. The preschool environment may include indoor plants and pets, such as birds, fish, chameleons, guinea pigs, lizards, or rabbits. Bringing nature indoors may also take the form of a terrarium (an open container with soil) and a collection of small plants and small animals, in which living things live indoors in as natural an environment as possible. The **terrarium,** or **vivarium,** could serve as "home" for visiting animals that the children have collected outdoors such as worms, snails, pill bugs, and caterpillars. Having a terrarium is an especially meaningful experience for children when they are involved in creating it, helping to collect terrarium materials (e.g., dirt, small plants, stones, and sticks), and to decide what animals and plants to include in it: "How do we make this a good place for snails?" "Why do we need to put in dirt?" "What plants should we include?" When actively involved in putting together the terrarium, children become engaged in observing and caring for living things in the terrarium and are more aware of ways to provide for the needs of animals and plants. In urban centers, or other

places with limited access to natural outdoor areas, bringing plants and animals inside will be very important. Check for zoning or legal restrictions due to local program policies before deciding which pets or plants to include in the preschool environment.

Engage children in close observations of living things. Invite children to closely observe small animals and various plants from their environment. Focus children's explorations on a particular aspect of living things and engage them in close observations of this aspect; for example, their physical structure, how they move, what they eat, where they live (what is their habitat), and how they protect themselves. Invite children to describe and record their observations using different methods and to share and discuss what they have learned about the plant or animal they observed. Use these opportunities to ask thought-provoking questions and encourage children to share their developing ideas and theories, whether in small or large groups.

- *Close observations of animals.* Children may explore in depth animals such as worms, snails, pill bugs, caterpillars, or insects, both in the outdoors and indoors, by bringing animals inside the room for a short period of time. For example, to engage children in deep explorations of the physical characteristics of living things, encourage children to look closely at the structure and body parts of the particular animal they observe: "What shape is the pill bug?" "What does it look like when it curls up?" "Look at the snail's antennae. What is the snail doing with them?" Probe children's thinking by posing questions: "What do you think the snail uses their antennae for?" "Why do you think it has a hard shell? What is it for?" Children can observe their animals closely over time and compare them to other animals, including themselves. It will help them recognize similarities and differences across different animals and between humans and nonhumans.

- **Close observations of plants.** Children should observe trees, bushes, flowers, and other plants outdoors, as well as indoors, by observing potted plants, sprouting seeds, or the terrarium in the room. To explore the physical structure of plants, for example, the teacher can encourage children to observe closely the distinct parts, including stems, trunks, branches, leaves, and roots: "What shape are the stems?" "What do they feel like?" "How are the leaves the same? How are they different?" "What do you notice about the roots?" Probe children's thinking by asking questions related to the function and purpose of different parts: "What do the stems do for plants?" "Why do you think plants have roots?" Such thought-provoking questions focus children's explorations on the distinct parts of the plant they observe and may engage them in thinking about ways in which the structures help them function and survive.

- **Explorations of fruits and vegetables.** Encourage children to explore a variety of fruits and vegetables. Explore their insides and outsides and discuss similarities and differences: "What does it look like on the outside?" "How does it feel?" "What do you predict is inside?" Children can sort and classify them based on different attributes. For example, which fruits have a hard peel and which ones do not, or which vegetables grow under the ground (e.g., carrot), and which ones grow above

the ground (e.g., cauliflower). Children can also discover that fruits including those we refer to as vegetables such as tomatoes and zucchini contain seeds inside, but vegetables (e.g., potatoes, carrots) do not contain seeds. A discussion about seeds could also lead to exploration of the life cycle of plants. Explorations of fruits and vegetables can also serve the purpose of increasing children's knowledge of nutritious food and healthful eating habits through opportunities for cooking and tasting food. For more information, see the *California Preschool Curriculum Framework, Volume 2,* chapter 3, "Health."

Invite children to share in-home experiences with living things. This is an area with a natural connection to home life. Encourage children to observe some of these same elements of animals and plants at home and bring in examples or do a "talk–share" about what they observed. For example, in a discussion about what different animals like to eat, children may share their experiences of feeding their pet (or the preschool pet they took home over the weekend). In discussing fruits or vegetables, children may share a fruit or a vegetable they tried at home for the first time or one that their family likes to eat. Family members may come to the preschool and share with children stories, pictures, or samples of plants or animals special to their culture (for example, a fruit or a vegetable unique to their kitchen). They can also teach the teacher and the children in the group the names of animals or plants in their home language. Such experiences enhance children's learning and build home–school connections.

Use books to enrich and extend children's study of living things. Children's books can extend children's firsthand scientific explorations and enrich their experiences. Include in the environment a selection of books that focus on living things, including fiction books, information and reference books, and books with clear and vivid images of the kinds of plants and animals children observe.

Some of the books should present living things in a scientifically accurate way, and not as they appear in fantasy. They should be engaging, informative, and relevant to the group's current interest. For example, books can illustrate the body structure or growth process and life cycle of living things through accurate images, and serve as resources for children and teachers. Make books accessible to children either in the book area or around the area where they observe plants and animals closely, and use them during small- or large-group time to support the discussion. Children may look at the images of animals and plants in the books and compare them to the living things they observe. Fiction books about plants and animals (e.g., *Tiny Seed*) can also enrich children's learning experiences about living things. The teacher can invite children to reflect about the content of the story and encourage them to act out and demonstrate with their bodies how the plant or animal has grown or changed.

VIGNETTE

Children were fascinated with their observations of the pill bugs at the outdoor exploration table. Mr. J invited children to use their hand lenses to observe them closely and documented their observations: "Look it is rolling up again." "It is moving now." He directed children's attention to one of the pill bugs that was not curled up and asked, "What shape is its body?" "How is it different from the one that is curled up?" Mr. J encouraged them to draw representations of their observations, of what the pill bug looks like, before and after it curls into a ball. Diana pointed to her drawing and explained, "First it looked like this, just straight," referring to a horizontal line, "and then it was round," and pointed to the circle she drew next to it. Maya showed with her body how pill bugs curl up. Mr. J encouraged other children to try to curl up like pill bugs, "Can you use your body to show me how the pill bugs curl up?" He helped Kashira curl her hand up, because she wore a leg brace and could not curl her body up. He then asked, "I wonder why pill bugs curl into a ball?" Sharon said, "Maybe because they are shy?" Mr. J asked, "Why do you think they curl up when they are shy? What makes you think that?" Kayla said, "I think it is because they get scared." Mr. J asked, "Why do you think pill bugs curl up into a ball when they are scared?" Tim jumped up, "Because they are afraid we are going to hurt them." Mr. J replied, "How does curling up into a ball help them protect themselves?" Tim answered, "Because they can hide inside," and Kayla said, "Because they look like a ball. They do not look like a bug anymore."

PLANNING LEARNING OPPORTUNITIES

▶ Mr. J wanted to focus children's exploration on pill bugs' behavior, particularly how pill bugs curl into a ball, and help them notice patterns of behavior and changes. He directed them to observe and document the phenomena closely and to notice the way the pill bug's body changes. Children communicated their observations through drawings and movement, demonstrating with their bodies how pill bugs curl into a ball. Mr. J wanted children to think deeper about these phenomena—*When* do pill bugs curl up? *Why?* Some of the children's theories were not correct (e.g., "Because it is shy"), but through questions, and gentle probing, children came to new understandings, more reasonable and sometimes more accurate than their previous understandings. As a follow-up, the teacher may show children how to do a little research on the Internet. Children can look at enlarged photos of pill bugs and learn more about them, for example, that they are not insects, that they prefer living in soil and under decaying leaves, and that these creatures are related to the armadillo. The teacher himself may be surprised.

VIGNETTE

The teacher cut open the avocado, and Danny got really excited. "I knew there was going to be a big seed inside." Ms. Wilson replied, "You did predict that there was going to be a big seed inside." She invited children to observe the inside of the avocado. Rena said, "It has this thing inside." Sara pointed to the empty half and said, "This is where it was." The teacher replied, "It is the avocado seed." She took out the seed and handed it to Rena. "Oh, it is slippery." Ms. Wilson put it on a tray and said, "It does feel very slimy." She invited children to observe the seed. "What does it look like? What does it feel like?" After she gave children time to observe the avocado seed, she pointed to the other fruits in the basket and said, "I wonder if these fruits are also going to have seeds inside. What do you think?" Rena said, "Maybe the orange will not have very big seeds." Danny said, "The avocado has a big seed inside, not the orange." Ms. Wilson asked, "What do you think is inside the orange?" The teacher invited the children to predict what kind of seeds are inside an orange, a mango, a butternut squash, a papaya, and a plum and wrote down their predictions. She then invited the children to cut open the fruits and check what was inside.

PLANNING LEARNING OPPORTUNITIES

▶ Ms. Wilson invites children to observe seeds in fruits that are cut open. She selected a variety of fruits, including ones that are familiar to the children in the group, such as mangos, papayas, and plums. Her goal is for children to focus on one way seeds are produced within fruits. She invites children to notice, discuss, and compare seeds of different fruits (scientifically, tomatoes, cucumbers, peppers, and zucchini are classified as fruits). Some seeds are small, and some are big. Some fruits have many seeds inside, and others (like the avocado) have only one. Seeds vary in size, shape, color, and number. By comparing seeds of different fruits, children will become aware of the variety of seeds within and across different kinds of foods. Children can also discover that carrots, potatoes, and other vegetables do not contain seeds.

Research Highlight: The Insides of Living Things

Traditionally, young children were described as externalists, focusing on external features of objects, and incapable of reasoning about internal nonobservable (nonobvious) aspects of things such as internal mechanisms of the human body and other animals.[59] Research in the last two decades has challenged this view, suggesting that by the age of four, children distinguish between animals, plants, and machines and display clear expectations for the kinds of things that are inside each of these categories of objects.[60] When asked about the content of various objects, they offer different answers for animate and inanimate things, typically reporting that animates have skin on the outside and blood, bones, and internal organs such as hearts or muscles on the inside, whereas inanimate objects have cotton, paper, buttons, and other "hard stuff" inside. By four years of age, children also appreciate the special importance of insides for an object's identity and how it functions. For example, they would agree that a dog is still a dog if you get rid of its fur, but not if you take out its insides, such as the blood and bones, so that all that is left is the outside. They also expect all dogs to have the same kind of insides.[61] Although children develop knowledge of internal parts between ages three and four, they do not see these internal parts as the causal explanation for familiar biological events such as movement or growth. As more concrete understanding of internal parts develops, an understanding of biological causes of behaviors arises, for example, that something inherent in bones, brain, and muscles cause animals to behave in particular ways.[62]

2.0 Changes in Living Things

A unique aspect of living things is their ability to grow and change. Living things change over time through stages of the life cycle, as they grow, develop, reproduce, and die. In order for living things to grow and develop, they must meet their basic needs. They need water, food, light, oxygen, and space to grow. Preschool experiences of caring for plants and animals—exploring growing plants and observing and studying animals as they grow and develop over time—deepen the children's understanding of how living things grow and change and what they need to grow and develop. By studying and comparing the needs of different animals and plants, children begin to realize that there are similarities and differences in how living things meet their needs and that some needs, such as food, water, and air, are basic to all living things.

Research Highlight: Growth and Change in Living Things

The notion of growth and change is fundamental to children's understanding of living things. From a very young age, children recognize that people, animals, and plants change over time due to growth and that these changes are specific to living things.[63] By the age of five, children realize that animals grow over time and can go through a metamorphosis.[64] Children understand some aspects of the life cycle of plants.[65] From a very young age, children also associate growth of plants and animals with feeding or watering. They understand that animals and plants have needs and require care. They may suggest that plants require rain and sunshine but overall have less understanding of what plants need in order to grow compared with animals.

VIGNETTE

After children were given time to explore lima beans, Mr. Adato asked them, "What do you think will happen to the lima beans if we plant them in our garden?" Sara predicted, "They will grow, and we will have more beans." Eric predicted that the lima beans will get bigger." Shawn predicted "If we water the beans, we will have a bean tree." Mr. Adato wrote the children's predictions and then read them to the group. He then asked, "What might we need to help them grow? What do you think our lima beans will need to grow?" Mr. Adato invited the children to share their ideas, so the children responded, "Water." "Soil." Mr. Adato said, "These are great ideas. Plants need water to grow, and many plants need soil to grow. What else do you think the lima beans need to grow?" The children said: "A garden." "A pot." "Dirt." "Rain." Mr. Adato recorded their ideas and asked, "Do you think they may need light?" One of the children said, "They need to be outside, because they need sunshine." Another child said, "No, they can grow inside." Mr. Adato suggested that they grow some beans inside the room in a pot and outside in the garden and find out what happens. He said, "Let's walk outside and find a good place in our garden for growing lima beans."

**PLANNING
LEARNING
OPPORTUNITIES**

▶ The teacher introduced children to the idea of planting lima beans (seeds) after they had time to explore the seeds and prepared them for their next learning experience: planting lima beans in the garden. He elicited children's predictions about what the lima beans will look like as they grow and focused the conversation on plants' needs, "What will our beans need to grow?" This raised their anticipation and involvement level in the upcoming planting project and also gave Mr. Adato an opportunity to find out and assess what they know, including some of the children's misconceptions. He accepted the children's ideas, even if some seemed incorrect and invited children to grow lima beans, both in the room and outside in the garden, to see what happens. Mr. Adato provided children with time to explore the lima bean pods and gathered children's thoughts, ideas, and predictions before beginning planting, making it a rich and more engaging experience for children.

Interactions and Strategies

Provide children with opportunities to care for plants and animals. Plants and animals in the preschool environment raise children's awareness of growth and change in living things and what is needed to survive. By observing adults caring for plants and animals and by actively participating in watering plants, feeding the class pet, or working in the garden, children become more aware of the needs of plants and animals and how they change over time. For example, a child may notice that the food tray of the class pet is empty and offer to feed it. "Teacher, may I give it some food?" Or she may notice that the soil in the pot is very dry and try to water the plant. She may also discover that if the needs of animals and plants are not met, they will die. "The leaves are yellow. It's dying."

Provide children with opportunities to observe and monitor plants' growth and development. Sprouting seeds and watching them grow, planting bulbs in the garden, or planting things indoors in pots made of recycled materials are activities that are typically used in early childhood programs when teaching about growing plants or gardening. Outdoor and indoor planting activities can become experiences of inquiry about plants, in which children ask questions, observe and explore plants closely, and track their changes and growth over time. By caring for plants and observing them

change from seed to plant, flower, and/ or fruit and back to seed, children learn about plants' needs and about the life cycle.

- **Provide children with a variety of planting experiences.** Invite children to start new plants in several differ- ent ways: from seeds, bulbs, tubers, and cuttings. By experiencing differ- ent ways to start new plants, children recognize that various plants may look very different but have similar needs.[66] Furthermore, children can compare and contrast what the growing process looks like in the seedling, bulb, and cutting they planted.

- **Invite children to experiment and test what plants need in order to live.** Children may have different ideas about what plants need to grow. Set up experiments and control the condi- tions to test children's ideas. Children can compare and contrast plants that are grown in light and those grown in a dark closet or those grown outside to those inside. They can grow seeds in different media such as sand, clay, potting soil, or garden soil and notice differences in plants' growth. They may also give plants different amounts of water—a small amount, a moderate amount, and a large amount (*Note:* Dif- ferences are more dramatic if there is no drainage from the pot.) One class even thought that plants, like children, might need water or milk or orange juice to thrive and tried out their ideas with surprising results.

- **Invite children to predict what plants will look like as they grow.** Engage children in a conversation about how their plants will grow: "What do you think it will look like when it grows?"

- **Encourage children to notice changes in their plants' growth.** "How is your plant different?" "How has it changed?" "Do you notice any buds?" "Does it have more leaves?" Encourage children to notice the way plants have grown and changed, and keep a record of children's observa- tions. Children can communicate their observations and ideas verbally or by drawing, pointing, and acting with their bodies.

- **Invite children to measure the growth of plants.** Engage children in thinking about ways to measure a plant's growth and keep track of the plant's changing height: "How can we measure how much it grew?" They may measure its height and keep a log of the plant's growth, using nonstandard measures such as unit blocks, paper strips, or a piece of string. Older chil- dren can also keep track of the plant's height using standard measuring tools such as a ruler or a cloth measuring tape, with the assistance of an adult. See the *California Preschool Curricu- lum Framework, Volume 1*, chapter 6, "Mathematics," for strategies to sup- port children's measurement concepts and skills.

- **Invite children to record the growth of plants.** Children can record the growth of plants, using different meth- ods, including, a personal notebook, a garden journal, or a group chart. They may draw a representation of the plant in their journal. A series of drawings with their notes would allow them to compare changes from week to week. They may also take photographs of the plant, with the assistance of an adult, to keep track of changes in the plant's development over time. They can also keep a log, or record on a chart, the

plant's height as measured on different days by gluing down strings cut to the measurement, or by writing down numbers, with adults' assistance.

- *Engage children in reflective conversations in small or large groups.* Invite children to share their observations and present their drawings or refer to other records of their plant's growth. Encourage children to talk about how the plant has changed and to reflect on what plants need: "How has it changed?" "What did you do to help it grow?" "What might we need to make this new seed grow?"

- *Involve families in children's planting and gardening experiences.* Parents and other family members may be invited to the preschool environment to take part in the planting experience. For example, they can bring in cuttings or seeds of vegetables or other plants that are unique to their culture. Or they can bring ones they grew up with, to share and plant with children. They may also share with the group key vocabulary words related to planting (e.g., *soil, roots, plant*), and the name of plants in the child's home language. Words in the child's home language can then be used in labeling plants (e.g., *radish, carrot*), and in children's journaling and group discussions.

A prominent display of the growing plants can generate conversations between children and family members when families visit the preschool. Such experiences bridge home and school and enhance connections with families.

Provide children with opportunities to observe changes and transformations in animals passing through stages of the life cycle. Providing children with the opportunity to observe the life cycle of organisms and see the transformations and changes enriches and enhances their learning experience and expands children's ideas of the different ways living things change over time. Some go through metamorphosis, but many do not. Land snails and guinea pig babies look like small versions of their parents when they are young. Other animals change and go through metamorphosis as they move through the life cycle. Painted-lady butterflies change from larva to butterfly in a few weeks, frog eggs develop into tadpoles that become frogs, and mealworms change into beetles. If possible, let children observe the life cycle of different animals. It generates in children a sense of wonder and excitement about the transformations they witness in the growth process.

- *Invite children to predict changes and closely observe animals passing through different stages of a life cycle.* Provide children with hand lenses and encourage them to observe closely and notice any changes. Model close observations, wonder aloud if they notice any changes, and encourage them to talk about what they see: "How did the baby caterpillar grow?" "What do you think will happen to them as they grow?" "What do you think this white "stuff" is?"

• *Invite children to record and document their observations of changing animals.* As children observe changes in an animal, encourage them to record their observations by drawing or through other forms of communication. Date their work and write down their observations in their journal. The teacher can use children's drawings and photos taken with a camera to create a class book that describes the life cycle of these animals. Some of the older children may decide to measure animals' changes in size. For example, they may pick a larva and measure it every couple of days, with the assistance of an adult in the room, and see how much the larva has grown. They may also predict and chart the number of days until the animal goes through transformation. For more information about strategies to support processes of recording and documenting, see the Scientific Inquiry strand, pages 166–169.

• *Encourage children to compare life cycles of different animals.* Engage children in a discussion about how other animals grow and change over the course of their life. If possible, provide opportunities for children to observe or read about different life

cycles, one that goes through metamorphosis and one that does not go through metamorphosis, and encourage children to compare the two. "What do baby snails look like when they grow? What do caterpillars look like when they grow?" Young children can also compare the life cycle of animals to their own process of growth and development.

Discuss the death of living things. As part of children's care and study of living things, they may come across the death of a plant, insect, bird, or a flower. Death is part of life, and children are aware of it. At the age of four, children have a basic understanding that living things can die, but they may still view death as temporary, reversible, and not universal to all living things. Understanding the concept of death continues to develop throughout their childhood. By the age of ten, children have a more solid understanding that death applies to all living things, including plants, humans, and animals; that all living things eventually die; and that dead things cannot physically come back to life. Preschool children may ask questions and show intense curiosity about dead insects and animals. Use incidents of death as opportunities to talk with children about death, address their questions from the scientific perspective of death, and explain to them that all living things die.

Death may be made more comprehensible to children by explaining it in terms of the absence of life functions familiar to young children. For example, when people die they do not breathe, eat, talk, or think; dogs do not bark or run; and dead flowers do not grow or bloom.[67] Family members may have different ways of explaining death to children (e.g., "The dog had to go away." "Nana is sleeping in heaven"). When the topic of death is discussed in preschool, parents and families should be informed of the discussions to be prepared to answer questions.

Invite children to investigate their own growth. Children have ideas about the process of growth in humans based on their own experience of growth from a baby to a toddler to a young child or through their experiences with younger siblings. Invite children to compare the stages of growth and change in the animal they observed to their own lives and experiences: "What about you? Do you grow like this?" This could be a good transition to invite children to investigate what happens to them when they grow. Some activities that have been used with young children by Gelman and other researchers include comparing baby pictures to recent pictures, having children visit an infant room and comparing their hand sizes and heights to babies', and recording changes in shoe sizes or height from when they started preschool to when they leave.[68]

Bringing It All Together

Ms. M invited the children in her group to observe the stages in the life cycle of silk-worms, hatching from eggs, growing as larvae, and spinning cocoons. She read the children a book about the life cycle of silkworms and showed them pictures of the metamorphosis. The next day, Ms. M showed the kids the box with silkworm eggs. She invited the children to observe them closely using hand lenses, "What do these eggs look like?" She helped some of the children hold the magnifiers and observe the silkworm eggs closely. She encouraged children to record their observations of the eggs by drawing them, and she wrote down their words: "They are tiny." "Many black eggs." Ms. M. asked the children, "What do you predict will happen to the eggs in a few days?" She wrote down their predictions. One of the children had brought in mulberry leaves to feed the silkworms. A few days later, the silkworms hatched. Ms. M invited children to observe the silkworms, and the children immediately noticed the change: "They move very slowly." "They are black." "They have hair."

The children were fascinated with the growth of the silkworms. They had been watching the larvae get bigger and bigger and were excited each time they noticed new changes. They would stop by the container to look at them and would share their observations with each other. "Look, this one is really big." "They stay on the leaf." "Maybe they need more leaves, I think they are hungry." They took turns cleaning the container and feeding the worms with mulberry leaves. They enjoyed watching them growing rapidly and molting. Ms. M encouraged the children to observe them closely and notice any changes. "Look how their head is white and green, but the rest of the body is still brown." "What do you think this white stuff is around them?" She invited children to record the growth and changes through drawings and words. Their drawings were dated, and later Ms. M put them into a book. At the end of each day, Ms. M invited the children to share their observations with the whole group during circle time. She asked them questions to focus the conversation and invited some of the children to share their drawings: "What did you notice when you observed the silkworms today?" "How are they different?" "What do you predict will happen next?" Children described the cocoons of the larvae, and it evolved into a discussion about what it is and how silk is produced. Ms. M also invited Lynn's mother, who works with textiles, to share with the group the story of how silk is used to make clothing. The mother shared with children items made of silk such as a silk dress and a silk scarf.

Observing the silkworms grow and change introduced children to the development of an animal through metamorphosis and allowed them to observe the changes and transformations over time. The children learned from direct observations about the life cycle of silkworms, what they need in order to grow, and how they grow and develop. In addition, books about silkworms served as an important resource for introducing children to the process and for learning some important information about how to care for silkworms. The use of inquiry skills was embedded in the process. Ms. M invited children to observe the silkworms closely using **observation tools,** to make predictions, to record their observations in their books, and to reflect and share their observations and ideas with others during group time. It also provided an opportunity to invite family members to the preschool to expand on their learning experience. Most importantly, it generated in children an excitement and fascination with a process of growth and change in nature.

Engaging Families

✔ Ask families about children's previous experiences, cultural beliefs, and theories about living things. Some children may have had contact with many living things, while others may have had little contact. Some may view certain living organisms as dangerous, scary, or elusive, while others may view certain living organisms as divine or sacred. Children's day-to-day interactions with the natural world and their sensitivity to the culture and belief systems of their communities influence their reasoning about concepts of living things. For example, there may be differences in the understanding of concepts such as, which things are alive, whether plants are alive, and the ability to view humans as animals. All of these are related to children's previous experiences (i.e., rural or urban), naming practices in their languages, and the cultural belief systems within their communities.[69] It is essential for teachers to talk with and listen to children's families to learn more about children's previous experiences, beliefs, and interests with regard to living things. They can also engage family members in teaching them and the children in the group key vocabulary words related to living things in the child's home language.

✔ Share with families children's experiences of inquiry in life sciences. Share with parents and family members how to provide children with opportunities to closely observe plants and animals and the strategies to encourage children to question, explore and investigate the characteristics of living things. Invite parents and other family members into the preschool or host a family night where families can learn about the science curriculum, observe documentation of children's work, and experience firsthand explorations of living things. Also, share with parents and family members the ongoing information and documentation of children's work through newsletters and the family communication bulletin board in the room.

✔ Involve family members as volunteers and rich resources in the study of life sciences. Parents or family members with certain expertise or interest (e.g., an avid gardener or a bird watcher) can be invited to the preschool to share their knowledge in a particular area of study. They can make presentations to children, share with children about what they do, set up exhibits, or engage children in different activities. They can also share tools, books, and stories related to their work or culture and assist as volunteers with explorations of living things outdoors or indoors.

✔ Support families in facilitating children's curiosity and learning about living things. Remind family members of the many opportunities to engage children in life science explorations outside the preschool environment. Such experiences provide the context for observing and learning about characteristics of living things. Provide family members with tips to guide children's explorations of living things, for example, what they may note about animals or plants when observing them together, key vocabulary associated with these experiences, sample questions to spark some conversations, and ways they can support children in expressing their thoughts. Share with family members simple activities they can do with their children such as planting seeds, building a terrarium, or looking for living things in their neighborhood. The teacher might also provide a list of suggested places they can visit such as the zoo, botanical gardens, aquariums, museums, and farms in their area and a list of children's books that are related to the life science concepts they are learning.

Questions for Reflection

1. Think about activities or projects related to life sciences that you were doing or are planning to do with the children in your group.
   - What is the purpose of these activities?
   - What concepts of life science do they focus on?
   - How do you develop children's inquiry skills in the context of these activities or projects?
   - How do you introduce the inquiry topic?
   - How did you, or will you, engage children in thinking about the key ideas or concepts of science underlying these projects or activities?
   - How do you find out about children's questions, ideas, and understandings related to these explorations?
   - How do you know when and how to draw an inquiry to a close?
2. How do you use the outdoors for engaging children in explorations of plants and animals? What could you add or change in the way you use the outdoors to enhance your life science curriculum? How will you bring living things inside as well?
3. How can you find out what ideas, interests, cultural beliefs, or fears the children in your group bring to their study of living things?
4. What tools, books, or other resources would you include in your environment to enhance children's observations and explorations of living things? How would you adapt some of these tools or materials to support the special needs of children in your group?
5. How can you engage families in the activity or project in meaningful and varied ways?

Earth Sciences

When children play with dirt, jump in puddles, collect rocks, observe the rain, or feel the heat of the sun, they have direct contact with aspects of the earth. Daily interactions and direct contact with objects and earth events provide children with the context to observe and explore properties of earth materials and to identify patterns of change in the world around them (for example, patterns of day and night, and changes in temperature). With teachers' guidance, children's everyday interactions and direct contact with objects and earth events can become rich, inquiry experiences of earth sciences. Teachers can provide children with opportunities to explore the physical properties of earth materials and to observe, record, and track changes in the weather and how it affects the living world. Exploratory interactions with earth materials and ongoing observations of earth phenomena enhance children's connection to nature and raise their awareness of the importance of caring for and respecting the natural world. The box below summarizes key concepts in earth sciences. The following section provides practical strategies to engage children in rich, focused explorations of earth materials and phenomena.

Key Concepts in Earth Sciences

In studying earth materials and phenomena, children become aware of key characteristics of earth:

- Earth materials (soil, sand, rocks, air, water) are part of the natural environment.
- Earth materials have different properties.
- There are patterns of change in earth phenomena (day/night; seasons).
- Natural objects in the sky (sun, moon) are not always in the same place.
- Temperature and weather changes can be tracked over time.
- Weather and seasonal changes affect the environment.
- People should respect and care for the environment.

1.0 Properties and Characteristics of Earth Materials and Objects

Earth materials are part of children's environment. Children have direct contact with soil, rocks, sand, air, and water through daily experiences. While playing outdoors, children may spontaneously collect rocks or dig in soil. They enjoy pouring and mixing water with dirt and sand. Through close observations and explorations of earth materials, children can learn about properties, how they are similar or different, and where earth materials can be found. For example, through close observation of sand, they may discover that it is made up of tiny pieces of rocks and that dry sand can be poured like a liquid. A closer look at rocks will reveal to children that rocks vary in size, shape, color, texture, and hardness. They may also begin to notice that soil, like sand, absorbs water and that different kinds of soils have different properties. They may notice that some areas around where they live have many rocks, and some areas do not have rocks. They learn about the geographical char-

acteristics of their home environment and become aware of whether they live in the mountains, near the beach, in a valley, or in the desert.

The preschool environment provides children with a variety of experiences to observe, explore, compare, and ponder about earth materials in their environment. The following strategies will broaden and deepen children's awareness and understanding of properties and characteristics of earth materials.

VIGNETTE

Ms. Tina observes the children playing at the sandbox. Ted fills up the bucket with water and pours it on the sand. Olivia and Ted watch as the water is absorbed by the sand. Next they begin to pile the sand into a mound. Olivia says, "It's like a mountain. Let's make it bigger." They add more sand and compact it together. Their mountain is beginning to take shape and gets bigger and bigger. Olivia says, "I am going to get water." She gets a small bucket and gently pours it on top of the mountain. She notices how the water creates a depression in the sand and then flows down. Ted says, "Like a river." He gets more water in the bucket and pours it again in the same place. The depressed part gets bigger. Ms. Tina gets closer and asks, "What happens when the water is flowing down your mountain?" Ted describes, "The water makes a hole in the mountain. Olivia says, "It takes the sand down." Ms. Tina said, "A little bit of water at the beginning helped to hold the mountain together, but pouring a large amount of water causes the sand to slip and slide away. It can also happen in nature, when water breaks down the land."

TEACHABLE MOMENT

▶ The sandbox is a great place to create different land forms such as mountains, valleys, craters, rivers, and lakes. Through playful hands-on experiences with sand and water, Ted and Olivia learn about their properties; for example, how water is absorbed in sand, and a stream of water causes the sand to drop and slide away. Ms. Tina raises their awareness of the phenomena they observe by asking them to describe what happened to the mountain. She then draws the connection to the phenomenon of erosion in nature, which is so prevalent on California's coastal shoreline.

VIGNETTE

Timothy was very excited this morning about the rock he brought from home. "Tell us about your rock," said Mrs. Hunt. Timothy told the group, "I found it when I went to the beach with my mom and dad, and I kept it in my pocket." Mrs. Hunt asked if he could pass around his white rounded pebble, so that everyone had a chance to look at it, and asked the group, "Have you seen a rock like this before?" One child said she saw one in her garden. Another child said he saw many rocks like this when he went to the beach. "What have you noticed about Timothy's rock? What does it look like? How does it feel?" The children were sharing their observations of the rock. They have mentioned that it is white and smooth, and it has one hole on the side. Mrs. Hunt wondered aloud, "What kind of rocks do you think we can find in our yard? I wonder if the rocks we have in our yard look similar to Timothy's rock." Later, while playing in the yard, Mrs. Hunt noticed that some of the children in the group were searching for rocks. Mrs. Hunt had joined the children in searching for rocks on the playground. She noticed how the children got excited with every rock they found and invited the children to put the rocks on a tray. By the time they had to go back inside the room, they had a collection of rocks to observe and investigate over the next several days.

TEACHABLE MOMENT

▶ Mrs. Hunt builds on children's emerging interest and excitement with rocks and plans to use it as a springboard for studying the rocks in their environment. By wondering aloud about the kind of rocks they may find in their yard, Mrs. Hunt raises their curiosity and also plants the idea that different locations may have different kinds of rocks. Smooth, rounded pebbles are usually found at the beach or near rivers or streams. Mrs. Hunt plans to do some research about rocks in their area, so she can guide and enrich children's investigations of rocks. She is not interested in teaching them the names of different rocks, as much as she wants them to recognize the characteristics of rocks in their area. She plans to invite children to observe them closely and classify and categorize them in different ways. They may also investigate how they change; for example, what happens to different rocks when they are put in water or scratched on their surface. Not all outdoor areas provide access to rocks. Children can collect rocks with their families over a period of time and bring them to the preschool environment, a nice way to engage families in children's explorations of earth materials.

Interactions and Strategies

Take children on a search for earth materials in nature. Children should be given opportunities to observe soil, rocks, water, and sand as they appear in nature, whenever possible. Take children on a search for natural materials around the area of the play yard, on a nature walk in the neighborhood, or a field trip in the area. Direct their attention to where earth materials can be found, what they look like in their natural setting, and what materials are part of the children's environment. A field trip in their area may provide them with opportunities to observe big rocks, high mountains, sand dunes, dirt and rocks at a construction site, or water in a stream, river, lake or ocean, depending on where they live. Invite children to go on a rock hunt (*Note:* Make sure there are no dangerous materials on the ground before children begin to collect natural materials. Prepare them for some of the things they might find that should not be collected but simply observed). Providing children with magnifying glasses, binoculars, and record-

ing materials will allow them to observe things more carefully and document what they see. Consideration should be made for children with special needs through assistance by teachers or peers or adaptation of materials so they are able to fully participate and make observations. Further explorations of rocks, sand, soil, and other natural materials they collect outdoors can be the focus of closer observations and investigations in the preschool setting.

Invite children to observe, compare and classify earth materials. Encourage children to observe earth materials closely, using their senses and with the help of magnifiers and other tools, to discover the physical properties. For example, in observing rocks, minerals, or crystals, encourage children to explore the color, shape, size, and texture.[70] "What does it look like? What color is this rock?" "How can we find out how big it is?" "How can we find out how much it weighs?" An examination of different kinds of rocks, sand, and soil allows for comparison and categorization of earth materials. Encourage children to come up with their own criteria for sorting and invite them to describe their sorting and classifying: "Tell me how you sorted these rocks. Why did you put these rocks together?" Activities of this kind not only highlight for children the variation in earth materials, but also introduce children to descriptive words and expand their vocabulary in a context that is meaningful for them. Consideration should be made for children with special needs through assistance by teachers or peers or adaptation of materials so they are able to fully participate and make observations. See the *California Preschool Curriculum Framework, Volume 1*, chapter 6, "Mathematics," for additional strategies to support children's sorting and classification skills, and chapter 4, "Language and Literacy," for strategies to support vocabulary and language skills.

Invite children to explore and experiment with earth materials. Exploring and experimenting with earth materials lead children to discover more of their properties. For example, when playing with rocks, children may discover that they can use certain rocks to draw on a sidewalk, that some rocks break more easily, or change color or texture when put in water. Children also discover what happens when water is poured onto soil or sand and how it affects the water and the sand. Wet and dry sand and soil do not behave in the same way. Wet sand behaves like mud, while dry sand behaves in some ways like liquid. Dry sand can be easily poured through a funnel to fill up a bottle, but it can be more challenging to try to fill the bottle with wet sand. Clay is another earth material that is derived from minerals. When adding water to solid clay, children may discover how it transforms into a soft, slippery material that can be cut, rolled, or flattened. They can also vary the amount of water they add to clay and notice how it affects its texture. Children may discover what happens to clay when it dries out and whether they can make it soft again.

Use opportunities to explore earth materials in the context of studying living things or when exploring other solid and nonsolid materials. Much of the explorations of earth materials can be a natural extension of children's explorations in physical and life sciences. Living things use earth resources to grow and survive. The study of plants, for example, provides an opportunity to explore properties of soil and to discuss with children the way soil helps plants grow. As children take part in putting together all the materials needed for creating a terrarium for their indoor plants, they may notice that the teacher puts gravel in the bottom of the terrarium and soil on top of the gravel. The teacher may use this as an opportunity to explore these earth materials with children: "How are gravel and soil different? Why do you think we need gravel at the bottom and soil on top? How do these materials help plants grow?" As children investigate the habitats of different animals, they notice that some prefer to live in soil, some live under rocks, and some live in water. This creates the opportunity to explore different earth materials and how they provide for the needs of different animals. The exploration of sand, soil, clay, water, and rocks can also be part of children's exploration of other solid and nonsolid materials (e.g., wood, play dough, rubber, metal), as described in the Physical Sciences strand.

Invite children to share in-home experiences with earth materials. Engage family members in children's explorations of earth materials and phenomena. For example, invite families to send in samples of rocks or soil from their neighborhood or from a trip to a different area. Teachers may also send home a journal for children to record in words or pictures what rocks, sand, soil or other natural materials they find outdoors.

VIGNETTE

Before going outside, Mrs. Cooper showed children a trowel and asked, "What do you think this is for?" Nikko said, "It's for digging in the mud." Hanna said, "My mom uses it for taking out the plants." Mrs. Cooper explained, "It is used for digging, and it's called a trowel. We are going to use this tool to dig up and collect some soil. I wonder what we are going to find in the soil, when digging in it. What do you predict we may find in the soil?" The children came up with different predictions: "Rocks." "Leaves." "A ladybug." "Old flowers." "Ants." "Seeds." Mrs. Cooper wrote down their predictions. Later, Mrs. Cooper brought outside several trowels and hand lenses. She helped the children use the trowels to dig in the dirt and collect some soil from the garden, which they put in a dishpan. After they collected enough soil for their plants in the dishpan, Mrs. Cooper invited them to observe more closely the soil they collected. She brought a sieve and showed the children how they could use it to sift the soil. She also provided them with tweezers to pick up decomposing plant and animal materials. The children looked curiously at the soil and, using their magnifiers, were excited to discover roots, small rocks, slugs, and even worms. During group time, Mrs. Cooper invited the children to describe what they discovered in the soil, and she made a list of all the things they found. She read the list and explained, "Soil is made up of all of these things. Small rocks, minerals, and plant and animal materials make up soil."

PLANNING LEARNING OPPORTUNITIES

▶ Mrs. Cooper recognizes an opportunity for exploration of soil, as part of her group's planting project. She prepares herself by reading about soil and learning about the main components of soil (e.g., minerals, organic matter, and living organisms). She introduces children to the trowel, a new tool they will use, and later she assists them in using it. Children's predictions about what they will find in the soil inform Mrs. Cooper of their ideas and thoughts, and increase children's curiosity and interest as they hear each other's predictions. Digging in the soil provides children with an immediate way to check their predictions, and it opens the door for more explorations of what they found in the soil.

2.0 Changes in the Earth

Young children have daily experiences and interactions with changes in the earth. They experience changes of night and day and may notice how the sun and the moon appear to move across the sky. Young children may assume that the sun and the moon are actually moving, as they do not yet understand that the earth rotates around on its axis once in 24 hours. They experience changes related to weather and know they need to dress differently when it is hot or cold outside. The children also notice when the rain falls or the wind blows, and the changes in the environment around them, such as the leaves falling down or puddles on the playground. Invite children to observe, record, and track changes in the earth that occur around them, such as the pattern of movement and change in the sun and the moon, changes in the weather and seasons, and the impact of weather and seasons on them, and on the environment around them. This practice requires systematic observations and recording, to identify patterns in the data and changes over time. The following strategies will increase and deepen children's awareness and ability to observe, describe, and track changes in the earth.

VIGNETTE

It was a rainy day, and Mr. Kim decided to take the children out to explore the rain. Before they went outside, Mr. Kim discussed the excursion with the group and asked for their ideas about what the rain may feel, sound, taste, and smell like, and where they think it comes from. After coming back inside, the children were all excited. They were still observing the rain through the window. Mr. Kim invited the children to share their observations of the rain and the clouds. "What did you notice about the rain?" Simon said, "I saw the rain falling on the ground." Reina said, "I felt the raindrops on my face. It tickled." Mr. Kim asked the children, "Can you show me with your body how the rain was falling down?" "It falls down like this," said Nicholas, and started jumping fast, rocking his feet on the floor. Mr. Kim said, "Oh, so rain is falling down from above (showing with his hands the direction in which the rain is falling). "Where do you think the rain is coming from?" John said, "It's falling down from the sky." Tommy said, "It is coming from the clouds." Mr. Kim invited children to observe the clouds again. "What do you notice about rain clouds?" Children looked outside and shared their observations: "They are up in the sky." "They are not white." "They are grey." "They have lots of rain inside." Mr. Kim said, "These are rain clouds. Scientists call them cumulonimbus clouds."

PLANNING LEARNING OPPORTUNITIES

▶ Mr. Kim guides the children to think about where rain comes from, and to notice what rain clouds (cumulonimbus clouds) are like. He did some basic research about different types of clouds and introduces the names in a meaningful context. Even though the children may be too young to understand how water droplets are formed in the clouds, they can begin to understand where rain comes from. The teacher encourages children to use all their senses to observe the rain and clouds. Such experiences help children to develop their ability to describe their observations, in words and through body movements, and to allow children who are nonverbal to participate and communicate their observations of the rain. Mr. Kim may also invite children to record their observations of the rain through drawings and dictations in their weather journals.

Interactions and Strategies

Engage children in observing and describing the sun and the moon and other natural objects in the sky. Invite children to observe the sky and describe what they see. Young children are aware that the sun, the moon, and the stars are in the sky but are not ready to understand the explanation behind patterns of movement and apparent changes in the sun and the moon. Their observations may lead them to draw wrong conclusions: that the sun comes up and goes down, the moon changes shape, and that the stars move to different parts of the sky. Teachers can invite observations and awareness without facilitating conversations on changes in the sun and the moon. For example, children may describe what they see when they look at the sky at night and compare it with the day sky. The teachers can ask questions to focus children's observations and facilitate the discussion about objects in the sky: "What does the moon look like?" "When you looked at the sky at night, what did you see?" You can also invite children to make predictions ("What do you predict we will see in the sky when we go outside?") and to record their observations of objects in the sky by drawing, or by creating other representations and by using different materials. Avoid magical demonstrations of earth phenomena, especially if they focus on concepts children are not yet ready to grasp; for example, showing movements of the earth in relation to the sun and the moon by doing the "flashlight around the globe" demonstration.

Provide children with opportunities to observe, record, and discuss the weather. Weather is driven by changes in temperature, air movement, and precipitation activity. Common weather phenomena in California include wind, rain, clouds, and in some areas fog and snow. Discussions about the weather can raise children's awareness to changes in temperatures and provide children with opportunities to use vocabulary to describe the types of weather they experience.

- ***Develop an awareness of the daily weather.*** During large- or small-group time, take opportunities to talk about the weather. Invite children to observe and describe the weather: "What do you see?" "How is the weather different from yesterday?" "What happens when the wind blows?" Children may start making predictions based on their observations. For example, by observing the sky, they may predict whether they think it is going to rain. Encourage children to label their observations, using words such as *windy, cloudy, foggy, rainy, sunny,* and to represent their observations in drawings or actions.

- ***Invite children to record and discuss changes in the weather.*** Recording the weather may take different forms: drawing a picture of the weather and describing it in words, recording the weather in their journal, or recording their observation on a weather chart (for example, using a picture with a drawing of clouds to indicate that it is a cloudy day). Children can also learn about the different types of clouds (e.g., cumulus, cumulonimbus, cirrus), and may observe the sky and record the clouds they are observing in their journals. The teacher may read the thermometer, a tool for measurement of temperature, with the children. For example, children may read an outside thermometer, with assistance from adults, and record observations in their journals or in a chart. Systematic recording of the weather in a chart allows children to look back at the data and learn about changes in the weather over time. Children discover that the weather may change from day to day and during the day, and they can identify and describe weather patterns. For example

they may say, "It rained three days this week," or "How many sunny days did we have this month?"

- ***Invite children to observe and discuss the effects of weather and seasonal changes on their life and the environment around them.*** Children notice that it is necessary to wear jackets in the winter, because it is cold outside, and they may need their boots and umbrella when it is raining. Weather can cause immediate changes in the environment. After the rain, children may notice puddles, or a stream of water in the yard. They may notice trails of water through the sand or soil. The wind may blow away leaves, toys, and other objects on the playground. On a hot day, children may notice that the slide is too hot to slide on or that the sand in the sandbox is hotter than usual. Provide opportunities for observations and discussions of the changes they notice in their environment.

With seasonal changes, there are noticeable changes in weather and temperature and some observable changes in plant and animal activity. For example, in the autumn, the leaves of some trees and plants may change color and fall down. Furry animals have thicker coats to keep them warm during the coming winter, and many birds travel to warmer places. In the spring, temperatures become warmer. Trees sprout buds and grow new leaves and flowers, and more birds and bugs are seen around. Draw children's attention to seasonal changes in their environment. Invite children to observe, record, and discuss changes in plants and animal activity. For example, children may observe a tree or a bush in the yard regularly throughout the year and track its changes over time: "Does it lose its leaves?" "Is it growing new leaves?" "Does it grow flowers or fruits?" "Which animals can be seen around the tree or use it as part of their habitat?" Children may record their observations of the tree or bush at different times of the year.

- *Engage families in children's explorations of weather and seasonal changes.* Invite children to share experiences related to weather and seasonal changes while at home and while on family trips to other areas. Parents and other family members should be part of children's explorations of weather and seasonal changes in the environment around them. Teachers may send home lead questions to guide in home observations with parents and other family members; for example, "Is it sunny or cloudy this morning?" "Is it windy?" Discussions with family members will provide children with opportunities to use vocabulary in either their home language or English or in both languages to describe the different types of weather they experience and the changes they notice in their environment.

VIGNETTE

During group time, Ms. Reese invited the children to record the weather. Tania said, "It is windy. When I came, I felt the wind on my face, and it moved my hair." Ms. Reese told the group, "Tania says that it is windy or breezy, because she felt the wind blowing her hair when she came in this morning. Let's look outside. How can we tell if it is still windy or not?" She opened the door, and the children could feel the wind coming in. Ms. Reese asked, "Is it a strong breeze or a light breeze?" The children agreed it was a strong breeze. Ms.

Reese told the group that there are special ways to tell if it is windy and to measure the strength of the wind. She showed the group a windsock that she had ordered in advance and explained to the children what it is. She told the children that she is going to hang it up high in the yard. "Together we will look at it and will be able to tell different things about the wind; for example, how fast it blows and in what direction it is going." Then she asked Tania, "Will you please help us record on our weather chart that it is windy today?"

PLANNING LEARNING OPPORTUNITIES

▶ A routine daily activity of recording the weather can become a rich experience in which children observe the weather outside and use the evidence to determine whether it is windy or not. Ms. Reese is prepared to help children understand and be curious about the weather. In this case, Ms. Reese presented children with a windsock and placed it in the yard, so that children would become aware of the tools that provide information about different features of the wind such as its direction and relative speed. At other times, she has planned questions to elicit children's observations or brought in other tools to measure temperature, wind, or rain. Her attention to this group activity has made it interesting for the children and herself.

VIGNETTE

Today, Rena's father came to school to share with the group some of his kites and to build a kite with the children. First, he invited the children to observe him flying one of his kites in the air, and then the children took turns flying the kite together with him. After they came inside, Rena's father asked the children, "So what do you think makes the kite fly up?" Children came up with different answers. "The wind touches the kite all around, and it goes up in the sky. It pushes the kite up, up, up, up in the sky." Another child said, "The air goes through the holes of the kite, and it moves the kite to the sky." Rena's dad invited children to notice the shape of the kite, and together they discovered that the kites he brought have a similar shape, "like a diamond." He also asked them why they think the kite needs to be light and not heavy, and one of the children said, "Because it needs to fly up." Rena's dad told them, "A long time ago, kites were invented in China. People used bamboo sticks and silk to make kites." He then invited children to build a kite. "Now we are going to build our own kite. What do you think we need to build a kite?"

PLANNING LEARNING OPPORTUNITIES

The children in this group observed how lots of things blew around on a very windy day. This was part of their exploration of air movement and how air can make other things move. Over a period of time, they investigated objects such as fans, parachutes, air propellers, and kites and talked about how some objects are moved by air. The teacher knew that Rena's father enjoys building and flying kites and invited him to share his expertise with the children. She always looked for ways to involve parents and family members to enrich children's learning experiences, and felt that after children had many different experiences related to air, they were ready for the visit. She called Rena's father, and they came up with a plan for his visit. After the visit, the teacher read children the book *Kite Flying* by Grace Lin, describing how an entire family participates in constructing a colorful dragon kite. Exploring kites with Rena's father incorporated elements from science, art, literacy, culture, and history. It was a powerful learning experience for the children and the teachers in the group, particularly for Rena who was very proud to help her father present his kites.

Preserving the Environment

Nature walks; studying and caring for plants and animals; playing with and exploring water, sand and rocks; observing weather and seasonal changes—are all experiences that enhance children's curiosity and love toward their natural environment, and build their disposition to participate in environmentally relevant activities in their everyday life. In addition, the preschool teacher can raise children's awareness of the importance of caring for and respecting the environment and engage children in practices related to its care.

Interactions and Strategies

Model and discuss respect for the environment. Young children can become sensitive to basic environmental issues, and develop pro-environmental attitudes and behaviors, especially if the adults in their environment model environmentally sensitive practices, and engage them in discussions about what we can do to protect our environment. Children can understand concepts such as recycling things, caring for animals, keeping the environment clean, and not wasting resources. These are concepts within their capacity to act and change. Air and water pollution and overcrowding are not issues that young children can actively prevent; and therefore are less appropriate to discuss in preschool. Model care and responsibility for the environment through everyday practices in the preschool environment, such as not leaving water running or lights on, reusing paper, recycling and utilizing recycled materials, and keeping the environment clean by picking up trash.

Engage children in caring for and protecting the environment through everyday routines in the preschool environment. Caring practices may include showing responsibility in turning off water after washing hands, taking turns in being the room's light keeper, saving paper and other materials, participating in sorting recyclable items, and going on a "trash hunt" to clean the yard. While outdoors in nature, remind them to act in a way that keeps animals and plants safe and to show respect for living and nonliving things in the natural environment. This would include observing rather than collecting insects and animals and releasing the ones they find and study back into their habitat.

Collect and use recycled materials. Invite children and families to collect and bring to class various kinds of recycled materials. Some of these items may be paper tubes (the ones inside of paper towel rolls), plastic containers of various kinds, bottle caps, sticks, straws, papers and others. While working with these materials, teachers can guide children to sort the materials by shape, material kind (e.g., plastic versus paper), where they come from, and why they need to be recycled. Use these materials with children in different art projects, putting together a construction project or a collage. An activity of "making paper," one in which children use recycled paper to make paper (soaking it in water and then grinding paper, squeezing it, and laying it out on a flat surface to dry), is a nice way to illustrate for children the use of recycled materials. They can draw or write on the paper they have made and even make a book. Such activities combine science, art, literacy, and social science.

Bringing It All Together

The children in Ms. B's group spend a lot of time exploring the outdoor environment. While outdoors, whether in the yard or on a walk outside, she talks with the children about the weather. She is always excited to draw their attention to different trees and plants, how they change or grow, and any birds or bugs that the children come across in their environment. There is one particular tree that the children in her group follow very closely and track its changes over time. The valley oak tree is native to California's valleys. In autumn its leaves turn a yellow or light-orange color and become brown by mid to late fall. By midwinter, the oak tree is leafless. In the spring, the oak tree sprouts new leaves, and in the summer, it has heavy, green foliage.

Every month the children observe the oak tree outdoors and keep records of how it changes from month to month. Ms. B. encourages children to make drawings of the tree, and together with the children, she takes photos of it once a month. While observing the tree, Ms. B invites them to share their observations: "What changes do you see?" "Why do you think the tree changed like that?" Through such discussions, Ms. B helps children to begin to draw the connection between the changes they observe in the tree and the changes in the weather and seasons. In the fall, children collected fallen oak acorns and leaves. They were fascinated with its deeply lobed leaves, and some of them made drawings of the oak leaves in their journals. They also observed the acorns and talked about what them and other trees around the yard that have dry fruit similar to the acorn. Ms. B creates a class book with the observational drawings, children's words, and photographs docu-menting the changes the children observe each month. By the end of the school year, the book will include their documentation of the tree in order of the seasons: fall, winter, spring, and summer (based on an example from Chalufour and Worth).[71]

This project illustrates the natural connection between earth sciences and life sciences. Through regular observations recorded of the valley oak tree throughout the year, children notice changes in the tree and how they coincide with weather and seasonal changes. Ms. B enhances children's awareness and involvement in the process by encouraging them to describe and record their observations and by making documentation materials visible to children. Documentation allows children to see the changes in the tree over time and provides the context for rich discussions and comparisons of current and previous images of the tree and ideas about why the tree or plant has changed. Experiences of ongoing observations in the outdoors enhance children's connection to nature and their awareness of changes in their natural environment.

Engaging Families

✔ Support families in facilitating children's curiosity and learning about their world. In the course of their daily life, children ask the adults around them for explanations about how the world works; for example, why the moon is sometimes invisible, how the seasons change, why the sun cannot be seen at night. Provide family members with tips to support children's awareness and understanding of their natural environment. For example, they can encourage children's inquiry about the natural world by providing key vocabulary (also in the child's home language, if possible) associated with these experiences. They may ask questions to spark some conversations. Give family members a list of recommended children's books and other resources to support children's understanding of the natural world. Talk with family members about their family's culture and stories about the weather, the moon and stars and other earth science content. When family members show curiosity and interest in learning about their natural environment, children follow their lead and demonstrate even greater interest.

✔ Share with families children's experiences of inquiry in earth sciences. Invite parents into the preschool or host a family night in which family members can learn about the science curriculum, observe documentation of children's work, and experience first-hand explorations of earth materials. Developing "What we are observing now" columns in the center newsletter, e-mail, or Web site announce-

ments, or notices on a bulletin board provide families with topics to discuss and ways to engage with their children. A list of open-ended questions to use with children is also helpful, along with some suggested activities. The teacher might also provide a list of suggested outdoor places to visit and children's books that are related to earth sciences (e.g., earth materials, objects in the sky, weather, and seasons).

✔ Involve family members as volunteers and rich resources in the study of earth sciences. Encourage family members to assist as volunteers with explorations of earth materials and phenomena. Family members with certain expertise or interest (e.g., geologist, naturalist) can be invited to the preschool to share their knowledge in a particular area of study. They can give presentations, tell children what they do, set up exhibits, or engage children in different activities. They can also share tools, books, and stories related to their work. Visits by parents and other family members enhance children's learning and the home–preschool connection.

Questions for Reflection

1. How do you use the outdoors for engaging children in explorations and observations of earth materials and phenomena? What could you add or change in the way you use the outdoors to enhance children's explorations of the natural world?
2. How does your preschool environment encourage children to initiate their own playful experiences with earth materials?
3. What other earth materials might you use to diversify the materials available in your preschool environment?
4. How do you engage children in observing and describing characteristics of the weather and its changing conditions (e.g., wind, rain clouds)?
5. What opportunities do you provide to encourage children to collect, explore, compare, and sort earth materials?
6. How can you engage children in yearlong observations of seasonal changes in their immediate environment?
7. How can you engage families in participating in your group's observations and investigations?
8. How do you support children in developing an awareness of the importance of caring and respecting the environment? How is respect for the environment reflected in the behaviors of the children in your group on a daily basis?

Concluding Thoughts

Young children have a sense of wonder and a natural curiosity about objects and events in their world. Through exploratory play and experimentation with objects and materials, they discover how to make their car go downhill faster or how to control the movement and flow of water. They are excited to find out what's inside a pumpkin, how trees change over the year, how the rain feels and smells, and why pill bugs curl into a ball. The preschool environment nurtures children's innate or natural dispositions to observe and seek information and guides their curiosity into opportunities to observe, explore, and inquire about objects and phenomena in their environment. Teachers provide children with a purposefully planned, play-based, supportive environment that expands their explorations. Children's explorations and guided investigations deepen children's understanding of concepts in science and develop their attitudes, skills, and language of scientific inquiry. While investigating concepts from physical, life, and earth sciences, teachers encourage children to ask questions, to observe and investigate, to predict and experiment with objects and materials, to draw conclusions, to document their work, and to share their observations and ideas with others. Such experiences not only develop children's scientific inquiry skills, but also provide the context for learning and developing their language (building vocabulary in English and in their home language), literacy, mathematics, and social skills. Science also offers a special avenue to include families in the curriculum and bridge the home and preschool cultures. Preschool science is inclusive and prepares children for the scientific skills and knowledge they encounter later in school. It fosters a joy of discovery, a positive approach to learning, and the development of skills and attitudes necessary for many areas of learning throughout life.

Map of the Foundations

Domain ⟶

Science

Strand ⟶

Earth Sciences

Substrand ⟶ **1.0 Properties and Characteristics of Earth Materials and Objects**

At around 48 months of age	*At around 60 months of age* ◀ **Age**
Foundation ⟶ **1.1** Investigate characteristics (size, weight, shape, color, texture) of earth materials such as sand, rocks, soil, water, and air.	**1.1** Demonstrate increased ability to investigate and compare characteristics (size, weight, shape, color, texture) of earth materials such as sand, rocks, soil, water, and air.
Examples ⟶ **Examples**	**Examples**
• Observes different rocks collected on a nature walk (using the senses of sight and touch). Sorts out all the smooth rocks. • Plays with rocks and discovers that she can use a rock to draw on a sidewalk. • Fills a bucket with soil and comments, "We need water to make it more squishy." • While playing in the sandbox, pours sand into a bottle and communicates to his friend in his home language, "I can fill up the bottle with sand all the way up." • While outside, observes a windmill spinning. Responds, "I can feel the wind. The air is pushing it." • A child who is visually impaired holds different rocks and communicates, "This one feels really smooth, but this one is not very smooth." • Uses a magnifying glass to observe sand and communicates, "I can see many tiny pieces." • Explains that sand and water are needed to make a sand castle.	• Pours water on sand and compares the dry sand with the wet sand (e.g., "The wet sand sticks together"). Demonstrates how to make a cake with wet sand by filling up the bucket and then turning it over. • Pours water in the sandbox to form craters, lakes, and dams. • Investigates the surfaces of different rocks and sorts the rocks based on how shiny they are. Communicates, "Here are very shiny rocks, and here are not so shiny rocks." • In explorations of air, observes a kite flying and communicates, "The wind blows really hard, and the kite goes really high into the clouds." • Collects soil from the garden and uses a magnifying glass to observe the container of soil closely. Describes and records, with adult assistance, observations: "The soil has tiny rocks inside. The soil has some yellow leaves and some leaves that turned almost black. The soil is a little wet and feels very soft."

Teacher Resources

Books

Brunton, P., and L. Thornton. *Science in the Early Years: Building Firm Foundations from Birth to Five.* Thousand Oaks, CA: Sage Publications, 2010.

The Young Scientist Series:

Chalufour, I., and K. Worth. *Discovering Nature with Young Children.* St. Paul, MN: Redleaf Press, 2003.

Chalufour, I., and K. Worth. *Building Structures with Young Children.* St. Paul, MN: Redleaf Press, 2004.

Chalufour, I., and K. Worth. *Exploring Water with Young Children.* St. Paul, MN: Redleaf Press, 2005.

DeVries, R., and others. *Developing Constructivist Early Childhood Curriculum: Practical Principles and Activities.* New York: Teachers College Press, 2002.

DeVries R., and C. Sales. C. *Ramps & Pathways: A Constructivist Approach to Physics with Young Children.* Washington, DC: National Association for the Education of Young Children, 2011.

Gelman, R., and others. *Preschool Pathways to Science: Facilitating Scientific Ways of Thinking, Talking, Doing, and Understanding.* Baltimore, MD: Paul H. Brookes Publishing, 2010.

Life Lab. *Sowing the Seeds of Wonder: Discovering the Garden in Early Childhood Education.* Santa Cruz, CA: Life Lab, 2010. An educator guidebook that provides insight and lessons for educators to help children develop a lifelong connection to the outdoors. A publication of Life Lab, Santa Cruz, California (http://www.lifelab.org).

Lind, K. K. *Exploring Science in Early Childhood Education.* 4th ed. Clifton Park, NY: Thompson Delmar Learning, 2005.

Martin, D. J. *Constructing Early Childhood Science.* Albany, NY: Thomson Delmar Learning, 2001.

Pollman, M. J. *Blocks and Beyond: Strengthening Early Math and Science Skills through Spatial Learning.* Baltimore, MD: Paul H. Brookes Publishing, 2010.

Sarquis, M., ed. *Marvelous Moving Things: Early Childhood Science in Motion.* Contributing authors: M. Neises, L. Hogue, and B. Kutsunai. Middletown, OH: Terrific Science Press, 2009.

Worth, K., and S. Grollman. *Worms, Shadows, and Whirlpools: Science in the Early Childhood Classroom.* Portsmouth, NH: Heinemann, 2003.

Web Resources

A Head Start on Science

A collaborative project between the Department of Science Education of California State University, Long Beach, and the Head Start Program of the Long Beach Unified School District. It includes information on training opportunities for teachers, sample activities, and other resources. http://www.csulb.edu/~sci4kids/

Center for Early Education in Science, Technology, Engineering and Mathematics, University of Northern Iowa

Supports early childhood educators in creating hands-on, interactive classroom activities that encourage children to develop and use scientific inquiry processes. The site provides information on teacher workshops, ideas for activities, and games. http://www.uni.edu/coe/special-programs/regents-center-early-developmental-education/ceestem

Children and Nature Network

The Children and Nature network supports people and organizations that work to reconnect children with nature. Includes resources for parents and educators. http://www.childrenandnature.org/

Exploratorium

The museum of science, art, and human perception in San Francisco. The museum's Web site offers plenty of resources, including hands-on activities, online exhibits, articles, videos, and more. http://www.exploratorium.edu

The Hawkins Centers of Learning

The Hawkins Room for Messing About with materials and ideas offers contemporary work on topics such as balance and rolling and access to articles and other resources. http://www.hawkinscentersoflearning.org/Contemporary_Work.html

KinderNature

A resource for early childhood educators, including activities, songs, games, an idea bank, book lists, and more. http://kindernature.storycounty.com

Life Lab Science Program

Helping schools develop gardens where children can create "living laboratories" for the study of the natural world. It includes valuable educators' training materials and resources and tips for starting a school garden. http://www.lifelab.org

Young Children articles on science, a journal of the National Association for the Education of Young Children (NAEYC), access to a list of articles about science in preschool. Search for "science." http://www.naeyc.org/yc/search

NASA Teacher Resource Site

NASA Education homepage. http://www.nasa.gov/audience/foreducators/index.html

National Science Teachers Association (NSTA)

The premier organization for science teachers of all grades. The site includes information on professional development, conferences, and institutes. http://www.nsta.org/

Nature Explore

A comprehensive program to connect children with nature. The Web site includes information about designing the environment, family activities, teachers' workshops, and other resources. http://www.arborday.org/explore

North American Association for Environmental Education (NAAEE)

The Web site has resources about environmental education programs and initiatives. http://www.naaee.net/ Teachers can also check out EE-link, a resource for exploring environmental education. http://www.eelink.net

Science NetLinks

Lessons, tools, resources, and benchmarks for science education. http://www.sciencenetlinks.com

Sid the Science Kid

The Web site for the PBS TV show "Sid the Science Kid" has a parent/teacher section that includes resources and activities to support children's learning process of different topics in science. http://www.pbs.org/parents/sid/

U.S. Department of Education, Office of Communications and Outreach. Helping Your Child Learn Science. Washington, DC: Ed Pubs, 2005. Booklet.

This booklet provides parents of children ages three through ten with information, tools, and activities to develop children's interest in the sciences. http://www2.ed.gov/parents/academic/help/science/index.html

Appendix: Suggested Materials

Scientific Tools

Observation Tools Tools to extend close observations	Magnifying glasses, hand lenses Binoculars Tweezers Microscope Trays (Collectors' trays)
Measurement Tools Tools for measuring length, height, weight, volume, and temperature	Tape measures, strings, unit blocks Rulers Scales (e.g., balance scale, bathroom scale) Measuring cups Measuring spoons Thermometer
Recording Tools Tools for recording and documenting information	Pencils, markers, crayons Science notebooks/journals Papers, posters Camera, computer Charts Felt board, magnet board Materials to create 3-D models

A Wide Range of Open–Ended Objects and Materials

Materials for Building and Construction Open-ended materials can be used in multiple ways and therefore allow for investigation, creativity, and problem solving.	*Sample Materials:* Blocks of various shapes, sizes, and materials (e.g., wood, foam, cardboard) Boxes Cardboard, planks, ramps Carpentry tools Gutters, hollow tubes Logs Nuts and bolts Screws Sticks Straws Wheels, wheeled objects Other construction materials

Collections of Objects and Reclaimed Materials For exploration of diverse materials and use in sorting, classifying, and ordering activities	*Sample Materials:* Bottles Boxes of various sizes Buttons Collection of balls of different sizes Collection of different types of animals (for sorting and pretend play) Collection of household tools made from metal, wood, plastic Collection of musical instruments Corks Fabrics (e.g., a collection of gloves made of wool, rubber, leather) Glass nuggets Metal lids Plastic lids Screws Shakers, maracas, castanets Styrofoam pieces Wind chimes Woodchips
A Variety of Substances/ Materials	Cooking utensils Corn starch Dough Eggshells Flour Liquids Salt Sugar
Natural Materials: Earth Materials Natural materials found on earth	Clay Crystals Minerals Rocks Sand Seashells Soil Tools to dig and explore soil (e.g., trowels, containers, magnifiers, trays) Tools to explore water (e.g., water table, clear plastic tubes, connectors, funnels, containers) Water
Natural Materials: Plant Materials Materials derived from plants and animals	Bark Cotton Feather Fruits Fur Leaves Seeds, seed pods (e.g., pinecones) Tree logs Twigs Vegetables

Living Things	
Plants*	Bulbs Indoor terrarium Garden area Garden tools Plants, tubers, cuttings Pots Seedlings Seeds (planted in soil or germinated with paper towels/cotton) Soil
Animals	Clear containers Organic material for animals (follow specific instructions for the care of different animals) Scientific tools Small animals (e.g., mealworms, land snails, earthworms, crickets, pill bugs, and the like)

Books	
Informational Books	Nonfictional, informational books about topics from the physical, life, and earth sciences.
Fictional Books	Literature books with connection to topics of science (e.g., weather, growth, life cycle, animals).

*Choose your plants carefully, as some plants are poisonous. More information about common poisonous houseplants can be found at http://www.nybg.org/hgc_online/fact_sheets_detail.php?id_fact_sheet=4.

Endnotes

1. National Academy of Sciences and National Academy of Engineering. *Nurturing and Sustaining Effective Programs in Science Education for Grades K-8: Building a Village in California: Summary of a Convocation* (Steve Olson, Rapporteur), ed. Jay B. Labov (Washington, DC: The National Academies Press, 2009).

2. E. S. Spelke, "Principles of Object Perception." *Cognitive Science* 14 (1990): 29–56; R. Baillargeon, "Physical Reasoning in Infancy," in *The Cognitive Neurosciences*, ed. M. S. Gazzaniga (Cambridge, MA: the MIT Press, 1995).

3. D. J. Martin, *Constructing Early Childhood Science* (Albany, NY: Delmar Thomson Learning, 2001).

4. K. Worth and S. Grollman, *Worms, Shadows, and Whirlpools: Science in the Early Childhood Classroom* (Portsmouth, NH: Heinemann, 2003).

5. Ibid.; see R. Gelman and others, *Preschool Pathways to Science: Facilitating Scientific Ways of Thinking, Talking, Doing, and Understanding.* Baltimore, MD: Paul H. Brookes Publishing, 2010; see C. Chaille and L. Britain, *The Young Child as Scientist: A Constructivist Approach to Early Childhood Science Education,* 3rd ed. (Boston, MA: Allyn and Bacon, 2003); see L. French, "Science as the Center of a Coherent, Integrated Early Childhood Curriculum," *Early Childhood Research Quarterly* 19, no. 1 (2004): 138–49.

6. National Association for the Education of Young Children (NAEYC), *Developmentally Appropriate Practice in Early Childhood Programs Serving Children from Birth through Age 8: A Position Statement of the National Association for the Education of Young Children* (Washington, DC: NAEYC, adopted 2009); National Association for the Education of Young Children (NAEYC) and National Association of Early Childhood Specialists in State Departments of Education, *Early Childhood Curriculum, Assessment, and Program Evaluation: Building an Effective, Accountable System in Programs for Children Birth through Age 8: A Joint Position Statement of the National Association for the Education of Young Children (NAEYC) and the National Association of Early Childhood Specialists in State Departments of Education (NAECS. SDE)* (Washington, DC: NAEYC, 2003).

7. National Research Council, and Kindergarten through Eighth Grade Committee on Science Learning, *Taking Science to School: Learning and Teaching Science in Grades K–8,* ed. R. A. Duschl, H. A. Schweingruber, and A. W. Shouse, Board on Science Education, Center for Education, Division of Behavioral and Social Sciences and Education (Washington, DC: The National Academies Press, 2007).

8. N. L. Gallenstein, *Creative Construction of Mathematics and Science Concepts in Early Childhood* (Olney, MD: Association for Childhood Education International, 2003).

9. R. Gelman and others, *Preschool Pathways to Science: Facilitating Scientific Ways of Thinking, Talking, Doing, and Understanding* (Baltimore, MD: Paul H. Brookes Publishing, 2010); K. Worth and S. Grollman, *Worms, Shadows, and Whirlpools: Science in the Early Childhood Classroom* (Portsmouth, NH: Heinemann, 2003).

10. D. C. Castro and others, "Language and Literacy Development in Latino Dual Language Learners: Promising Instructional Practices," in *Contemporary Perspectives on Language and Cultural Diversity in Early Childhood Education: A Volume in Contemporary Perspectives in Early Childhood Education,* ed. O. N. Saracho and B. Spodek (Charlotte, NC: Information Age Publishing, 2010).

11. National Committee on Science Education Standards and Assessment and National Research Council, *National Science Education Standards.* Center for Science, Mathematics and Engineering Education (Washington, DC: National Academy Press, 1996).

12. National Association for the Education of Young Children (NAEYC), *Developmentally Appropriate Practice in Early Childhood Programs Serving Children from Birth through Age 8: A position Statement of the National Association for the Education of Young Children* (Washington, DC: NAEYC, adopted 2009).

13. K. Worth and S. Grollman, *Worms, Shadows, and Whirlpools: Science in the Early Childhood Classroom* (Portsmouth, NJ: Heinemann, 2003).

14. C. Chaille and L. Britain, *The Young Child as Scientist: A Constructivist Approach to Early Childood Science Education.* 3rd ed. (Boston, MA: Allyn and Bacon, 2003).

15. R. Gelman and others, *Preschool Pathways to Science: Facilitating Scientific Ways of Thinking,Talking, Doing, and Understanding* (Baltimore, MD: Paul H. Brookes Publishing, 2010).

16. D. J. Martin, *Constructing Early Childhood Science* (Albany, NY: Delmar Thomson Learning, 2001).

17. P. Brunton and L. Thornton, *Science in the Early Years: Building Firm Foundations from Birth to Five* (Thousand Oaks, CA: Sage Publications, 2010); D. J. Martin, *Constructing Early Childhood Science* (Albany, NY: Delmar Thomson Learning, 2001).

18. C. Chaille and L. Britain, *The Young Child as Scientist: A Constructivist Approach to Early Childhood Science Education,* 3rd ed. (Boston, MA: Allyn and Bacon, 2003).

19. K. Worth and S. Grollman, *Worms, Shadows, and Whirlpools: Science in the Early Childhood Classroom* (Portsmouth, NH: Heinemann, 2003).

20. J. K. Bernhard and V. Pacini–Ketchabaw, "The Politics of Language and Educational Practices: Promoting Truly Diverse Child Care Settings," in *Contemporary Perspectives on Language and Cultural Diversity in Early Childhood Education: A Volume in Contemporary Perspectives in Early Childhood Education,* ed. O. N. Saracho and B. Spodek (Charlotte, NC: Information Age Publishing, 2010).

21. R. Gelman and K. Brenneman, "Science Learning Pathways for Young Children," *Early Childhood Research Quarterly* 19 (2004): 150–58.

22. C. E. Landry and G. E. Forman, "Research on Early Science Education, in *The Early Childhood Curriculum: Current Findings in Theory and Practice,* 3rd ed., ed. C. Seefeldt (New York: Teachers College Press, 1999).

23. N. L. Gallenstein, *Creative Construction of Mathematics and Science Concepts in Early Childhood* (Olney, MD: Association for Childhood Education International, 2003).

24. R. Gelman and others, *Preschool Pathways to Science: Facilitating Scientific Ways of Thinking, Talking, Doing, and Understanding* (Baltimore, MD: Paul H. Brookes Publishing, 2010).

25. Ibid.

26. Ibid.

27. Ibid.

28. Ibid.

29. D. J. Martin, *Constructing Early Childhood Science* (Albany, NY: Delmar Thomson Learning, 2001).

30. J. K. Bernhard and V. Pacini–Ketchabaw, "The Politics of Language and Educational Practices: Promoting Truly Diverse Child Care Settings," in *Contemporary Perspectives on Language and Cultural Diversity in Early Childhood Education: A Volume in Contemporary Perspectives in Early Childhood Education,* ed. O. N. Saracho and B. Spodek (Charlotte, NC: Information Age Publishing, 2010).

31. R. Gelman and others, *Preschool Pathways to Science: Facilitating Scientific Ways of Thinking, Talking, Doing, and Understanding* (Baltimore, MD: Paul H. Brookes Publishing, 2010).

32. Ibid.

33. M. Fenichel and H. A. Schweingruber, *Surrounded by Science: Learning Science in Informal Environments,* Board on Science Education, Center for Education, Division of Behavioral and Social Sciences and Education (Washington, DC: National Academies Press, 2010).

34. S. Blum-Kulka, *Dinner Talk: Cultural Patterns of Sociability and Socialization in Family Discourse* (Mahwah, NJ: Lawrence Erlbaum Associates, 1997).

35. M. A. Callanan and L. Oakes, "Preschoolers' Questions and Parents' Explanations: Causal Thinking in Everyday Activity,"

Cognitive Development 7, no. 2 (1992), 213–33.

36. R. A. Reiser, M. A. Tessmer, and P. C. Phelps, "Adult-Child Interaction in Children's Learning from *Sesame Street.*" *Educational Communications and Technology* 32, no. 4 (1934): 217–33; M. A. Callanan and J. L. Jipson, "Explanatory Conversations and Young Children's Developing Scientific Literacy," in *Designing for Science: Implications from Everyday, Classroom, and Professional Settings,* ed. K. Crowley, C. D. Schunn, and T. Okada (Mahway, NJ: Lawrence Erlbaum Associates, 2001).

37. M. Bang, D. L. Medin, and S. Atran, "Cultural Mosaics and Mental Models of Nature," *Proceedings of the National Academy of Sciences of the United States of America* 104, no. 35 (2007): 13868–74.

38. K. Crowley and others, "Shared Scientific Thinking in Everyday Parent–Child Activity," *Science Education* 85, no. 6 (2001): 712–32.

39. O. N. Saracho, "The Interface of the American Family and Culture" in *Contemporary Perspectives on Language and Cultural Diversity in Early Childhood Education: A Volume in Contemporary Perspectives in Early Childhood Education,* ed. O. N. Saracho and B. Spodek (Charlotte, NC: Information Age Publishing, 2010).

40. I. Chalufour, K. Worth, and Education Development Center, *Building Structures with Young Children* (St. Paul, MN: Redleaf Press, 2004).

41. K. Worth and S. Grollman, *Worms, Shadows, and Whirlpools: Science in the Early Childhood Classroom* (Portsmouth, NJ: Heinemann, 2003).

42. I. Chalufour, K. Worth, and Education Development Center, *Building Structures with Young Children* (St. Paul, MN: Redleaf Press, 2004); I. Chalufour, K. Worth, and Education Development Center, *Exploring Water with Young Children* (St. Paul, MN: Redleaf Press, 2005).

43. K. Worth and S. Grollman, *Worms, Shadows, and Whirlpools: Science in the Early Childhood Classroom* (Portsmouth, NH: Heinemann, 2003).

44. M. Bullock, R. Gelman, and R. Baillargeon, "The Development of Causal Reasoning," in *The Developmental Psychology of Time,* ed. W. J. Friedman (New York: Academic Press, 1982); E. S. Spelke and others, "Origins of Knowledge," *Psychological Review* 99, no. 4 (1992): 605–32.

45. K. Inagaki and G. Hatano, *Young Children's Naïve Thinking about the Biological World* (New York: Psychology Press, 2002).

46. J. H. Flavell, F. L. Green, and E. R. Flavell, "Young Children's Knowledge about Thinking," *Monographs of the Society for Research in Child Development* 60, no. 1, serial no. 243 (1995): v–96; A. Gopnik and H. M. Wellman, "The Theory Theory," in *Mapping the Mind: Domain Specificity in Cognition and Culture,* ed. L. A. Hirschfeld and S. A. Gelman (New York: Cambridge University Press, 1994).

47. M. Bullock, R. Gelman, and R. Baillargeon, "The Development of Causal Reasoning," in *The Developmental Psychology of Time,* ed. W. J. Friedman (New York: Academic Press, 1982); E. S. Spelke and others, "Origins of Knowledge," *Psychological Review* 99, no. 4 (1992): 605–32.

48. M. Bullock, R. Gelman, and R. Baillargeon, "The Development of Causal Reasoning," in *The Developmental Psychology of Time,* ed. W. J. Friedman (New York: Academic Press, 1982).

49. A. Gopnik and others, "Causal Learning Mechanisms in Very Young Children: Two-, Three-, and Four-Year-Olds Infer Causal Relations from Patterns of Variation and Covariation," *Developmental Psychology* 37, no. 5 (2001): 620–29.

50. Cited from L. E. Schulz and E. B. Bonawitz, "Serious Fun: Preschoolers Engage in More Exploratory Play When Evidence Is Confounded," *Developmental Psychology* 43, no. 4 (2007): 1045–50.

51. C. Kamii and R. Devries, *Physical Knowledge in Preschool Education: Implications of Piaget's Theory* (New York: Teachers College Press, 1993).

52. C. Chaille and L. Britain, *The Young Child as Scientist: A Constructivist Approach to Early Childhood Science Education,* 3rd ed. (Boston, MA: Allyn and Bacon, 2003); R. DeVries and others, *Developing Construc-*

tivist Early Childhood Curriculum: Practical Principles and Activities (New York: Teachers College Press, 2002).

53. B. Zan, R. Edmiaston, and C. Sales, "Cooking Transformations," in *Developing Constructivist Early Childhood Curriculum: Practical Principles and Activities*, R. Devries and others (New York: Teachers College Press, 2002).

54. K. Worth and S. Grollman, *Worms, Shadows, and Whirlpools: Science in the Early Childhood Classroom* (Portsmouth, NH: Heinemann, 2003).

55. R. Devries and others, *Developing Constructivist Early Childhood Curriculum: Practical Principles and Activities* (New York: Teachers College Press, 2002).

56. D. J. Martin, *Constructing Early Childhood Science* (Albany,NY: Delmar Thomson Learning, 2001).

57. I. Chalufour, K. Worth, and Education Development Center, *Discovering Nature with Young Children* (St. Paul, MN: Redleaf Press, 2003); Ibid.

59. J. Piaget, *The Origins of Intelligence in Children*, trans. M. Cook (New York: International Universities Press, 1952); S. Carey, *Conceptual Change in Childhood* (Cambridge, MA: MIT Press, 1985).

60. G. M. Gottfried and S. A. Gelman, "Developing Domain-Specific Causal-Explanatory Frameworks: The Role of Insides and Immanence," *Cognitive Development* 20, no. 1 (2005): 137–58; K. Subrahmanyam, R. Gelman, and A. Lafosse, "Animate and Other Separably Moveable Objects," in Category-Specificity in Brain and Mind, ed. E. Fordes and G. Humphreys (London: Psychology Press, 2002).

61. S. A. Gelman and H. M. Wellman, "Insides and Essences: Early Understandings of the Non-obvious," *Cognition* 38 (1991): 213–44.

62. G. M. Gottfried and S. A. Gelman, "Developing Domain-Specific Causal-Explanatory Frameworks: The Role of Insides and Immanence," *Cognitive Development* 20, no. 1 (2005): 137–58

63. K. Inagaki and G. Hatano, *Young Children's Naïve Thinking about the Biological World* (New York: Psychology Press, 2002).

64. K. S. Rosengren and others, "As Time Goes by: Children's Early Understanding of Biological Growth in Animals," *Child Development* 62, no. 6 (1991): 1302–20.

65. A. K. Hickling and S. A. Gelman, "How Does Your Garden Grow? Evidence of an Early Conception of Plants as Biological Kinds," *Child Development* 66, no. 3 (1995): 856–76.

66. I. Chalufour, K. Worth, and Education Development Center, *Discovering Nature with Young Children* (St. Paul, MN: Redleaf Press, 2003).

67. E. A. Grollman, *Explaining Death to Young Children* (Cincinnati, OH: Forward Movement Publications, 1998).

68. R. Gelman and others, *Preschool Pathways to Science: Facilitating Scientific Ways of Thinking, Talking, Doing, and Understanding* (Baltimore, MD: Paul H. Brookes Publishing, 2010).

69. S. R. Waxman and D. Medin, "Experience and Cultural Models Matter: Placing Firm Limits on Anthropocentrism," *Human Development* 50, no. 1 (2007): 23–30; S. Atran and D. Medin, *The Native Mind and the Cultural Construction of Nature* (Cambridge, MA: The MIT Press, 2008); M. Bang, D. L. Medin, and S. Atran, "Cutural Mosaics and Mental Models of Nature," *Proceedings of the National Academy of Sciences of the United States of America* 104, no. 35 (2007): 13868–74.

70. K. K. Lind, *Exploring Science in Early Childhood Education*, 4th ed. (Clifton Park, NY: Thomson Delmar Learning, 2005).

71. I. Chalufour, K. Worth, and Education Development Center, *Discovering Nature with Young Children* (St. Paul, MN: Redleaf Press, 2003).

Bibliography

Atran, S., and D. Medin. *The Native Mind and the Cultural Construction of Nature.* Cambridge, MA: The MIT Press, 2008.

Baillargeon, R. "Physical Reasoning in Infancy." In *The Cognitive Neurosciences.* Edited by M. S. Gazzaniga. Cambridge, MA: The MIT Press, 1995.

Bang, M., D. L. Medin, and S. Atran. "Cultural Mosaics and Mental Models of Nature." *Proceedings of the National Academy of Sciences of the United States of America* 104, no. 35 (2007):13868–74.

Bernhard, J. K., and V. Pacini-Ketchabaw. "The Politics of Language and Educational Practices: Promoting Truly Diverse Child Care Settings." In *Contemporary Perspectives on Language and Cultural Diversity in Early Childhood Education: A Volume in Contemporary Perspectives in Early Childhood Education.* Edited by O.N. Saracho and B. Spodek. Charlotte, NC: Information Age Publishing, 2010.

Blum-Kulka, S. *Dinner Talk: Cultural Patterns of Sociability and Socialization in Family Discourse.* Mahwah, NJ: Lawrence Erlbaum Associates, 1997.

Brunton, P., and L. Thornton. *Science in the Early Years: Building Firm Foundations from Birth to Five.* Thousand Oaks, CA: SAGE Publications, 2010.

Bullock, M., R. Gelman, and R. Baillargeon. "The Development of Causal Reasoning." In *The Developmental Psychology of Time.* Edited by W. J. Friedman. New York: Academic Press, 1982.

Callanan, M. A., and J. L. Jipson. "Explanatory Conversations and Young Children's Developing Scientific Literacy," in *Designing for Science: Implications from Everyday, Classroom, and Professional Settings.* Edited by K. Crowley, C. D. Schunn, and T. Okada. Mahwah, NJ: Lawrence Erlbaum Associates, 2001.

Callanan, M. A., and L. Oakes. "Preschoolers' Questions and Parents' Explanations: Causal Thinking in Everyday Activity." *Cognitive Development* 7, no. 2 (1992), 213–33.

Carey, S. *Conceptual Change in Childhood.* Cambridge, MA: MIT Press, 1985.

Castro, D. C., and others. "Language and Literacy Development in Latino Dual Language Learners: Promising Instructional Practices." In *Contemporary Perspectives on Language and Cultural Diversity in Early Childhood Education: A Volume in Contemporary Perspectives in Early Childhood Education.* Edited by O.N. Saracho and B. Spodek. Charlotte, NC: Information Age Publishing, 2010.

Chaille, C., and L. Britain. *The Young Child as Scientist: A Constructivist Approach to Early Childhood Science Education.* 3rd ed. Boston, MA: Allyn and Bacon, 2003.

Chalufour, I., K. Worth, and Education Development Center, Inc. *Discovering Nature with Young Children.* St. Paul, MN: Redleaf Press, 2003.

———. *Building Structures with Young Children.* St. Paul, MN: Redleaf Press, 2004.

———. *Exploring Water with Young Children.* St. Paul, MN: Redleaf Press, 2005.

Crowley, K., and others. "Shared Scientific Thinking in Everyday Parent-Child Activity." *Science Education* 85, no. 6 (2001): 712–32.

DeVries, R., and others. *Developing Constructivist Early Childhood Curriculum: Practical Principles and Activities.* New York: Teachers College Press, 2002.

Fenichel, M., and H.A. Schweingruber. *Surrounded by Science: Learning Science in Informal Environments.* Board on Science Education, Center for Education, Division of Behavioral and Social Sciences and Education. Washington, DC: The National Academies Press, 2010.

Flavell, J. H., F. L. Green, and E. R. Flavell. "Young Children's Knowledge about Thinking." *Monographs of the Society for Research in Child Development* 60, no. 1, serial no. 243 (1995): v–96.

French, L. "Science as the Center of a Coherent, Integrated Early Childhood Curriculum." *Early Childhood Research Quarterly* 19, no. 1 (2004): 138–49.

Gallenstein, N. L. *Creative Construction of Mathematics and Science Concepts in Early Childhood.* Olney, MD: Association for Childhood Education International, 2003.

Gelman, R., and K. Brenneman. "Science Learning Pathways for Young Children." *Early Childhood Research Quarterly* 19, no. 1, (2004): 150–58.

Gelman, R., and others. *Preschool Pathways to Science: Facilitating Scientific Ways of Thinking, Talking, Doing, and Understanding.* Baltimore, MD: Paul H. Brookes Publishing, 2010.

Gelman, S. A. *The Essential Child: Origins of Essentialism in Everyday Thought.* London: Oxford University Press, 2003.

Gelman, S. A., and H. M. Wellman. "Insides and Essences: Early Understandings of the Non-obvious." *Cognition* 38 (1991): 213–44.

Gopnik, A., and others. "Causal Learning Mechanisms in Very Young Children: Two-, Three-, and Four-Year-Olds Infer Causal Relations from Patterns of Variation and Covariation." *Developmental Psychology* 37, no. 5 (2001): 620–29.

Gopnik, A., and H. M. Wellman. "The Theory Theory." In *Mapping the Mind: Domain Specificity in Cognition and Culture.* Edited by L. A. Hirschfeld and S. A. Gelman. New York: Cambridge University Press, 1994.

Gottfried, G. M., and S. A. Gelman. "Developing Domain-Specific Causal-Explanatory Frameworks: The Role of Insides and Immanence." *Cognitive Development* 20, no. 1 (2005): 137–58.

Grollman, E. A. *Explaining Death to Children.* Cincinnati, OH: Forward Movement Publications, 1998.

Hickling, A. K., and S. A. Gelman. 1995. "How Does your Garden Grow? Evidence of an Early Conception of Plants as Biological Kinds." *Child Development* 66, no. 3 (1995): 856–76.

Inagaki, K., and G. Hatano. *Young Children's Naïve Thinking about the Biological World.* New York: Psychology Press, 2002.

Kamii, C., and R. DeVries. *Physical Knowledge in Preschool Education: Implications of Piaget's Theory.* New York: Teachers College Press, 1993.

Landry, C. E., and G. E. Forman. "Research on Early Science Education," in *The Early Childhood Curriculum: Current Findings in Theory and Practice.* 3rd ed. Edited by C. Seefeldt. New York: Teachers College Press, 1999.

Lind, K. K. *Exploring Science in Early Childhood Education.* 4th ed. Clifton Park, NY: Thompson Delmar Learning, 2005.

Martin, D. J. *Constructing Early Childhood Science.* Albany, NY: Thomson Delmar Learning, 2001.

National Academy of Sciences and National Academy of Engineering. *Nurturing and Sustaining Effective Programs in Science Education for Grades K-8: Building a Village in California: Summary of a Convocation.* Steve Olson, Rapporteur. Edited by Jay B. Labov. Washington, DC: The National Academies Press, 2009.

National Association for the Education of Young Children (NAEYC). *Developmentally Appropriate Practice in Early Childhood Programs Serving Children from Birth through Age 8: A Position Statement of the National Association for the Education of Young Children.* Washington, DC: NAEYC, Adopted 2009.

National Association for the Education of Young Children (NAEYC), and National Association of Early Childhood Specialists in State Departments of Education. *Early Childhood Curriculum, Assessment, and Program Evaluation: Building an Effective, Accountable System in Programs for Children Birth through Age 8: A Joint Position Statement of the National Association for the Education of Young Children (NAEYC) and the National Association of Early Childhood Specialists in State Departments of Education (NAECS/SDE).* Washington, DC: NAEYC, 2003.

National Committee on Science Education Standards, and Assessment and National Research Council. *National Science Education Standards.* Center for Science, Mathematics and Engineering Education. Washington, DC: National Academy Press, 1996.

National Research Council, and Committee on Science Learning, Kindergarten through Eighth Grade. *Taking Science to School: Learning and Teaching Science in Grades K-8.* Edited by R. A. Duschl,

H. A. Schweingruber, and A. W. Shouse. Board on Science Education, Center for Education, Division of Behavioral and Social Sciences and Education. Washington, DC: The National Academies Press, 2007.

Piaget, J. *The Origins of Intelligence in Children.* Translated by M. Cook. New York: International Universities Press, 1952.

Reiser, R. A., M. A. Tessmer, and P. C. Phelps. "Adult-Child Interaction in Children's Learning from Sesame Street." *Educational Communications and Technology* 32, no.4 (1984): 217–33.

Rosengren, K. S., and others. "As Time Goes By: Children's Early Understanding of Biological Growth in Animals." *Child Development* 62, no. 6 (1991): 1302–20.

Saracho, O. N. "The Interface of the American Family and Culture," in *Contemporary Perspectives on Language and Cultural Diversity in Early Childhood Education: A Volume in Contemporary Perspectives in Early Childhood Education.* Edited by O. N. Saracho and B. Spodek. Charlotte, NC: Information Age Publishing, Inc., 2010.

Schulz, L. E., and E. B. Bonawitz. "Serious Fun: Preschoolers Engage in More Exploratory Play When Evidence is Confounded." *Developmental Psychology* 43, no. 4 (2007): 1045–50.

Spelke, E. S. "Principles of Object Perception." *Cognitive Science* 14 (1990): 29–56.

Spelke, E. S., and others. "Origins of Knowledge." *Psychological Review* 99, no. 4 (1992): 605-632.

Subrahmanyam, K., R. Gelman, and A. Lafosse. "Animate and Other Separably Moveable Objects." In *Category-Specificity in Brain and Mind.* Edited by E. Fordes and G. Humphreys. London: Psychology Press, 2002.

Waxman, S. R., and D. Medin. "Experience and Cultural Models Matter: Placing Firm Limits on Anthropocentrism." *Human Development* 50, no. 1 (2007): 23–30.

Worth, K., and S. Grollman. *Worms, Shadows, and Whirlpools: Science in the Early Childhood Classroom.* Portsmouth, NH: Heinemann, 2003.

Zan, B., R. Edmiaston, and C. Sales. "Cooking Transformations." In *Developing Constructivist Early Childhood Curriculum: Practical Principles and Activities.* By Devries and others. New York: Teachers College Press, 2002.

Glossary

Introduction

scaffolding. A process by which adults or capable peers provide supportive structures to help children learn and play. Scaffolding is helpful when children are faced with a challenge that they can solve with a simple hint, question, or prompt.

History–Social Science

anecdotal notes. Short accounts of particular incidents or events.

anti-bias literature. Books that address race and ethnicity, along with consideration of gender, language, religious diversity, sexual orientation, physical and mental abilities, family structure, and socioeconomic class through the use of authentic examples and experiences.

authentic objects. Items from a variety of settings (e.g., cultural, historical, linguistic) that reflect real-world experiences.

authentic questions. Open-ended questions asked with the purpose of learning children's ideas, experiences, and perspectives.

autobiographical memory. Memory for personal events in one's life.

barter. To trade by exchanging things of value rather than money.

chronological. Sequences in order of time (such as putting the birthdays of family members in chronological order).

civics. Study of the privileges and obligations of citizens.

consensus building. Activities that help children come to agreement, such as by discussion, encouraging children to listen to others' views, restating different points of view, and so on.

consumer. A person who uses (and thus may purchase) something of value, such as an object or a service.

cultural artifacts. Any items created by humans that give information about the culture of the items' creators and users.

ecology. The field of biology concerned with the relationship between organisms (including humans) and the environment.

economic exchange. Giving one thing of value for another thing of value, such as giving money to a shopkeeper to purchase food.

ecosystem. A physical environment in which plants, animals, and (sometimes) humans live and interact.

intuitive. Obtaining understanding by one's own natural reasoning, rather than learning from another.

mental "scripts." Understanding of steps in familiar routines, such as what occurs when going to a restaurant, getting ready for bed, and so on.

persona dolls or puppets. Dolls or puppets that represent diverse backgrounds and experiences, have a particular identity (e.g., a name, family history, and other traits), and are used to discuss issues that may relate to classroom situations.

print artifacts. A genuine print document (e.g., bus schedule, city map, menu) used to extend children's classroom learning.

pro-social. Positive and cooperative. Sharing with another child is an example of pro-social behavior.

spatial. Pertaining to space.

timeline. Understanding of the sequence in time in which events occurred, such as that grandparents were born before parents were, or that a tree begins as a small seedling and becomes larger over time.

tourist approach. A superficial educational approach that does not make diversity a routine part of the classroom environment and daily learning experiences.

Science

animate objects. Animate objects are living things with the capacity to impart motion or activity. The term refers to animals (including humans) and is distinguished from inanimate objects such as plants or nonliving objects (e.g., a car or a rock).

cause and effect. Cause is what makes something else happen (e.g., kicking the ball), and effect is what happens as a result of the cause (e.g., the ball rolled).

classify/classification. The sorting, grouping, or categorizing of objects according to established criteria.

communication. The skill of expressing ideas, describing observations, and discussing findings and explanations with others, either orally, through sign language, or in written form (e.g., drawings, charts, pictures, symbols).

compare and contrast. Looking at similarities and differences in real objects and events.

constructivist approach. According to this approach, children construct knowledge and build theories through active experimentation and interaction with objects and people in their environment, rather than passively taking in information.

documentation. Different forms of recorded information, including drawings, photographs, written transcripts, charts, journals, models, and constructions.

earth materials. Naturally occurring materials found on earth, including minerals, rocks, soil, and water.

earth sciences. The study of the earth, which includes topics related to properties of earth materials (i.e., soils, rocks, and minerals), the ocean, weather, and forces that shape the earth. Major components of earth sciences are geology and oceanography.

habitat. The home, place, or environment where an organism or a biological population normally lives.

hypothesis. A proposed explanation for an observable phenomenon that can be tested by an experiment. A confirmed hypothesis supports a theory.

inferences. Logical assumptions or conclusions that are based on observations but are not directly observed.

investigation. Part of the process of scientific inquiry that involves asking a question and conducting systematic observations or simple experiments to find an answer.

life cycle. The series of changes in the growth and development of humans, animals, or plants.

life sciences. The study of living things, including plants and animals, their characteristics, life cycles, habitats, and their interrelationships with each other and the environment. The life sciences encompass biology, physiology, and ecology.

living things. Living organisms that have the capacity for self-sustaining biological processes such as growth, breathing, reproduction, and responding to stimuli. Examples of living things are humans, animals, and plants.

measurement tools. Simple tools used to measure length, volume, or weight. Examples include rulers, scales, measuring cups, and spoons.

observation. The process of gathering information about objects and events using the senses of sight, smell, sound, touch, and taste, and noticing specific details or phenomena that ordinarily might be overlooked.

observation tools. Tools to extend observations, such as magnifying glasses.

open-ended questions. Questions that do not have a single right answer or that cannot be answered with yes or no.

patterns. Regularities or elements in events or objects that repeat in a predictable manner.

physical characteristics of objects. Attributes or properties of objects, such as the size, color, shape, and material the object is made of.

physical properties. Observable features of a material, such as how it looks (e.g., shape, color), feels (e.g., solid, liquid, texture), or behaves (e.g., sinks in water).

physical sciences. The study of nonliving matter and energy. These sciences deal with physical properties and transformations of substances, as well as the nature of motion, force, and energy (e.g., mechanical energy, heat, sound, light, electricity). The two major branches of physical sciences are physics and chemistry.

prediction. A guess or estimation that is based on prior observations, knowledge, and experiences.

predisposition. A tendency or inclination for something. In the context of early childhood science, young children have the predisposition—the inclination and capacity—to learn abstract concepts from biology and physics.

reclaimed materials. Any materials that have been used before and are reused. Examples include hollow tubes, corks, lids, planks, and empty bottles.

record. To set down information or knowledge in writing, drawing, or other permanent forms for the purpose of preserving evidence or tracking data over time.

scientific inquiry. The diverse ways in which scientists explore and develop knowledge and understanding of scientific ideas. The process involves making observations, posing questions, planning investigations, using tools to gather information, making predictions, recording information, and communicating findings and explanations.

simple machines. Six mechanical devices that make it easier to move or lift something: levers, wheels on axles, pulleys, inclined planes, wedges, and screws. These are the elementary building blocks of many complicated machines used in daily life.

sorting. Grouping together objects with similar properties or that belong to the same category.

STEM. An acronym that stands for science, technology, engineering, and mathematics.

substance. Any material with a definite chemical composition (e.g., water, salt, sugar, gold).

terrarium/vivarium. An enclosed environment, such as a transparent open container, where small animals and plants are raised and kept in natural conditions for observation and study.

variation and diversity. Differences among individuals of the same species; for example, humans vary in physical structure, behavior, and physiological characteristics. Diversity represents the variety or differences that exist among organisms.

OSP 13 130558

12-002 PR12-0013 4-13 50M